Free Cash, Capital Accumulation and Inequality

Investment is the engine of growth. In consequence, the social welfare of the populace depends on the expectations of uncertain profitability as understood by the agents of a wealthy few who decide upon levels of investment. As private wealth is intimately tied to the investment process, the importance of wealth concentration goes far beyond considerations of equity. In recent years, private economic power has become increasingly concentrated as more of the population has become dependent upon an elite pursuing private ends. In this context, this book examines the role of capital accumulation in various historical contexts.

Over seventy years ago, Michal Kalecki derived the mathematical relationship between government deficits, the external trade account and free cash—defined as the gross profit over and above that portion ploughed back into new investment. Since then, the free cash literature has remained largely within an industrial organizational context where free cash theory has helped to explain mergers. In contrast, this book revisits Kalecki's free cash construction at the macro and global level and explores the various causes and effects of free cash on the economy. As part of this examination, the author highlights the historical uses of free cash in imperialist adventures, mergers and speculative endeavors. In addition to developing a new relative valuation measure of capital accumulation, he also utilizes a neo-Kaleckian model to help explain the U.S. slowdown in investment since the late 1960s, the increasing inequality of wealth and income, and the recent speculative episodes associated with the spillage of free cash. Finally, based on these models, the book argues for heightened taxes on the wealthy and an increased role for government investment in health care and energy.

Free Cash, Capital Accumulation and Inequality offers an explanation as to how wealth and income inequalities have fashioned, and been fashioned by, various historical episodes right up to the present. It will be of great interest to those studying and researching in the field of economic analysis.

Craig Allan Medlen is Professor of Economics at Menlo College, in California. He graduated with a B.A. in Economics from University of California Berkeley in 1966 and received his Ph.D from U.C. Santa Barbara in 1973.

Routledge Frontiers of Political Economy

240 The Political Economy of Lula's Brazil
Edited by Pedro Chadarevian

241 Resisting Financialization with Deleuze and Guattari
Charles Barthold

242 Class and Property in Marx's Economic Thought
Exploring the Basis for Capitalism
Jørgen Sandemose

243 Economics, Ethics and Power
From Behavioural Rules to Global Structures
Hasse Ekstedt

244 Supranational Political Economy
The Globalisation of the State-Market Relationship
Guido Montani

245 Free Cash, Capital Accumulation and Inequality
Craig Allan Medlen

246 The Continuing Imperialism of Free Trade
Developments, Trends and the Role of Supranational Agents
Jo Grady and Chris Grocott

247 The Problem of Political Trust
A Conceptual Reformulation
Grant Duncan

For more information about this series, please visit: www.routledge.com/books/series/SE0345

Free Cash, Capital Accumulation and Inequality

Craig Allan Medlen

Routledge
Taylor & Francis Group
LONDON AND NEW YORK

First published 2019
by Routledge
2 Park Square, Milton Park, Abingdon, Oxon OX14 4RN

and by Routledge
52 Vanderbilt Avenue, New York, NY 10017, USA

First issued in paperback 2020

Routledge is an imprint of the Taylor & Francis Group, an informa business

British Library Cataloguing-in-Publication Data
A catalogue record for this book is available from the British Library

Library of Congress Cataloging-in-Publication Data
Names: Medlen, Craig.
Title: Free cash, capital accumulation and inequality / Craig Medlen.
Description: 1 Edition. | New York : Routledge, 2019. | Series: Routledge frontiers of political economy | Includes bibliographical references and index.
Identifiers: LCCN 2018019883 (print) | LCCN 2018028629 (ebook) | ISBN 9781315168289 (Ebook) | ISBN 9781138051447 (hardback : alk. paper)
Subjects: LCSH: Cash flow. | Saving and investment. | Income distribution. | Equality.
Classification: LCC HF5681.C28 (ebook) | LCC HF5681.C28 M43 2019 (print) | DDC 330.12/2—dc23
LC record available at https://lccn.loc.gov/2018019883

ISBN 13: 978-0-367-58633-1 (pbk)
ISBN 13: 978-1-138-05144-7 (hbk)

Typeset in Times New Roman
by Swales & Willis Ltd, Exeter, Devon, UK

Contents

List of figures vi
List of tables vii
Acknowledgments viii

1 Prologue and preview 1

2 Michal Kalecki's derivation of free cash 13

3 Hobson's choice: free cash export or domestic redistribution 22

4 Free cash and the stock bubble of the 1920s 38

5 Veblen's Q-Tobin's Q and relative valuation 51

Appendix 1 Expansion of cash through new investment 82

6 Stagnation and free cash: a neo-Kaleckian model 83

7 The multinational escape 112

Appendix 2 Multinational deficits and parents' embeddedness 131

8 Free cash, relative valuation and inequality 133

9 Crossing the boundary line 147

Index 174

Figures

4.1 Wide free cash and mergers 43
5.1 Tobin's Q 59
5.2 Capital's share and the Merger/New Investment ratio 63
5.3 Corporate output/corporate fixed investment 66
5.4 Cash/I; Cash/Y 67
5.5 Corporate investment and income growth rates 73
5.6 Investment stagnation and marginal Q proxies 74
6.1 Free cash as a fraction of corporate investment 89
6.2 High income rates 91
6.3 Corporate taxes as a fraction of profit and cash 93
6.4 Government debt and federal debt relative to GDP 95
6.5 Mortgage and consumer debt/income 98
6.6 Rates of return (stocks and bonds) 102
7.1 Multinational sales/exports of goods 116
7.2 Ratios of affiliates/parents 119
7.3 Multinational sales/U.S. exports (goods) to affiliates 122
7.4 Foreign U.S. sales/U.S. imports 122
7.5 The multinational trade deficit 123
7.6 Trade deficit (goods) and the decline in the dollar 124
8.1 Free cash and spillage 136
8.2 Capital spillage 137
8.3 Capital/income (output) ratios 141
8.4 Capital/Y; Cash/Y 143

Tables

4.1 Free cash in the 1920s 42
A2.1 Trade deficit components: correlations on trend 131
A2.2 Multinational parents' embeddedness: value added, capital expenditures, R&D 132

Acknowledgments

Acknowledgment of help and advice is an exercise in remembrance, and in this case, a matter of comradery and some laughter. Acknowledging her own role in having fun, Diana, my best friend and wife, would quip "Acknowledgment always comes before the book." She would often inquire, "Want to talk economics again?"

Remembrance extends over decades. My exposure to the importance of class arrangements came by way of Carl Landauer, who, in the 1960s, taught a course in Marxian economics at U.C. Berkeley and to Paul Sweezy who encouraged my early inquiries into the young Marx. Exposure to Veblen and other economic forerunners was brought to me by William F. Kennedy, at U.C. Santa Barbara. His one-on-one course with me in the history of economic thought drilled home the notion that economics and history were inexorably bound together in a way that could not be unraveled. A simple idea, and the starting point of any critical assessment of mainstream economics which, in violation of this most important idea, abstracts economics from historical context.

For help in research, I am very much indebted to the library staff at Menlo College, particularly Anne Linvill who, with patience and good cheer, sought materials through inter-library loan and web sources. Other professional helpmates, whose editorial remarks have helped distill ideas in the present work include Paul Davidson, Christian Wolf, Glen Atkinson, Laurel Busch, Richard V. Adkisson, Vicki Taggart, Christopher Brown, Jan Kregel, L. Randall Wray and Richard Sturn. I particularly wish to acknowledge the help of Julio López, whose correspondence and wonderful book on Michael Kalecki (co-authored by Michaël Assous) guided me away from a number of what otherwise might be called "original errors."

Various parts of the book are built on previous articles that I have written. Chapter 3 expands upon my article "A Historiographical Exhumation of J.A. Hobson's Over-Saving Thesis: General Theory Versus Historiography," *The European Journal of the History of Economic Thought*, October 2012; large parts of Chapter 4 on the 1920s stock bubble are dependent on "Industrial Aspects of the Stock Bubble of the 1920s: Free Cash and the Federal Reserve," *Journal of Business and Economics in Times of Crisis*, January 2012; excerpts in Chapter 5 dealing with Q theory and relative valuation are taken from

"The Trouble with Q," *Journal of Post-Keynesian Economics*, Summer 2003; "Veblen's Q-Tobin's Q," *Journal of Economic Issues*, December 2003; "The Bubble Machine: Relative Capital Valuation, Distributive Shares and Capital Gains," *Journal of Economic Issues*, March 2007; "Marginal Q: An Institutional Search for an Unobservable Variable," *Journal of Business and Economics in Times of Crisis*, Spring 2015; the focus on corporate taxes in Chapter 6 takes its lead from "Free Cash, Corporate Taxes and the Fiscal Deficit," *Journal of Post-Keynesian Economics*, Fall 2015; Chapter 7 builds on "Two Sets of Twins? An Exploration of Domestic Saving-Investment Imbalances," *Journal of Economic Issues*, September 2005; "The Great Escape: The Multinational Trade Deficit in Historical Perspective," *Journal of Economic Issues*, March 2018. My work on Thomas Piketty in Chapter 8 relies in part on my article "Piketty's Paradox, Capital Spillage and Inequality," *Journal of Post-Keynesian Economics*, Winter 2017.

Finally, my often-brief encounters and correspondence over the years with Paul Sweezy, John Bellamy Foster, Marvin Lee, Don Harris, James O'Connor, Phillip Anthony O'Hara and hundreds of students have cemented my conviction that serious economics can be (and should be) combined with friendship and light-hearted levity. To these persons, I extend my thanks.

1 Prologue and preview

Capitalism is a growth system. In the face of ongoing technological advance, and competition by rivals, business firms adapt and expand. The supply of labor, growing both through productivity advance that expands output per head and population growth, requires new outlets for labor absorption. In the absence of planning that would reduce the number of working hours per person and maintain a level of pay that would allow a reasonable standard of living, labor absorption requires growth.

The engine of growth is investment. Businesses are going concerns and need ever-growing markets. New products and modifications of older vintages are part of a cycle of innovation and obsolescence. Saturation of markets is an ever-present threat, particularly for large firms in mature markets. Automobiles *need* to be replaced. Along with the deterioration of the automobile stock, self-driving and electric cars will provide for the necessary expansion of markets. In addition to new space-related research endeavors, existing weapon systems *need* to undergo a process of profitable obsolescence to maintain a growing market for defense contractors. In certain industries, such an energy, quantum computing and aircraft development, the future path of product development is quite uncertain and a range of investment options is pursued simultaneously. Often the gestation period for product development is long, requiring a constantly changing investment mix with a corresponding sales effort devoted to market enlargement. Market enlargement, in turn, requires enough new state expenditures and investment across the economy to generate the income necessary to purchase the expanded level of output.

Apart from profit-maximizing pricing requirements, this necessity for ongoing growth pushes aside all other factors that might intercede. The term "sustainable development" is often used to indicate a new ecological awareness. Under present conditions, sustainable development means—first and foremost—investment in the service of profitable growth.

On the productivity front, investment carries productivity advances whereby machines replace labor. Such technological unemployment is quite painful for those displaced. But growth is facilitated by such displacement, as those displaced are available for employment elsewhere. Absorbing the displaced entails expanded markets and a corresponding amount of accompanying investment. Thus, investment enlarges the capital stock and the capacity to produce while simultaneously expanding income. Paralleling the mixed blessing of labor displacement, this expanded capacity requires more income generation so as not to develop excess capacity. Excess capacity is deadly. If generated in sufficient amounts, excess capacity stifles new investment. Such stifling begets the onslaught of economic downturn, instigating a degenerative cycle of more excess capacity, accompanying unemployment and the economy's inability to recover. Along with increased state expenditures, investment is a main generator of expanded income. In consequence, the necessity for investment growth is imperative. And, in paradoxical fashion, this growth must be in sufficient amount to avoid the idle capacity that the new investment threatens to enlarge.[1]

Investment depends on the willingness of the wealthy and their agents to invest in pursuit of profit. In consequence, the social welfare of the populace depends on the expectations of uncertain profitability as understood by the corporate agents of a wealthy few. As will be documented immediately below, investment expenditures are quite concentrated, with a relative handful of major firms carrying forth the lion's share. This economic power of the few over the many is oftentimes expressed negatively as the power of the giants to engage in monopsony, in the power to leverage financial weight, and in the ability to extract state funds for bailouts and contracts. But more often the power of the giants is simply taken for granted as the natural consequence of an existing social order where the sales of individual firms often exceed the production of nations. These giants are the gravitational center of a business system with radial arms that expand outwards in a network of millions of dependent businesses and individuals. In the nature of the case, this corporate center must remain profitable and growth-driven in order to feed the outer orbits of business and the larger society. Corporate power is thus understood as facilitating power and, by reason of its all-encompassing nature, beyond fundamental change, beyond fundamental challenge.

Upon reflection, this mega-dependency of all upon the giants might appear obvious. But the enormity of the economy renders invisible any detailed picture making up the complex whole. Just a few of the innumerable connections illustrate the point. The non-corporate business sector—comprised in large part by smaller businesses—invests around 20 percent of total business investment.[2] Such businesses employ millions. In 2012, enterprises with a total workforce of less than five hundred, employed almost half of total business employment; those with less than one hundred employed over one-third (Caruso, 2015, p. 2). Those who work for auto repair shops, local road workers, stop-and-shop gas stations, used car facilities, shopping malls depend directly or indirectly on the great auto and oil firms that collectively employ over a million workers worldwide. In the production of all types of pipe, toys, paint, carpeting, asphalt for roofs and roads, major corporations devoted to the production of oil, rubber, chemical and plastic are omnipresent. In addition to the firms engaged in designing and manufacturing medical equipment, large corporate health facilities and locally owned hospitals, physicians and health workers depend upon the great pharmaceutical companies, insurance firms and drug chains. Metal fabricators of all types and sizes are reliant on firms such as U.S. Steel, Anaconda Copper and International

Nickel, who, in their specialty products, require material imports from all over the globe transported by ships that, in turn, embed the very metals whose imports are being transported. Interlocking connectedness of major firms and an extended business network is the rule. A search for exceptions would be futile.

The corporate ecosystem also extends into government expenditures and procurement of revenues. State and local government revenues depend not just on taxes levied on income, property and sales but on the gas tax and assorted fees levied by state departments of motor vehicles, whose redeployment expands the transportation tributaries of roads and highways. Direct investment at the federal level is comparatively small. But its procurement of high-tech weaponry and other outputs reach into large-scale contractors and university facilities whose research and development facilitate and sponsor large amounts of private investment in industries as wide-ranging as defense, space, telecommunications, nuclear power, biotechnology and aircraft procurement. The leasing arrangements of public land areas by timber and mineral companies, together with assorted other subsidies to large firms, buttress the enlargement of aggregate demand which the federal government generates through contracts, transfer payment mechanisms and entitlement programs. The employment of military staff in the U.S.'s 700+ military bases and naval fleets, together with the military and policing aid to various governments, protect the shipping lanes and resource-rich areas from which major U.S. firms profit and to which investment flows. These corporate benefits include not just the procurement of material resources—oil, copper, tropical foodstuffs and the like—but also labor resources which, through U.S. multinational affiliates and others, supply imports into the global distribution channels largely dominated by major firms.

As private wealth is intimately tied to the investment process, the importance of wealth concentration goes far beyond considerations of equity. Unlike a not-too-distant past where a good part of the U.S. population had direct access to the means of livelihood through the ownership of land and artisan shops, the current workforce depends overwhelmingly upon wages and salaries. In recent years, there has developed a new interest in income and wealth disparities. This interest has directed intellectual energy to uncovering the causes of the recent rise in inequalities and to the functional outcomes associated with the rise. But behind this discussion lies the larger social question of investment as a primary driver of social consequence and its use for private ends.

This larger question is not new. Robert Heilbroner describes the over-arching theme of capital accumulation and the quest for profit as the "great drama" underlying the works of major forbearers such as Adam Smith, J.S. Mill, Marx and Keynes. Heilbroner might also have mentioned more recent theorists, such as Joseph Schumpeter, Michal Kalecki, Joseph Steindl, Paul Baran and Paul Sweezy. All recognized that the "vital accumulation process hinges on the ability of a capitalist class to extract profit from the system." All understood the importance of property rights and the division of "functions between the realm of business and that of the state—a division of functions that takes for granted the priority of accumulation as a necessary condition for a stable social order." All understood capitalism "as a social formation in which the accumulation of capital becomes the organizing basis for sociopolitical life" (Heilbroner, 1985, pp. 142–143).

The importance of the "great drama" of capital accumulation and the private nature of its appropriation remains doubly true when more and more of the populace is dependent on a proportionately smaller elite exempt from public accountability. Investment outlays and wealth ownership are highly concentrated. From the early 1970s to the present, the top 200 publicly listed non-financial firms have put into place approximately 65–70 percent of the total corporate investment of those listed, with the top 50 generating approximately 40 percent and the top 25 generating one-third (Grullon, Hund and Weston, 2018, p. 5). These megafirms sit on top of over a million corporations that collectively put into being about 80 percent of total business investment.[3] In 2007, approximately 6 percent of households owned over 80 percent of the outstanding stock, with the top 1 percent owning over 50 percent (Kennickell, 2009, p. 63). From 1929—the first year in which the U.S. government records gross saving—until the present, gross corporate profits in the United States have generated the largest part of gross saving, with some part of personal saving derivable from such profits.[4] As will be discussed in Chapter 2, these aggregate profits derive primarily from aggregate investment expenditures.

At the level of wealth taken as a totality, wealth has become increasingly more concentrated. In 2013, the top 1 percent of family units held between 36 and 42 percent of total wealth,[5] with the largest gains over the preceding decades going to those at the very top of the wealth pyramid. The hierarchical concentration narrows as if dictated by a mathematical fractal. From 1978 until 2012, the top 1 percent roughly doubled its share of total wealth. The top one-tenth of 1 percent tripled its wealth share to claim half of the top 1 percent's share, with the top one-hundredth of 1 percent claiming half of that (Saez and Zucman, 2016, pp. 552–553).

Examining the quest for gross profits provides us with a wide window to inquire into the distribution of income and wealth. The window also invites inquiry into the historical framework of capital accumulation and alternations in government policy. The distribution of income and wealth is both cause and effect of the saving-investment process. In the absence of explicit planning, demand for product and investment ultimately derives from the class arrangements that determine income and wealth. In contrast to wealthier families where savings make up a much larger portion of their income than others, most working-class families consume the vast portion of their income with some substantial portion consuming more than their income (Medlen, 2008, p. 859). Correspondingly, alternations in income distribution alter consumption, investment and growth. A tilt in income distribution towards working-class families, for example, would bolster aggregate consumption, induce larger amounts of investment and additional employment. It might also, by reason of expanded production, enlarge aggregate profits.

Despite the fact that the main saving-investment process surrounds the corporate form of profit-plowback, elementary mainstream economics—as exemplified in modern textbooks—still retains the tautological but now archaic understanding that saving is simply the reverse side of consumption. In understanding saving as a "residual," this portrayal of saving reflects a much earlier period of artisan and mercantile accumulation where "abstinence" from consumption allowed an embryonic accumulation of capital. Profit seeking and abstinence were part of the same artisan framework.[6] As tautology, saving-as-residual is true by definition. But in the modern period of (say) the last 150 years when the very rich could not possibly consume their income—even if they single-mindedly attempted to try—and where the bulk of saving is generated through corporate gross profits, understanding saving as a residual is to substitute tautology for understanding.

Modern government policy operates in the service of expanding investment and so underpins the quest for private gain. It does so through assorted subsidies and subventions, tax breaks and government contracts, and a monetary policy designed to facilitate the financing of private investment opportunities whose availability—apart from significant downturn—is simply assumed. This availability assumption is largely predicated on faith, which boom times heavily reinforce. This facilitation of investment is unconsciously founded on the assumption that the pursuit of profit through investment is the only way—or, at least the only way meriting discussion—in which employment and income can be dispensed to the underlying population. The social goal of high employment and income generation is tied inexorably to the private pursuit of profit. The institutional arrangements for profit-seeking investment are simply taken for granted as a boundary line that is not to be violated.

The boundary line dictating that investment be undertaken by private parties is tantamount to understanding that direct government production and investment—as opposed to government expenditure—be shrunk to an irreducible minimum. The boundary line requires that government should not produce goods and services that could otherwise be provided through private markets. The widest possible area for profit-making should be preserved. This understanding is rarely expressed explicitly. Rather, prevailing discussion concerns government *interference* with private markets, as opposed to the possibility of *direct government production*, a possibility that only rarely materializes. Economists of conservative persuasion are the main carriers of this markets-only ideology. Societal maintenance, a strong defense budget and sufficient policing to maintain civilized society are to be supported by government. And that is all. Regarding public policy, this triad constitutes the limits of conservative imagination. Government services, such as educational services, might well be modified to allow private initiative through vouchers; regulations tailored to protect the environment and workers should be minimized so as to allow maximum growth; any and all measures in support of self-reliance—particularly the reduction of entitlements that might interfere with such reliance—are to be encouraged; even government sponsorship of health care is understood to stifle private initiative.[7]

Those committed to an active fiscal policy conceive of a larger role for government in managing aggregate demand. But here, again, deference is paid to the for-profit core of the investment process. Fiscal advocates often critically assess the outsized U.S. military expenditures which make up the bulk of federal expenditures on consumption and investment. But outside of infrastructure development, paying bills for health and education, and expanding transfer payments, fiscal advocates rarely suggest actual projects that would direct government production. Demand management is itself the goal, providing incentives for profitable investment that *might* result in satisfactory if not full employment.

Those who advocate larger government expenditures often invoke the fiscal advocacy associated with John Maynard Keynes. This invocation typically calls for enlarged amounts of government spending to maintain employment, rather than any prescription for government production. Keynes's own view was more nuanced. In Robert Skidelsky's understanding, Keynes tried to carve out a "middle" way whereby public enterprises devoted to the general welfare would coexist with privately owned productive facilities (Skidelsky, 1995, pp. 219–241). Keynes was a pragmatist whose advocacy for assorted projects and policies largely depended upon immediate context. For example, in the mid-to-late 1920s, Keynes supported Lloyd George in his call for state construction and advocated a "big construction program of capital works—in housing, road building and electrification" (p. 185). In his *General Theory of Employment, Interest and Money* (1936), Keynes contemplated the future possibility of a "somewhat comprehensive socialization of investment" (p. 378). But for all of this, Keynes's advocacy of state intervention remained quite vague. For the direction of state involvement Keynes referred to the "common will, embodied in the policy of the State" (p. 377). Keynes's placement of State policy in the service of the "common will" begged the question of what the common will consisted of and, most importantly, how the common will related to the disproportionate state power exercised by the dominant classes carrying out the investment process.

Free cash

Free cash is the cash (profit after tax plus depreciation) left over after new business investment. From a societal perspective, free cash measures how much remuneration the wealthy receive after carrying out their social role in providing employment and income through investment. Free cash derives from capitalists' consumption that partially self-funds through security payouts, with the remainder available for speculative purposes, mergers, stock repurchases and capital export. As will be discussed, free cash has been involved in imperialist expansion as well as being foundational in an assortment of speculative excesses. The last part of this book shows how free cash has expanded in recent decades and makes an argument for a larger governmental role in production and investment. It also makes an argument for higher taxes on the wealthy so as to minimize the speculative episodes that have periodically imploded in downturns. High taxes on cash would simultaneously rectify—at least in part—the greatly expanded rise of inequality of income and wealth that has arisen partly as a result of free cash spillage in the stock market. High taxes on cash would also allow for much greater monetary means for governmental investment projects aimed at a variety of human needs underserved by existing markets.

As a term, free cash was first coined by Michal Jensen in understanding the leveraged buyout movement of the 1980s (Jensen, 1986).[8] But as a macro concept for understanding free cash generation across the entire economy, free cash owes its mathematical formulation to Michael Kalecki (1899–1970), who, in the 1930s, understood that government deficits and export surpluses would generate gross profits (cash) in excess of new investment and capitalists' consumption. I provide a skeletal model of Kalecki's formulation in Chapter 2, and an expanded version in Chapter 6, where I explore the relationship of both government deficit spending and non-corporate deficit spending to free cash. Kalecki's understanding that government deficits expand the savings pool stands in stark contradiction to the familiar "Twins Deficit" thesis whereby government deficits are alleged to crowd out investment through the siphoning-off of saving.

Kalecki's formulation of free cash and deficits was constructed under the conditions of the Great Depression. In consequence, he did not spell out the full ramifications of how free cash could be spilled in domestic markets through mergers, dividends and speculative endeavors. But he did understand that imperialist adventures were partially caused by the inability of capitalists to dispose of free cash without capital export. I take up the issue of imperialism in Chapter 3 where I explore John Atkinson Hobson's early theory of imperialism. Hobson applied free cash theory (without the name) to not only European colonial expansion but also to the neo-colonial expansion of the U.S., exemplified most spectacularly in the territorial grab associated with the Spanish–American War. Hobson also understood the monopolization process of the late nineteenth century as a generator of free cash and so linked monopoly to imperialism. In a theme also taken up by Thorstein Veblen—Hobson's contemporary—Hobson understood that monopoly generated free cash by restricting output and investment in the service of higher prices and profits.

Over the next decades of the twentieth and twenty-first centuries, outlets for free cash turned inwards towards mergers and speculation. For the 1920s, I estimate in Chapter 4 the free cash that drove the second merger wave that swallowed over 7,000 firms through acquisitions (Thorp, 1931, p. 78); Soule, [1947] 1975, p. 142), and provided a source of stockbroker loans outside of traditional banking conduits (Kindleberger, 1973, p. 113). Beyond certain limits, cash could not profitably be invested in new facilities within the recently formed oligopolistic structures. As a consequence, free cash drained into acquisitions. In the 1920s, mergers were particularly prevalent in utilities and manufacturing when the associated forces for expansion like the automobile and suburbanization drove the larger boom. In addition to providing stock market cash through loans, free cash contributed to the stock bubble of the decade through acquisition premiums accorded to targeted firms. Free cash also contributed to the manic psychology accorded to the prospect that any stock purchase might soon be a target. Willard L. Thorp noted that for the 1920s decade a major factor was "undoubtedly the large profits which many concerns have made during the period of expansion . . . It is not surprising that the expansiveness of the businessman during periods of prosperity often expresses itself in the merger movement and large business organizations."[9]

The 1920s was the first boom superimposed on quasi-monopoly foundations, established earlier in the Great Merger Wave of 1895–1904. Utilizing an analysis first employed by Thorstein Veblen, I explore in Chapter 5 how this transformation into monopoly pricing power split apart a new discounted stream valuation of capital from a more traditional form of capital valuation based on replacement costs. The replacement valuation of capital descended from earlier competitive conditions. In Veblen's analysis, the higher valuations accorded to firms with monopoly power indicated their ability to restrict production and investment. These higher valuations also registered the speculative excesses that were to blow up in 1929.

In the prosperity after World War II, Veblen's dichotomization of capital valuation—expressed as the ratio between stock valuation and replacement cost (Tobin's Q)—served as the basis of an investment theory. Rather than being a simple indicator of monopoly power, higher Qs would allegedly drive investment ahead. Entrepreneurs and existing firms could reap stock gains by producing new assets and selling them on the stock market. I show that Tobin's Q theory fails a basic empirical test in reference to firms' choice of expansion between mergers and investment. I formulate a new theory of mergers based on *relative* valuation and show that when a higher distribution of income flows towards capital the value of older capital acquired through mergers rises relative to new investment. This accords well with a free cash theory of mergers. Extra cash means extra monetary means for consolidation. This result also suggests a tie-in between stagnation of investment, stock market gains and wealth inequality. Monies flowing towards mergers are monies flowing towards owners of targeted firms, who, in respect of existing fact, are disproportionately wealthy. And so the great circle: higher income inequality—when returns to capital expand relative to output—drives wealth inequality.

In Chapter 6, I discuss the declining growth rate of investment dating from the late 1960s and relate this stagnation to the post-WWII oligopoly-stagnation theses of Joseph Steindl, Paul Baran and Paul Sweezy. These theses hark back to the monopoly-stagnation theses of Hobson and Veblen. Along with oligopoly-stagnation theorists, I argue that the most recent stagnation is the result of long-term forces. In turn, I examine the simulative impact of both government and consumer debt and mathematically derive a neo-Kaleckian model that helps explain the post-WWII rise of government and consumer deficit spending, free cash and its speculative effluent. Government deficits are understood as a response to the massive lowering of taxes on the wealthy and the need for stimulation under stagnant investment growth. Consumer debt is understood as a predictable response to a flattening of wages, induced by a very large decline in manufacturing employment, stagnant investment growth and the globalization of production.

In light of the U.S. multinationals' expansion of the last half century, I argue in Chapter 7 that Kalecki's specification of free cash, deficit spending and the trade balance needs a major reformulation. For the period prior to World War II and immediately thereafter, U.S. export surpluses created free cash in the way that Kalecki had formulated. However, unlike this earlier period where trade predominated, multinational production and use of import supply lines are now the dominant ways in which large firms seek out foreign markets and generate cash. In *the absence of the cash-generating domestic* deficits of the U.S. government and private parties, the large and growing trade deficits of the last forty years would have cut into domestic free cash. But with enlarged and growing cash flows generated through deficit spending, cutbacks on investment due to multinational production and use of imports may actually have expanded free cash aggregates over and above the levels that would have otherwise obtained. I argue that this multinational generation of free cash is structurally located and has been (and is now) largely immune to exchange-rate declines in the value of the dollar.

The simultaneous rise of deficit spending in all its forms and the offshoring of production and investment allows for understanding the recent rise in free cash. As free cash provides the wherewithal for mergers, such a composite also allows for an understanding of the increasing concentration of industry and monopoly power associated with the recent stagnation of corporate growth.

Chapter 8 deals with the recent rise of inequality of income and wealth and shows how free cash spillage gives additional credence to Thomas Piketty's thesis relating inequality to the capital/output ratio and the rate of return on capital. The neo-Kaleckian model is put to additional use in showing how deficit spending of all types is spilled into the stock market, expanding inequality while at the same time lowering rates of return on equity, interest rates and increasing the prices of speculative assets. As these lowered interest rates were a primary factor in generating the most recent housing bubble, a neo-Kaleckian understanding allows additional insight into the Great Recession commencing in the latter part of 2007.

The final chapter argues for a larger governmental role in the investment process. The chapter illustrates the case with short sketches of how government investment in health and energy could significantly raise the standard of living of people while simultaneously providing for additional employment and security. Following on John Kenneth Galbraith's understanding that human "needs" should be distinguished from "wants," I advocate government investment targeting the satisfaction of "needs." With such targeting, human welfare would not depend upon the magnitude of growth but rather its direction. The present ongoing drumbeat for enlarged growth reflects the view that existing investment patterns are not to be altered; indeed, given the legacy assets of major corporations, such patterns will not be altered unless the government redirects the general course. Under existing arrangements, enlarged growth is the only mechanism that can trickle down to sustain employment and welfare. I argue that with public investment directed towards human needs, a slowing down of the rate of growth would not only be compatible with an expansion of human welfare but would also allow for an ecologically sound economy. I argue too that such government direction over the investment process would be best accomplished with high taxes on the wealthy. Such taxes could not only finance a better national economy but would simultaneously fight inequality and claim the free cash that drives speculation.

In reference to health, I propose a parallel government health system comprised of tuition-subsidized medical schools, government pharmaceutical establishments, and a partial buyout of existing hospital facilities. Buyouts of hospitals and other health facilities would minimize political opposition and should be employed when possible. A parallel government health system need not replace the existing for-profit system but would induce competition that would lower health costs across the board. The federal government has the financial wherewithal to carry this project forward. Most importantly, health, along with food and shelter, are recognized to be at the base of the needs structure. To ration health in accordance with income—as is done presently—is as unnecessary as it is debasing.

In reference to energy, I propose a government buyout of vested interests to facilitate a national grid freed from overlapping jurisdictions and devoted to solar energy. As the fuel is free, solar energy could totally revamp the growth process. Applied to the aging railroad systems of the U.S. and to newly fabricated mass transit systems, solar energy would cheapen transportation costs and allow expanded production in areas now characterized as industrial wastelands. In contrast to the present situation where the migratory displacement of labor towards new job hubs devastates existing communities, bringing jobs to people would allow communities to be rehabilitated and preserved. Needless to say, massive solar networks would move society towards sustainability and ecological health.

A final comment: apart from a discussion surrounding J.A. Hobson's early thesis of imperialism and the multinational dimension of U.S. production, the book focuses almost exclusively on the U.S. economy. It should be noted, however, that the recent slowdown of U.S. growth finds an overseas parallel in the vast bulk of OECD countries. The U.S. falling tax rates on the wealthy also finds an overseas parallel. Whether recent U.S. free cash expansion finds a global counterpart is a question still to be answered.

In reference to the development of inequality, the present book's U.S. focus leaves major gaps. Financial flows across borders—amounting to trillions of dollars a day—have generated a super-large speculative arena and a new concentration of global wealth. Some have begun the trek of understanding this new globalization of financial gain and the global divergence of income and wealth.[10] Others will certainly follow.

In reference to government investment processes related to needs, there is the further question of agency—the question of how to politically confront the massive inertia and resistance of propertied interests and others committed to a markets-only understanding of how a modern economy should work. This is indeed a gap. I have no ready answers. Proposals directed towards health and energy, however, do take up those industries that would have the most extensive implications for enhancing human welfare. Accordingly, the possible engagement of large numbers of people in advocacy for such change is greater in these critical industries than in others. Certainly, the argument for government production is most easily made when the implications for enhancing human betterment is maximal.

The markets for goods and services related to "wants"—particularly the "higher wants" relating to ostentatious automobiles, luxurious homes, jewelry and the like—would be shrunk if sufficiently high taxes were employed on exorbitant wealth and high incomes. Such shrinkage would have the adventitious consequence of freeing up resources that could be directed towards basic human needs.

Notes

1 See the discussion in Evsey D. Domar, 1957, especially Chapter 5. In the simplest model, the capacity to produce depends proportionately on the capital stock, so that changes in capacity depend proportionately on changes in the capital stock, or levels of investment. In contrast, changes in the ability to buy depend on the Keynesian multiplier multiplied by changes in investment, or the *change in the change of the capital stock.* For changes in the ability to buy to equilibrate with changes in capacity, investment growth would have to be proportional to the saving/income ratio multiplied by the capacity/capital stock ratio. Expansion of the saving/income ratio—in rough measure the expansion of gross profits to the total economy—and the growth of more efficient capital—reflected in a rise in the capacity/capital stock ratio require a faster rate of investment growth to avoid excess capacity. Such a rigid specification of growth requirements gives at least a partial understanding of why under-utilized capacity might well be normal and why the economy needs government stabilization measures designed to expand purchasing power.

2 Total fixed non-residential business investment from the Department of Commerce; corporate investment from the Federal Reserve, *Flow of Funds Accounts.* Subtraction of the latter from the former allows a calculation of non-corporate business investment.

3 See endnote 2; number of corporations specified are "C" corporations. "S" corporations make up close to 4 million firms.

4 In 2016, undistributed gross profits (retained earnings plus depreciation changes) were almost twice the gross saving of households and institutions. As saving from dividends derive from gross corporate profit, this approximate two-fold difference should be considered a conservative estimate (table 5.1, Department of Commerce).

5 Differing estimates depend on various methodologies. Emmanuel Saez and Gabriel Zucman (2016) cite the higher figure; Jesse Bricker et. al. (2016) cite the lower.

6 Like other conceptions that misguide inquiry, this understanding is not entirely false. Wealthy families do have personal savings and can, as individual entities, sell off stock to others. Today, consumption is the central core of macroeconomic theory, not the pursuit of profit. In the simplest model, consumption is functionally related to the level of income. Investment, government spending and net exports are understood as "exogenous." More complex models allow investment to be determined by income and the interest rate. Equilibrium is established when saving and investment equilibrate. The categories of consumption investment, government and net exports allow a separate discussion and categorization of each, leading the student of economics to the taxonomical conclusion that the economy is indeed a complex arrangement of interdependent economic items.

7 A full accounting of alleged government oversteps can be found in Milton and Rose Friedman's *Free to Choose*, 1980.

8 Jensen was interested in various industries and firms, not the macro economy. In Jensen's definition, free cash was monies left over after capital expenditures, where capital expenditures were not necessarily confined to new investment propelling growth. Free cash, as used in the current book, is calculated only in reference to new investment.

9 Cited in Reid, 1968, p. 67.

10 See, for example, Galbraith, 2008, 2012; Thompson, 2008; Stiglitz, 2015.

References

Bricker, Jesse, Alice Henriques, Jacob Krimmel and John Sabelhaus, "Measuring Income and Wealth at the Top Using Administrative and Survey Data," *Brookings Papers on Economic Activity*, Spring 2016.

Caruso, Anthony, "Statistics of U.S. Businesses: Employment and Payroll Summary 2012," U.S. Department of Commerce, Economics and Statistics Administration, U.S. *Census Bureau*, February 2015.

Domar, Evsey, D. *Essays in the Theory of Economic Growth*, Oxford University Press, New York and Oxford, 1957.

Friedman, Milton and Rose Friedman, *Free to Choose: A Personal Statement*, Harcourt Brace Jovanovich, New York and London, 1980.

Galbraith, James K. *Inequality and Instability: A Study of the World Economy Just Before the Great Crisis*, Oxford University Press, Oxford, 2012.

Galbraith, James K. "Global Inequality and Global Macro Economics," in *Global Inequality*, edited by David Held and Ayse Jata, Polity Press, Cambridge, 2008, pp. 148–175.

Grullon, Gustavo, John Hund and James P. Weston, "Concentrating on Q and Cash Flow," *Journal of Financial Intermediation*, Vol. 30, Issue C, 2018, pp. 1–15.

Heilbroner, Robert L. *The Nature and Logic of Capitalism*, W.W. Norton & Co., New York and London, 1985.

Jensen, Michael, "Agency Costs of Free Cash Flow, Corporate Finance and Takeovers," *American Economic Review*, Papers and Proceedings, 1986, pp. 322–329.

Kennickell, Arthur, "Ponds and Streams: Wealth and Income in the U.S., 1989 to 2007," working paper, Board of Governors, January 7, 2009.

Keynes, John Maynard, *The General Theory of Employment, Interest and Money*, Harcourt, Brace Jovanovich, New York, [1936] 1964.

Kindleberger, Charles P., *The World in Depression, 1929–1939*, University of California Press, Berkeley and Los Angeles, 1973.

Medlen, Craig, "Galbraith Preference Mappings: Needs and Want, Evidence from the 2005 Budget Study, Notes and Communications," *Journal of Economic Issues*, Vol. XLII, No. 3, September 2008, pp. 853–862.

Reid, Samuel Richardson, *Mergers, Managers, and the Economy*, McGraw-Hill Book Company, New York, 1968.

Saez, Emmanuel and Gabriel Zucman, "Wealth Inequality in the United States since 1913: Evidence from Capitalized Income Tax Data," *Quarterly Journal of Economics*, Vol. 131, No. 2, 2016, pp. 519–578.

Skidelsky, Robert, *John Maynard Keynes, The Economist as Savior, 1920–1937*, Penguin Books, New York, 1995.

Soule, George, *The Prosperity Decade: From War to Depression 1917–1929*, M.E. Sharpe, Inc., New York, [1947] 1975.

Stiglitz, Joseph E., *The Great Divide: Unequal Societies and What We Can Do About Them*, W.W. Norton & Co., New York and London, 2015.

Thompson, Grahame F. "Global Inequality, the 'Great Divergence' and the Supranational Regionalization," in *Global Inequality*, edited by David Held and Ayse Kaya, Polity Press, Cambridge, 2008, pp. 176–203.

Thorp, Willard L., "The Persistence of the Merger Movement," pp. 74–89, *American Economic Review*, Papers and Proceedings of the Forty-third Annual Meeting, Vol. XXI, No. 1, March 1931.

2 Michal Kalecki's derivation of free cash

Free cash studies have inevitably discussed inherent limits on new capital expenditures relative to cash generated. Such studies have focused mainly on mergers and acquisitions in particular historical periods, relating industrial formations to methods of financing.[1]

At a macro level, however, free cash explanations surrounding specific industrial and historical considerations appear unduly narrow, particularly in light of the ubiquitous spread of oligopoly formations across the economy and across time. For as long as growth proceeds upwards, the monopoly power invested in oligopolistic formations *will tend* to generate excess cash. Monopoly pricing power allows high returns. Monopolistic pricing power also involves restriction of production and investment in support of administered prices and high markups. At least since the 1920s, oligopoly formations exhibiting monopoly pricing power have permeated virtually the whole of the economy outside of residential construction, trade in services and the ground floor of agriculture.[2] In consequence, a case-by-case explanation of free cash generation can only fall short in explaining how *aggregate totals of free cash* expand and how such expansion furthers merger activity and capital spillage in general.

The key to understanding the macro-generation of aggregate free cash totals surrounds not just the oligopoly formations of modern industry, but the consumption level of the capitalist class and the deficit spending of both government and private parties. In grappling with understanding the Great Depression of the 1930s, Michal Kalecki was the first to express this insight in reference to government deficits. He noted that "A budget deficit has an effect similar to that of an export surplus. It . . . permits profits to increase above the level determined by private investment and capitalists' consumption" (Kalecki, [1933] 1971, p. 85). During the Depression, merger and speculative activity came to a near-halt. So Kalecki understandably did not foresee the full importance of free cash for understanding mergers and speculative activity. In Kalecki's view, government deficits provided both remedial sustenance through additional purchasing power and an expansion of profits that might be directed, under favorable circumstances, towards additional investment.

Reasoning from the simplest possible thought experiment, Kalecki first assumed a closed economy without government or trade and with the working class consuming all of the wage bill:

Production (Y) consists of consumption (C), divided between workers' consumption (Cw) and capitalists consumption ($C\pi$) and investment (I), which generates income divided between gross profit (profits (π)+ depreciation (Dep)) and (wages (W)). Under the assumption that all workers' wages are consumed (W = Cw):

$$(1) \quad Y = Cw + C\pi + I = W + (\pi + Dep) = W + C\pi + I$$

$$\text{Or: (1a)} \quad \pi + Dep = C\pi + I$$

This latter identity does not distinguish between cause and effect. But Kalecki reasoned that capitalists cannot determine their profit. But they *can make decisions on investment and consumption* and if current gross profits are inadequate to finance these decisions, these decisions can still be financed through debt. Accordingly, "capitalists earn what they spend" (Feiwel, 1977, p. 85).

This last point deserves emphasis. Total output (Y) as in (1) above depicts the division of income into its components, with the capitalists' share arising out of their behavioral (causal) activity. Consequently, Kalecki transforms what would otherwise be just an identity into a short-term model.

From (1a), it is apparent that a certain amount of capitalists' consumption will be mirrored by an exact amount of Free Cash, defined narrowly as (π + Dep – I). Capitalists' consumption thus provides aggregate excess cash for firms to dispose of or to be returned in funding the consumption.

Kalecki extended the concept of gross profit generation by showing that in addition to investment, government deficit spending and export surpluses (modified here as a positive Current Account[3]) allow for both the expansion of aggregate gross profits and the generation of *gross profits in excess of new investment and capitalists' consumption.*[4] To show this, modify (1) above to include government expenditures financed through taxes (T) and the fiscal deficit (FD) and the Current Account (CA) and allow W* and (π +Dep)* to be after-tax receipts of workers and capitalists respectively.

$$(2) \quad Y = Cw + C\pi + I + T + FD + CA = W^* + (\pi + Dep)^* + T$$

Simplifying and again noting the assumption that workers consume all their income. (i.e. Cw = W*),

$$Cw + C\pi + I + FD + CA = W^* + (\pi + Dep)^*$$

$$(2a) \quad (\pi + Dep)^* = C\pi + I + FD + CA$$

To summarize: "capitalists earn what they spend" plus the spending associated with government deficits and the current account. Note that a negative current account subtracts from profits.

We can rearrange (2a) to arrive at Free Cash, defined in this model as net of corporate taxes:

$$\text{(2b)} \quad \text{Free Cash} = ((\pi + \text{Dep})^* - \text{I}) = \text{C}\pi + \text{F.D.} + \text{CA}$$

An expansion of government deficit spending and/or a positive current account generates free cash over and above capitalists' consumption. Investment need not expand for additional cash to flow into businesses.

It should be noted that the free cash model (2b) is a stripped-down model. In Chapter 6, I enlarge the model to encompass personal saving, non-business investment such as residential construction and deficit spending outside of the government sector. I will show how non-government deficit spending—such as consumer deficit spending—has an analogous effect to government deficit spending in enlarging free cash.

The free cash model (2b) is a stripped-down model also in that it neglects the impact of productivity advance—particularly the advance carried forth by new investment. In other writings, Kalecki was quite explicit about the impact of technological change,[5] particularly over the longer run. But in his short-term modeling of income determination—as represented by the model above—he abstracted from its impact. This neglect is equivalent to understanding a particular vintage of investment in one period as equivalent to another of the same magnitude in another period. Productivity advance, however, allows an expanded level of output and an expanded level of income receipts. It also allows for an expansion of free cash. In particular, an enlarged income accruing to capitalists will expand their consumption and, in accordance with (2b), will enlarge free cash quite independently of any enlargement of deficit spending or the current account.

Although limited to short-term income determination, Kalecki's model gives insight into how government deficit spending and a positive current account *might* enhance stability. A neoclassical perspective relies on a plow-back of saving into more productive investment to generate growth. But it assumes that a willingness to save will in fact be translated into investment. Under conditions of excess capacity, the Kaleckian perspective disallows any such optimistic assumption as an automatic response. Under a Kaleckian understanding, deficit spending and current account surpluses encourage investment by enhancing aggregate demand. They also allow for a measure of free cash that permits investment in future periods to expand beyond current levels, *without requiring firms to take on additional debt to finance such investment.* This is not to deny that savers and investors are often different and that debt enables the conversion of savings into investment. But at the aggregate level, free cash constitutes internally generated funds that could be placed into future investment.

Government deficit spending and a positive current account therefore allows (but does not guarantee) a reduction in private debt and risk in pursuit of capital expansion. Kalecki never stressed the point but his free cash conception links inexorably to his "Principle of Increasing Risk."[6] Tracy Mott summarizes Kalecki's "Principle" noting that the "size of the [firm's] own capital" is the limiting factor on the expansion of the firm. This limit arises

> because the more of one's own wealth tied up in a particular fixed investment, the more danger one [is] exposed to in the event of failure and the more trouble one would be under in case of a sudden need for liquidity.

This emphasis on "increasing risk" helps in understanding the priority of internal cash flow financing as opposed to outside financing. Debt is both dangerous and liquidity absorbing as interest is paid out. Equity finance, is safer but "dilutes the value of the investment to the original shareholders (Mott, 2010, pp. 5–6).

Although certainly helpful in understanding the priority of internal financing, the "Principle of Increasing Risk" certainly needs qualification. Confronted with the possibility of market saturation, mature firms need to inject additional liquid capital—often in large amounts—to maintain and expand markets. As going concerns, firms often require new investments geared towards innovation simply to stay alive. That said, free cash allows for additional firm expansion through the reduction of risk. Of course, there is no assurance that such expanded investment will take place, or that debt will be correspondingly reduced with additional cash flow. Indeed, the latter chapters of the present work show that investment growth has slowed considerably over the last few decades with expanded amounts of corporate debt underpinned by the use of free cash as a collateral base. In that government deficits generate the free cash that supports corporate leverage, there exists a hierarchy of debt layering whereby sovereign debt allows an increasingly risky upper layer of corporate obligations. The latter chapters also show that the larger part of recent free cash generation has been directed towards mergers and speculative ends.

Investment is self-funding

The Kaleckian analysis above is an extended and class-based version of the Keynesian propositions that investment is self-funding and that government deficits help stabilize an unstable economy. Kalecki and Keynes worked independently so it should not be thought that Kalecki simply modified Keynes's analysis. But in showing that investment creates gross savings (the lion's share of saving is either gross profit (profits plus depreciation) or derives from gross profit through security payouts), both theorists reversed the causal sequence of the saving-investment process. This reversal of causality qualifies as the most important advance in comprehending the saving-investment process at the aggregate level under conditions of excess capacity. In contrast to the micro-view of the firm where investment derives from gross profits (saving) and its future prospects, Keynes and Kalecki understood that at the macro-level of an underemployed economy, investment created the saving necessary to fund the investment.

The circumstances of the Great Depression gave birth to this new understanding. Saving could only be realized if there was sufficient income to save. Investment drove the economy and the growth of income. In consequence, high investment was one with high incomes and thereby high saving. In Keynes's critique of the classics, Keynes maintained that the causal presumption of savings driving investment required an unwarranted assumption that resources of labor and capital were fully utilized. Such an assumption meant that every "decline in consumption meant an increase in investment to absorb the labor released. The rate of investment is then governed by the desire of the community to save." But with underutilized resources, "It is the rate of investment which governs the rate of saving and not *vice versa*" (Robinson, [1942] 1991, pp. 65–66).

In addition to showing how investment is self-funding, Kalecki's formulation of free cash also shows how capitalists' consumption could be self-funding through payouts in dividends and interest. As shown by the free cash formulations in both (1a) and (2b), a growing level of capitalists' consumption will appear on the income statements of businesses as an enlargement of gross profits in excess of new investment. This excess cash is now available to fund the high level of capitalists' consumption from which the free cash derives. This possibility of consumption funding does not mean that capitalists' consumption is necessarily financed through free cash, or that free cash is disgorged towards dividends and interest in any exact measure. Such finance might well involve other sources such as debt. In addition to interest and dividends, free cash might well be spilled in merger activity, or be available for capital export, or, in more recent decades, spilled in stock repurchases. As businesses can use free cash as an indicator of economic health and collateral for debt, free cash generation also permits cash spillage in excess of free cash through debt financing. As will be shown in Chapter 8, the simultaneous rise of free cash and debt has been particularly prevalent in recent decades.

The self-funding nature of investment and consumption is instructive in terms of depression economics. It is also instructive in clarifying the relationship of monopoly power and the associated cash making up the bulk of saving. In contrast to the price competition of the mid-nineteenth century, the later trusts and monopoly structures dating from the latter part of that century aimed to increase profits (saving) by crimping production and investment. Unlike the microeconomics of the firm whereby investment restriction acts to maintain monopoly pricing and profit, at the macro level, such crimping of investment stifles growth and profit. The fallacy of composition obtains. Individual monopolies and oligopolistic structures exhibiting monopoly pricing power can grow profits while restricting investment if the overall economy grows. But if the aggregate economy is infused with monopoly power, both investment and profits (saving) would tend to decline along with the economy. Given Keynes's reputation as the main theorist of the Great Depression, it is somewhat ironic that he never inquired into how the industrial structure might bring on stagnation. Kalecki came closer to the mark by relating the "degree of monopoly" to the division of income, whereby an expansion of monopoly led to an expansion of profits and investment slowdown ([1952] 2009, pp. 11–41).[7]

In relating spending propensities to the class division of income, the Kaleckian version of the investment-driven savings process constituted a distinct improvement over that of Keynes. By pointing to the high levels of worker consumption and the discretionary nature of capitalist investment, Kalecki's analysis pointed to how planned investment could sustain the economy, without the uncertainties associated with private accumulation.[8] No longer dependent on the prospects and risks attendant to obtaining private profit, planned investment could maintain economic growth without interruption. Keynes's analysis pointed in the same direction, particularly in Chapter 12 of the *General Theory* where he discusses the precariousness of assessing future investment prospects under a "State of Long-Term Expectation." But Keynes himself could never embrace a socialist outcome other than to suggest that if taxation and monetary policy and "perhaps other measures" failed, "a somewhat comprehensive socialization of investment will prove the only means of securing an approximation to full employment." This offhand remark was accompanied by the proviso that a quasi-socialist outcome would be a last-ditch measure and would not preclude "all manner of compromises and of devices by which public authority will co-operate with private initiative" (Keynes, [1936] 1964, p. 378).

Kalecki's sharp-edged notion that consumption and purchasing power would expand with a redistribution of income towards wages was also implicated in Keynes's analysis. But Keynes never emphasized this aspect of his theory. Keynes introduced an aggregate "propensity to consume" that would decline with expanded income across the entire economy. But in contrast to the Kaleckian version of class-based consumption where wages were assuredly spent, Keynes provided his famous psychological law rooted in the "community": "that when aggregate real income is increased aggregate consumption is increased but not so much as income" (Keynes, [1936] 1964, p. 27). This diminishing "propensity to consume" with income certainly suggests the possibility of a class-based analysis, with the aggregate propensity to consume enlarged with an increased wage bill relative to gross profits and assorted incomes flowing into the upper classes. But by framing the "propensity to consume" in light of the whole economy, Keynes's analysis bypassed any explicit analysis of the distribution of income and its macro-implications. This omission is glaring in light of Keynes's multiplier analysis. As the power of the multiplier effect depends critically on the propensity to consume, one might have expected Keynes to recommend an income redistribution towards wages in the service of expanding the multiplier. But no such recommendations are to be found in Keynes's work.

Apart from understanding how government deficits can create free cash, the Kaleckian identity (2b) is important for understanding how a positive current account (Kalecki's "export surplus") relates to foreign debt. A positive current account means that the world owes the "export surplus" country. Such a surplus thus involves foreign debt. A country's imports are another's exports. So any *exclusive trade among the advanced world* producing largely substitutable products would simply be a "beggar-thy-neighbor" war, with each nation attempting to expand production and profits at the expense of the other. Net importers would arrive at debtor status as a derivative of their inability to compete. However, with colonialism or any type of foreign domination of others, a rich developed country *can put debt on the colonial sphere, so as to generate* a positive current account with that colonial sphere. So, in this case, cause and effect are reversed—instead of positive current accounts causing external debt, external debt can lead to positive current accounts. Kalecki expressed this important idea without elaboration, no doubt because he saw that

> The connection between "external" profits and imperialism is obvious. The fight for the division of existing foreign markets and the expansion of colonial empires, which provide new opportunities for export of capital associated with the export of goods, can be viewed as a drive for export surplus, the classical source of "external" profits. Armaments and wars, usually financed by budget deficits, are also a source of this kind of profits.
>
> (Kalecki, [1933] 1971, p. 85)

Kalecki never fully examined the empire-building that resulted in World War I and which spilled over into the World War II. But his reference to the "classical source" of "external" profits certainly referred to the territorial expansion by the European powers and the United States.

To the generation of "external" profits and its relationship to free cash we now turn to J.A. Hobson's theory of imperialism. Of necessity, this inquiry will be quite limited in scope, relating Hobson's theory of imperialism to the maldistribution of wealth and income within the advanced capitalist spheres, the monopoloid structures within modern capitalism, and the tendency to depression arising out of these monopoloid structures. Hobson's analysis of a tendency to depression is particularly important. His analysis was, as Keynes acknowledged in a critique contained within the *General Theory*, prefatory to Keynes's own work.[9] As will be shown, however, Keynes edited out of his own analysis the Hobsonian thesis of how monopoly related to imperialism. Keynes also understood Hobson's theory as an "underconsumption" theory as opposed to an "underinvestment theory" due to monopoly power.

Notes

1 The merger wave of the 1920s involved a great deal of horizontal mergers that were largely carried out by second-tier firms. Dominant firms left over from the Great Merger Wave were under the watchful eye of the Justice Department. The thinking at the time was that consolidation at a secondary level might allow expanded competition with the giants (Stigler, 1950). A similar anti-trust concern influenced the conglomerate merger wave of the 1960s. Conglomeration would expand overall concentration, but the octopus legs of the conglomerates tended to lessen concentration ratios in each industry entered. Free cash, however, could explain a large part of the 1960s merger wave (Mueller, 1969). In the buyout wave of the 1980s, high amounts of leverage were associated with large amounts of free cash. Such leverage justified its existence by directing free cash outward from acquiring corporations that could not use it toward target corporations that could. With debt finance, interest on bonds substituted for dividends with the advantage that interest paid reduced corporate taxes. By the late 1980s, debt-financed mergers left a third of them bankrupt (Holmstrom and Kaplan, 2001, p. 128). Over recent decades, banking consolidations can be partially explained by the expansion of finance in general and the proliferation of non-financial firms like General Electric and the great auto firms into financial services.

2 I say "ground floor" because while crops and farms often involve thousands of firms and parties, the narrows of food distributors, seeds, pesticides and agricultural equipment are largely dominated by oligopoly structures.

3 The current account deals with exports and imports of goods and services, but also with income and transfer remittances.

4 The mathematics in this section follows the logic of Kalecki, [1965] 2009, pp. 45–51.

5 See, for example, Kalecki, "A Theorem on Technical Process," [1941] 1991.

6 Kalecki credits M. Breit for the basic formulation of the "Principle of Increasing Risk" (Kalecki, [1937] 1990, p. 289).

7 The Keynesian revolution in thought surrounding the Great Depression came at the same time as theories of imperfect completion and oligopoly were being developed. For stagnation theorists like Paul Baran and Paul Sweezy, the key to situating the Keynesian revolution in history was to understand how the Depression related to the restrictionist tendencies of monopoly power. For clarifying remarks relating monopoly power to the Keynesian revolution, see Paul Sweezy ([1963] 1964, pp. 305–314); Baran and Sweezy (1966, pp. 54–58).

8 Joan Robinson, a friend of Kalecki, once noted that "The planning of investment is the key to economic control." Her reference was both to the former Yugoslavia and, in a somewhat too optimistic assessment, the "capitalist countries" that "now accept the necessity for planning" (Robinson, 1969, p. 186).

9 In a listing of just Hobson's 'most important works,' G.D.H. Cole (1940) lists forty books that Hobson wrote, not including the numerous works that Hobson contributed to various journals. Hobson's writings treat not just strictly economic themes, but social, political and psychological issues dealing with whole realms of culture, political accommodation and wars. Among a variety of other topics, Hobson wrote on the Boer War, the Egyptian question relating to the Suez Canal and the cotton imports flowing into Britain, the relationship of India and the Dominions to the larger Empire, the inter-imperialism of major powers in relation to China and South Africa, the aftermath of World War I, the elements making for progressive taxation and the difficult question of how tropical resources and foodstuffs could be garnered without imperialism. For readers interested in a recent and detailed overview of Hobson's development over time as well as the extensive literature surrounding Hobson's views to those of others, consult Cain (2002).

References

Baran, Paul and Paul Sweezy, *Monopoly Capital*, Monthly Review Press, New York, 1966.

Cain, P.J., *Hobson and Imperialism: Radicalism, New Liberalism, and Finance 1887–1938*, Oxford University Press, Oxford, New York, 2002.

Cole, G.D.H., "Obituary: J.A. Hobson," *The Economic Journal*, Vol. 50, No. 198/199, June–September 1940, pp. 347–360. Published by Wiley on behalf of the Royal Economic Society.

Feiwel, George R., *The Intellectual Capital of Michal Kalecki*, University of Tennessee Press, Knoxville, 1977.

Holmstrom, Bengt and Steven N. Kaplan, "Corporate Governance and Merger Activity in the United States: Making sense of the 1980s and 1990s," *Journal of Economic Perspectives*, Vol. 15, No. 2, Spring 2001, pp. 121–141.

Kalecki, Michal, *Selected Essays on the Dynamics of the Capitalist Economy 1933–1970*, Cambridge University Press, Cambridge, UK, 1971.

Kalecki, Michal, *Collected Works of Michal Kalecki*, Vol. 1, Clarendon Press, Oxford, 1990.

Kalecki, Michal, *Collected Works of Michal Kalecki*, Vol. II, Clarendon Press, Oxford, 1991.

Kalecki, Michal, *Theory of Economic Dynamics, An Essay on Cyclical and Long-Run Changes in Capitalist Economy*, Monthly Review Press, New York, [1952] 2009.

Keynes, *General Theory of Employment, Interest and Money*, Harvest/HBJ Book, Harcourt Brace Jovanovich, San Diego, CA, New York and London, [1936] 1964.

Mott, Tracy, *Kalecki's Principle of Increasing Risk and Keynesian Economics*, Routledge Studies in the History of Economics, Taylor and Francis, New York and Oxford, 2010.

Mueller, Dennis, "A Theory of Conglomerate Mergers," *Quarterly Journal of Economics*, Vol. LXXXIII, No. 4, November 1969, pp. 643–659.

Robinson, Joan, *An Essay on Marxian Economics*, Orion Editions arranged with the Macmillan Press, Ltd., Philadelphia, PA, [1942] 1991.

Robinson, Joan, "Socialist Affluence," in *Socialism, Capitalism & Economic Growth*, edited by C.H. Feinstein, Cambridge University Press, Cambridge, UK, 1969.

Stigler, George J. "Monopoly and Oligopoly by Merger," *The American Economic Review, Papers and Proceedings*, May 1950, Vol. XL, No. 2, pp. 23–34.

Sweezy, Paul, "The First Quarter Century," in *Keynes General Theory: Reports of Three Decades*, edited by Robert Lekachman, St. Martin's Press, Macmillan & Co. Ltd., New York and London, [1963] 1964.

3 Hobson's choice

Free cash export or domestic redistribution

Today, it is rare to hear a defense of outsized wealth and income inequality. But when a defense *is* mounted, it typically runs along lines familiar to persons living one hundred years ago. Superior merit is sometimes invoked, as tautologically evidenced by market outcomes or by asserting natural inequalities as to talent, brains and ambitions. Much less often and with much less credence, such merit is subliminally understood to be mysteriously transferable from inherited wealth. Most often, however, the defense runs along functional lines. At the level of the individual or firm, investment derives from savings. Consequently, there must be an economic class sufficiently wealthy so as to abstain from the consumption of its total income. Transforming this necessary condition into a larger virtue proceeds by way of an assessment that investment prospects are large and a conviction that in regard to private saving there can be no such thing as too much. The nineteenth century provides the benchmark. In a famous passage in the *Economic Consequences of the Peace*, Keynes wrote that

> Europe was so organized socially and economically as to secure the maximum accumulation of capital . . . Society was so framed as to throw a great part of the increased income into the control of the class least likely to consume it. The new rich of the nineteenth century were not brought up to large expenditures, and preferred the power which investment gave them to the pleasures of immediate consumption. In fact, it was precisely the *inequality* of the distribution of wealth which made possible those vast accumulations of great wealth and capital improvements which distinguished that age from all others.
>
> (Keynes, [1920] 1988, pp. 18–19; original emphasis)

Keynes was outlining not just the facts of inequality but its justification. Growth depended on a "double bluff or deception." The mass of the people would, through deference to authority or otherwise, tolerate a small portion of the "cake," on the understanding that the larger part of the cake would accrue to the capitalist class that would invest. The acquiescence of the masses mirrored an understanding that all persons could benefit from growth. As Keynes put it, "The duty of 'saving' became nine-tenths of virtue and the growth of the cake the object of true religion" (p. 20).

Keynes's description of nineteenth-century capital accumulation depicted a time when profitable prospects brought in "immense accumulations of fixed capital" (p. 19). In emphasizing the point, Keynes compared the "railways of the world" to the pyramids of Egypt, and obliquely referred to ancillary investments surrounding the conversion of sail to coal power and the development of factories based on steam (p. 19). Keynes also noted that the export of European capital to the world allowed the import of cheap food from North America and assorted materials and resources that sponsored domestic development. Although Keynes did not explicitly discuss the larger colonial question, he did mention that the interest receipts of exported capital helped the reinvestment process to allow

> as a reserve . . . against the less happy day when the *industrial labor of Europe* could no longer purchase on such easy terms the produce of other continents, and when the due balance would be threatened between its historical civilizations and the multiplying races of other climates and environments. Thus the whole of the European races tended to benefit alike from the development of new resources whether they pursued their culture at home or adventured it abroad.
>
> (pp. 22–23, emphasis added)

In noting the benefits accruing to industrial labor through the export of capital, these early writings of Keynes argued that the inequality surrounding the saving-investment process benefited the whole of society. Keynes's optimistic assessment could be challenged on several levels. Keynes's depiction avoided any discussion of the territorial captivity of native peoples and the associated violence that maintained imperial empires. That capital export might benefit "the whole of the European races" meant that sections of labor could be (and would be) ideologically absorbed to maintain their place within the capitalist orbit. It was in this vein that Lenin comprehended how the "super profits" acquired through the export of capital permitted the "bribery" of a new labor aristocracy (Lenin, [1917] 2011). Keynes never discussed the ideological absorption of the proletariat into the social fabric of capitalism. But given Keynes's subsequent revulsion against the Bolshevik experiment and his belief that the given social order was the only socially acceptable order available, such ideological absorption was fully in line with his desire for social maintenance and peace. In an essay written five years after *The Economic Consequences of the Peace*, Keynes wrote that "the *Class* war will find me on the side of the educated *bourgeoisie*" (Keynes, [1925] 1963, p. 324; original emphasis). For Keynes—ever the pragmatist—historical circumstances changed policy prescriptions; but for the nineteenth century, Keynes was fully convinced that capital export served the social order taken as a whole.

Others would register exception. Apart from Marxists, like Lenin, Nikolai Bukharin and Rosa Luxemburg, there were a variety of reformist critics of capital export who suggested that territorial expansion and a concomitant development of finance and commerce in the hinterland was just one way—and a depraved way—of achieving a higher level of material welfare.[1] Of these critics, John Atkinson Hobson was the most noteworthy. In *Imperialism* ([1902] 1965), Hobson distinguished between the older colonial structures and the new imperial reach that absorbed large areas of newly acquired lands that were inhospitable to European culture and commerce. Hobson argued that if only the mal-distribution of income within Europe was rectified in favor of the lower classes, domestically expanded markets could substitute for territorial expansion. Higher wages would feed mass consumption power and encourage larger amounts of investment. After first detailing the extensive growth of European domination over new territories in the latter part of the nineteenth century and minimizing or dismissing explanatory hypotheses such as extended commercial advantage and population growth that would account for such expansion, Hobson came to the conclusion that the wealthy had much too much wealth and income. Unable to profitably dispose of their excess saving on domestic investment due to the domestic poverty of the general population, and unable to consume enough themselves to maintain demand, the wealthy and their agents looked towards new domains for the investment of surplus capital. As this capital could not be profitably invested on the home front, such monies *constituted free cash as measured by domestic investment opportunities*.

The natural outgrowth of too much inequality was a tendency to depression. According to Hobson, the middle classes might well apportion their income in accordance with the interest rate, but the very rich, who owned the large firms and landed estates, could not possibly consume any additional income. Indeed, the rejection of more consumption by the rich constituted "an instinctive rejection of the *injurious* effort to incorporate . . . surplus in . . . current expenditures" (emphasis added). For Hobson, it was "likely that a large and growing proportion of the total volume of saving in England and in the Western world . . . [was] . . . of this order" (Hobson, 1914a, p. 100). Hobson's formulation was rooted firmly in the class structure and in the industrial matrix to which the class structure was appended. Without foreign markets or a drastic restructuring of inequality that would bolster enough consumption power, depression was in the offing.

Hobson thus turned Keynes's justification of nineteenth-century inequality on its head. This was the result not of corrected error but a shift forward in time and a corresponding shift in historical context. As A.K. Cairncross notes:

> In the middle of the nineteenth century the building of British railways and towns took nearly the whole of Britain's savings. A trickle of capital found its way abroad, partly to finance railway-building on the Continent, partly in commercial and banking ventures and partly in speculative loans to foreign governments, generally in the Near East or in South America. It was not till after 1870 that the trickle began to assume really formidable proportions and the growth of capital came to centre on overseas development.
>
> (Cairncross, [1953] 2015, p. 2)

That the domestic absorption of savings prior to 1870, "took nearly the whole of Britain's savings," suggests a petering out of domestic investment opportunities, leading to foreign outreach. This understanding receives additional support when consideration is given to the sunk capital in traditional industries that could only maintain profitability through new territorial expansion. Expanded foreign investment centered primarily on steam transportation, both in railways and ships; utilities, such as electric facilities, tramways and telegraph facilities, and other infrastructure development, such as docks and harbors, mining, and materials of all kinds (p. 2). Over the time period from 1870 to 1914, "Britain herself had invested abroad about as much as her entire industrial and commercial capital, excluding land and that one tenth of her national income came to her as interest on foreign investments (p. 3).

This one-tenth of the national income meant that while capital exports were large, the flow of derived income was even larger. In the period 1903–13, capital export from Britain absorbed some 7 percent of British income (Kenwood and Lougheed, 2001, p. 28). "Over the longer period between 1870 and 1914, Britain's net export of capital totaled 2,400 million [pounds]" (Sweezy, 1969. p. 194). But in the same years, Sweezy writes, the sum total of "interest, dividends and other remittances amounted to no less than 4,100 [pounds]."[2] This generation of free cash required larger and larger markets for its absorption. Hobson's dilemma—either expanded markets abroad or substantial redistribution of income towards common people—was not relieved by expanded territorial acquisitions. The British outreach towards new acquisitions put Britain on a treadmill whereby the expansion of markets simply generated the need for more.

Hobson's thesis is open to the critique that, apart from the white settler colonies and dominions of Britain, the new territorial claims of the late nineteenth century absorbed but a small fraction of the total capital export of Britain and the advanced nations in general. But, as noted above, any futuristic understanding had to anticipate places for further growth. Railroad mileage had largely peaked in Britain around 1870. And although rail expansion had not yet peaked in Canada, Australia, Argentina, Brazil and Mexico, they had certainly leveled off in the turn to the twentieth century (Rostow, 1978, pp. 452, 458, 511, 494). As other nations played industrial catch-up to Britain in the latter part of the nineteenth century, it became increasingly difficult for Britain to export to more advanced nations as production became largely substitutable. Consequently, a larger percentage of British capital exports went to British Dominions, India and Latin America.

The export of British capital to the United States was also considerable, making up roughly one-fourth to one-fifth of capital export from mid-century to World War I (pp. 28–30). But even here, as shown most particularly in the substitution of U.S. rail subscriptions for that of the British (Hobson, [1914b] 2012, pp. 152–153), there was a displacement of British investment, anticipating the U.S.'s post-war capital export position. Such displacement put additional pressure to obtain the monetary receipts necessary for the procurement of U.S. production, particularly agricultural production. As Keynes had noted in reference to ample food imports into Europe, capital exports allowed a "general reduction in the price of imports" (Keynes, [1919] 1988, p. 7). Such reductions in wage goods permitted higher profits, as employers could pay a lower wage than otherwise.

In addition, capital exports allowed expanded trade in general which bolstered home demand. Balance of trade figures show that apart from the United States, France and Russia, British exports of goods to the Empire and Latin America followed the pattern of India whereby exports consistently outpaced imports (Cairncross, [1953] 2015, p. 189), if only by small amounts. This contrasted sharply with the general balance of merchandise trade that consistently showed negative balances from the mid-1820s onward (Tiberi, 2005, pp. 34–38) and which Hobson himself had recorded from 1870 to World War I (Hobson, [1914b] 2012, p. 170). Moreover, in terms of cyclical ups and downs, capital exports corresponded to Hobson's understanding that foreign markets alleviated the tendency to depression: "There is also plenty of evidence that it was foreign rather than home investment that pulled Britain out of most depressions before 1914" (Cairncross, [1953] 2015, p. 188).

Capital export in general and territorial expansion in particular sustained European growth. In the course of their duties, colonial administrators would assume large administrative and military responsibilities that would protect joint-stock investments in sponsoring rail, shipping and other infrastructure facilities whose building and assembly would require additional investments both in the hinterland and in Europe. Interest on colonial debt would be earned by European imports from resource-rich colonial lands and flow back to financiers and the wealthy. Saturated rail and steel facilities within Europe would find extended markets in the larger colonial and neo-colonial world.[3] Shipping facilities could expand to transport both exports of European product to the protectorates and the imports necessary to pay service costs. The military apparatus necessary to protect shipping and the artificial colonial lines drawn up by European powers also absorbed savings, while providing military careers for officers of prominent social standing. Those of ecclesiastical persuasion could temporarily leave their domestic pulpits and find newly conquered foreign peoples to convert.

Hobson would understand the parties attached to the new imperialism as "parasites," (Hobson, [1902] 1965, Ch. 4). But given the overarching context of imperialist expansion, it was unclear as to whom would be exempt from Hobson's parasitic classification. In addition to the arms dealers and the military itself, and the financiers and shippers and the great manufacturers geared to export, there was the large proportion of the labor force devoted to trade. Hobson asserted that the proportion of labor devoted to trade was *only a fifth to one-sixth* of the total labor force including the portion of labor in ancillary trades (Hobson, [1902] 1965, p. 28). Hobson would minimize the importance of this very large ratio by not only omitting Keynesian multiplier effects—of which he was apparently unaware—but by suggesting that

> There is no necessary limit to the quantity of capital and labour that can be employed in supplying the home markets, provided the effective demand for the goods that are produced is so distributed that every increase of production stimulates a corresponding increase of consumption.
>
> (Hobson, [1902] 1965, p. 29)

Hobson's parasitic conception of virtually the whole of British society, or at least a sufficiently large part to implicate the whole economy, was in essence a call for a new social system and a corresponding redistribution of income towards the laboring classes.

Lack of internal markets drove imperialist expansion. But that was not the whole of Hobson's analysis. Trade, if contained exclusively within the advanced nations, would, at least in time, mean increasing competition among substitute products. Britain's early lead in the industrialization process allowed a rapid catch-up among nations in the latter part of the nineteenth century. But increasingly as other nations industrialized—the Scandinavian group, France, Belgium, Germany and the United States—and became more and more self-sufficient, trade among advanced nations increasingly approximated a zero-sum game. I say "approximate." The comparative advantage of North America, France and Southern Europe in foodstuffs counterbalanced Britain's lead in industry. But in the competitive race among advanced nations, an important *marginal* advantage would accrue to those nations that could establish newly formed markets in the hinterland. Hobson avoided the term "comparative advantage," as the term suggested developed trading markets, voluntary labor markets and a whole range of commercial institutions notably lacking in the newly acquired territories. But Hobson did understand the pull towards resource-rich territories that could produce tropical foodstuffs, rubber, tin and other geographically located products. This pull spoke for the possibility of trade with the underdeveloped regions. But it also spoke to the problems of how to exploit the non-market areas without imperialism.[4]

The tariff hikes of the late nineteenth century also pushed for more territorial grab. Until very late in the nineteenth century, Britain stood out for free trade the longest, as free trade benefited the strongest. But even Britain came to adopt a protectionist stance when rivals started to carve into foreign markets. These tariff hikes were self-defeating, as the limitation of imports for one country limits exports for the next. So here again, the new advantage would go those nations most aggressively engaged in colonial expansion. Enlarged export markets in the Dominions and particularly in the new territories required debt both for purchasing exports and for enforcing debt servicing. Under the colonial whip, debt could be imposed or at least subsidized and protected through military and policing arrangements.

These subventions of money and military support deserve emphasis. In his doctoral thesis ([1914b] 2012), Hobson discussed in detail the many defaults on sovereign state debt and private ventures throughout the world—railroads and governments in the southern United States, governments, such as Greece, Egypt and Turkey, where the "administration of their debts [were] partially or wholly taken out of their hands" (p. 127), the municipal defaults in Argentina (p. 128), not to mention the "rubbish" bonds of other South American states, such as Ecuador, Paraguay and Peru (p. 147). In contrast, Hobson notes the case of Indian railroads whereby the Government of India

> granted all land required, free of expense for ninety-nine years, to companies incorporated by Act of Parliament in England, and guaranteed interest, generally at 5 percent, upon the capital employed. The necessary stimulus to private enterprise was thus applied, and by July 1858 seven distinct companies were engaged in constructing lines under the guarantee system.
>
> (p. 135)

For Hobson, colonialism, with all of its assorted ramifications, was a net liability. As a British citizen, he argued that if the new hinterland was to be dominated by imperialist forces, other nations should do it. Britain could maintain free trade and by its shipping and commercial advantages, Britain could still maintain access to the world and the products of others' protectorates (Hobson, [1902] 1965, Ch. 5). This reversion into nationalism was, for Hobson, a partial escape from his own intellectual difficulties. He could never reconcile his belief that all of the world's resources should be available to all with the fact that many of these resources were located in non-market societies not subject to conventional trade. Understandably, he was quite unable to understand how the "art of self-governance" (European style) and self-promoted trading relations could be developed by non-Western cultures in any short period of time. This dilemma—in conjunction with his belief that the world's resources needed to be developed—may explain why, in the Economic Interpretation of Investment (1911), Hobson eventually came to understand that "imperialism is a necessity, if transitory, stage on the way to democracy and internationalism" (Cain, [1999] 2013, p. v).

The problem of underdevelopment helps also to explain why Hobson put finance at the center of imperialist expansion. Newly acquired areas could not engage in self-sustaining trade. Michal Kalecki's comment, that the fight for "new opportunities for [the] export of capital associated with the export of goods, can be viewed as a drive for export surplus, the classical source of 'external' profits" (Kalecki [1933] 1971, p. 85), puts the export of free cash and trade in a unified association. But in the imperialist reach into a hostile world, such free cash export, with state-sponsored military backup, must come first to establish and maintain future trade. Hobson developed this finance thesis over time. But perhaps his best sketch was contained in *Democracy After the War* ([1917] 2013) published during the height of World War I. Unlike "traders," who might be denied a certain market and can turn to the next, financiers have a vested stake, which is a

> fixed and lasting one . . . bound up with the general prosperity or failure of the country. Their economic interest in that foreign country may be as great as or greater than in their own, and what happens as to good or evil in that country may be more important to them than anything likely to happen in

> their own. If, therefore, any action of their Government, any stroke of foreign policy, can improve the security of that distant country, it improves their securities, and even if a threat of war or an act of war is needed to obtain that object, what matter? The people pay the cost with their lives and their money, the investor and financier reap the gain.
>
> (p. 83)

Hobson's historiography of industry

Hobson's inquiries into imperialism involved not just foreign investment but a historiography of industry that related stages of industrial development to the over-saving process and imperialism. This historical account developed along the timeline of his own intellectual growth. His early thoughts, in *The Physiology of Industry* ([1889] 1956), written in conjunction with A.F. Mummery, broke with the notion that saving was an unquestioned good. According to Hobson and Mummery, capital investments were rigidly dictated by consumption requirements. Correspondingly, there could be too much capital—understood as fixed installations—relative to consumption power. Implicitly, the work dealt with competitive markets where output and investment could not be controlled and where even the attempt would prove nugatory, given the plethora of firms competing for market position. In the view of Hobson and Mummery, depressions were the inevitable result of uncoordinated capital investments relative to purchasing power.

Evidence of over-capacity indicated that realized saving exceeded the profitable use of capital. *The Physiology of Industry* thus implicated inadequate consumption power relative to the capital stock and therefore clearly pointed towards the redistribution of income advocated by Hobson in his later works. In focusing on over-saving, Hobson and Mummery did note that "labourers . . . are the chief sufferers from the saving habits of the rich" (Hobson and Mummery, [1889] 1956, p. 182). But this insight did not extend to the advocacy of remedial measures directed towards altering the distribution of income.

In this early work, Hobson and Mummery understood saving as "realized" saving in the form of additions to the capital stock. It was this identification of saving with additional accumulation that formed the basis of Keynes' famous critique in the *General Theory* (1936). Keynes credits Hobson and Mummery as predecessors in understanding over-saving but only to remark that they did not properly emphasize the distinction between planned saving and planned investment and, consequently, could not understand the nature of an under-full employment equilibrium. According to Keynes, the

> root of Hobson's mistake . . . [was] . . . his supposing that it is a case of excessive saving causing the actual accumulation of capital in excess of what is required, which is, in fact, a secondary evil which only occurs through mistakes of foresight; whereas the primary evil is a propensity to save in conditions of full employment more than the equivalent of the capital which is required.
>
> (pp. 367–368)

Keynes's critique, by invoking the "propensity to save" rather than realized saving and, most importantly, the possibility of "foresight," suggested at least the possibility of industrial control—or attempts at industrial control—over saving and investment. Given the anarchical nature of a modern economy, industrial control could not be affected at the macro-level of the economy without the controlling hand of government. But the attempt to maximize gross profits (business saving) through the control of production and investment at the level of the industry is certainly one with formations exhibiting monopoly power. In his *General Theory* critique, Keynes mentioned that Hobson's later works "contained his 'root' error" (Keynes, 1936, p. 370),[5] but Keynes was remiss in neglecting Hobson's later inquiries into the changing nature of the industrial structure, most particularly the movement into a monopoly phase of capitalism. Concerned as he was with General Theory rather than history, Keynes omitted any commentary on Hobson's understanding of a changing industrial structure.

Hobson was the author of one of the main contemporary texts in economic history, *The Evolution of Modern Capitalism* (1894). In this text and in other works following, most particularly *The Problem of the Unemployed* (1896), *Imperialism* (1902), *The Industrial System* (1910) and *Work and Wealth* (1914), Hobson inquired into the unfolding of the nineteenth century into the twentieth. In Hobson's view, this temporal transition was equivalent to the unfolding of competitive capitalism into a new type of capitalism that was infused with monopoly power (Hobson, 1894, pp. 128–185). According to Hobson, in the competitive phase of the nineteenth century, new capital vintages introduced by new firms dictated both a rapid obsolescence of existing capital and overcapacity in the sense that consumption could not keep pace with the productive power of industry (p. 149). This over-saving as excess capacity would be manifest either as idle plant and equipment that would hamper further investment, or as overproduction, which would drive prices below the level at which profits could be earned (Hobson, 1896, pp. 61–63). This unprofitability would, in itself, prevent further investment and stifle recovery through the ruinous effects on industry. Even with excess capacity, new entrants might enter an industry as the newcomers who at least had a chance of acquiring a profitable portion of the existing market. But Hobson's favorite theoretical tool—the fallacy of composition—instructed him that such new investment would undercut the industry taken as a whole. For unless markets expanded sufficiently, the new entrants would take markets away from others (pp. 85–86). Keynes's critique—quoted above—that 'the root of Hobson's mistake . . . [was] . . . his supposing that it is a case of excessive saving causing the actual accumulation of capital in excess of what is required' was, from an historical standpoint, not a mistake but a condition characteristic of the nineteenth-century economy and of competitive structures in general.

In Hobson's succession of works, he explored the development of an organic industrial system riddled with a vast mixture of business firms, small and big, competitive and monopolistic. In his *Evolution of Modern Capitalism* (1894, pp. 113–116) and later in *The Industrial System* (1910, pp. 183–196), Hobson concentrated mainly on the creation of large, monopolistic firms evolving out of an earlier competitive stage. But he also noted a variety of industries populated by numerous small business firms. These included fishing, agriculture, luxury and fashion trades, retail trade, arts and the professions. He noted also that even in those industries that tended towards gigantism (milling, manufacturing, wholesale commerce, insurance and finance), the concentration of capital often proceeded in a milieu, where smaller and medium-size firms persisted. Nevertheless, he understood that, in these key industrial sectors, the tendency to monopoly operated as an inexorable force. The evolutionary dynamic of capitalism consisted of a weeding-out of inefficient firms, the growth of larger firms driven by economies of scale in manufacturing and distribution, and the monopolistic binding-up of firms through mergers, trusts, pools, cartels and associations (Hobson, 1894, pp. 172–181).

Keynes' version of over-saving was conceived at a time when oligopolistic and monopolistic elements had entered the industrial structure and when large amounts of savings were made up of or derived from gross profits. Under a condition where monopolistic practices could restrict output and investment in the quest for higher profits, there might well by—to repeat Keynes' words—"a propensity to save in conditions of full employment more than the equivalent of the capital which is required." Unlike Hobson, Keynes did not direct his inquiries towards the relationship of saving to industry, relegating saving to the residual left over from consumption. In contrast, Hobson was intrigued by the growth of saving and its apparent correlation with monopoly power.[6] In *The Problem of the Unemployed* (1896), Hobson groped towards understanding how competition gave rise to firms superior "in the arts of competition" and how these firms would restrict investment and output in the service of increased profitability. Technological advances, embodied in new investment, would be introduced at a slower pace to maximize total return, understood as the comparative result between what the combined capital would lose as a result of obsolescence and the expanded profitability due to the cost savings obtainable through new capital installations (Hobson, 1896, pp. 85–86).

In *Imperialism* (1902), Hobson develops these insights, particularly in Chapter VI, which he tellingly entitles "The Taproot of Imperialism." Far from omitting the case where savings tended to outpace investment (as Keynes charged), Hobson examines in some detail the industrial setting where this phenomenon takes place. In the modern trust, free cash is generated. A trust "cannot normally find inside the 'trusted' industry employment for that portion of the profits which the trust-makers desire to save and invest." To the possible charge that new inventions would require savings, Hobson wrote: "New inventions and other economies of production or distribution within the trade may absorb some of the new capital, but there are rigid limits to this absorption" (Hobson, [1902] 1965, pp. 75–76). In reference to the payouts accruing to the wealthy stockholders and managers, Hobson wrote that the captains of industry were the recipients of an "enormous amount of wealth," but

> No luxury of living to which this class could attain kept pace with its rise of income, and a process of automatic savings set in on an unprecedented scale. The investment of these savings in other industries helped to bring these under the same concentrative forces.
>
> (Hobson [1902] 1965, pp. 74–75)

In *Imperialism* (1902), Hobson's remarks on trustification pertained to the U.S. industrial structure. But his analysis would apply equally well to the case of Germany. The German cartels, formed behind protectionist walls, not only protected German industry on the domestic front, but allowed for a degree of export dumping. As fixed costs could be covered by high domestic prices, German industry could lower prices to compete on world markets. Coming from behind even held a technological advantage as new capital installations could be of the most efficient vintage.

Hobson maintained that the free cash generated from monopolistic practices combined with traditional foreign debt to further the export of capital and imperialist conquest. In this connection, it is not surprising that Lenin, in his "popular outline" *Imperialism: The Highest Stage of Capitalism*, gives credit to Hobson's *Imperialism*, "with all the care that, in my opinion, that work deserves" (Lenin, [1917] 2011, p. 7). For some scholars, like John Strachey, the likeness of the imperialist theories of the two allowed one to link them together as "The Hobson-Lenin Explanation" of imperialism (Strachey, 1960, Ch. VI). The commonality of the two in understanding imperialism and its accompanying militaristic buildup is unmistakable. World War I confirmed that rival empires born of imperialism could lead inexorably to the most major conflagration imaginable. The War also confirmed that the territorial expansion that was one with increased industry and free cash was, in its own way, a zero-sum game. Not even the partial concessions and compromises made by monopoly groups across boundaries could maintain the peace. These compromises were extensive: the French–German split over Morocco; the division of Persia into spheres of influence by Britain and Russia; the joint financial ventures in China where the Four-Power group of Britain, Germany, France and the United States morphed into the Six-Power group with the addition of Russian and Japan; the compromises over the split-up of the Ottoman Empire, and the mobilization of rival forces in Egypt and the financing of the Suez Canal, among others.

Militaristic expansion was tied inexorably to the motor force of capital accumulation that required continued expansion without end. In Schumpeterian fashion, imperialism is often understood as expansion for its own sake, arising out of war machines whose existences constituted their own ends rather than means. Hobson conceded that the military apparatus fed upon itself, but it was basically ancillary to the capital-accumulation mechanism of perpetual motion. Hobson did not deny that a whole range of motives fed into the military animus. Such motives involved political prestige, animal propensities towards violence, patriotic allegiance, and even a "zest for hazard and adventure and . . . passion for physical self-assertion and personal prowess" (Hobson, [1917] 2013, p. 35). He was also acutely aware of war habits of thought, stressed repeatedly by Joseph Schumpeter that were "artificially preserved in the life of the leisured ruling caste and in the popular pastimes" (p. 35). These sentiments were ingrained over centuries and would rise to the surface under any wartime pretext. But Hobson distinguished "the volume and intensity of . . . motives from their management and direction" and put the guidance and direction of all the militaristic sentiments in the service of capital accumulation that "fuse . . . and exploit them" (p. 37).

Hobson bemoaned the jingoism, militarism and nationalist fervor that was part of imperialism and which contributed to World War I. But, in *Imperialism* (1902) and in works written prior to the actual outbreak of hostilities, he did not actually forecast the War. Rather, his prescription for redistributed wealth and income was primarily a plea for more equality within the advanced nations. His plea was consistently reformist. In a foreshadowing of Keynes, Hobson advocated higher taxes on the wealthy and unspecified state-generated employment projects. Although his reformist prescriptions remained vague, he was fully convinced that a rational reformist program based on income redistribution would alleviate the ugly choice of a jingoistic and warlike expansion of capital export or depression resulting from deficient domestic markets born of inadequate consumption due to the poverty and deprivation of the underlying population. Such a restructuring would certainly mean social control over the main industrial and financial forces. In short, any such control would have to overthrow the ruling groups tied to modern industry and finance so as to dictate collective investment decisions.

But Hobson could never bring himself to advocate such an overthrow. In *Democracy After the War* (1917), in the penultimate chapter entitled "The Conquest of the State," Hobson tried to specify the conditions whereby the common peoples' interests would be advanced in a "democratic" State. Given that parliamentary representatives and judiciary magistrates were all aligned with or came from the upper classes, he understood existing democracy as "sham self-government" (p. 185). But despite the title of the chapter, the "Conquest" remained curiously apart from the issue of collective ownership of property, even of the infrastructure variety. After a momentary focus on the class structure of the existing State, and his assertion that "Industrial and social safety and progress . . . demand the successful capture of the State by the people" (p. 183), Hobson did not address the social control necessary to carry out collective investment. Instead, Hobson called for more and better education for all. This education would further critical thinking and transcend the existing education for commoners that tended towards the type necessary for clerks and those engaged in menial tasks. Such would presumably prepare the common people for taking up the important administrative tasks within a new socialized state.

Hobson's call for a pacifistic reformist state did not escape criticism, even from those critics, who, like Thorstein Veblen, were otherwise sympathetic. In commenting on Hobson's earlier call for reformation, contained in *The Problem of the Unemployed* (1896) Veblen categorized Hobson's remedial elements of a "Reformed Distribution of Consuming Power," "taxation of 'unearned' incomes, higher wages [and a] shortened working day," as "palliatives." Such a movement could only be "chimerical," in that "public policy is with growing singleness of purpose guided by business interests with a naïve view to an increase in profits" (Veblen, [1904] 1978, p. 257). Politics was firmly in the grip of business and at least for the foreseeable future, could be assumed to remain so.[7]

The United States: a partial test of mass purchasing power?

It was in the U.S. that mass markets formed in the most extended way. Curiously, Hobson did not discuss the development of these mass markets, perhaps deferring to his case that the free cash of U.S. firms could only find sufficient outlets through imperialism. But I believe that the U.S. case offers a partial test of Hobson's thesis that *relative* equality generates purchasing power and development.

Unlike the tenant farmers and the urban proletariat of Europe who had to pay some large part of their earnings to estate owners and landlords, a large part of the U.S. population obtained their food and home from their own land and labor. Having basic needs met, farm income could be devoted to the purchase of manufactured products. This enormous homeland advantage of mass markets elicited commentary as early as Adam Smith. Despite England being a far richer country, he noted that "The wages of labor . . . are much higher in North America than in any part of England" (Smith, [1776] 1981, p. 87). The land constituted an escape valve whereby the alternative to manufacturing labor was the farm. In consequence, wages rose. Such high wages also "enhanced the incentive to substitute capital for labor, machines for men" (Landes, 1998). This allowed the rapid catch-up of U.S. manufacturing. By the turn into the twentieth century, U.S. production exceeded all other nations, including Britain (Beaud, [1981] 2001, p. 143).[8]

U.S. exceptionalism in terms of home-grown mass markets cements Hobson's understanding that higher income among the lower echelons of the population drives growth. U.S. exceptionalism also provides a contrast to Europe in terms of capital export. Given the European class structure and its inability to create mass markets, capital export was necessary for European growth. Not so America. In sharp contrast to Europe, the great advantage of the United States was that expansion filled out the borders of the continent, involving a kind of people's imperialism whereby settlers established themselves on the lands of Native Americans, and the lands of Mexico. High remuneration and the self-help surrounding the provision of needs provided the consuming power that allowed mass purchases of sewing machines, pot-bellied stoves, rifles and farm implements. This advent of mass markets and the production of standardized products even acquired a new name: the "American system."

Large-scale U.S. capital imports during the nineteenth century facilitated U.S. capital accumulation, particularly in railroads. These railroads made U.S. land into real estate. Over a quarter of a million miles of track were laid by the time of World War I (Nelson, 1959, p. 81) These extensive lines allowed farmers access to urban and world markets, drove numerous ancillary markets in steel, steam, coal, hydraulics and dimensioned lumber, and facilitated a new retail trade that allowed Sears and other catalogue merchandisers access to the farm belt. In the last two decades of the nineteenth century, railroad construction made up nearly half of U.S. private investment (Baran and Sweezy, 1966, p. 226). In this enormous market-enlarging field, the U.S. followed Britain in a timeline sequence that eventually ended in saturation.[9] Corresponding to the vastly enlarged lands of the United States, the building of railroads tapered off later than Britain. Growth slowed down in the 1890s and after a momentary rebirth around the turn of the century fell considerably after the Panic of 1907 (Baran and Sweezy, 1966, pp. 226–227).

The export of food and other staples to Europe allowed U.S. debts to be easily serviced. But as industrialization proceeded and as rail building slowed down, one could detect at least the prospects of future U.S. capital export. This prospect became increasingly evident as trustification and consolidation of numerous industries took hold from around 1870 to the turn into the twentieth century. A variety of commentators, such as Thorstein Veblen, noted that industrial trustification was one with a tendency to "chronic depression' (Veblen, [1904] 1978, pp. 250–251). That the crash of 1907 followed a merger wave that encompassed some half of the U.S. capital stock was a stark reminder that monopoly can trigger depression and retard growth in recovery.

This descent into stagnation was interrupted by war orders coming in from Europe. Subsequent to the War, the automobilization and suburbanization of the 1920s provided vast new markets and propelled the economy out of the severe downturn of 1921. The "American system" moved into the next century. A survey commissioned by the Ford Motor Company found that in 1929, Americans had 19 automobiles for every 100 inhabitants "compared to 2 for every 100 persons in France and Britain." This same survey found that "out of 100 working families, 98 owned an electric iron, 76 a sewing machine, 51 a washing machine, 49 a phonograph . . . 36 a radio and 21 a vacuum cleaner" (Beaud, [1981] 2001, p. 182).

Notes

1 Bernard Porter (2008) provides an extensive summary treatment of various reformers and a comparative treatment of their views to those of Hobson.

2 Sweezy calculated the total from figures tallied from A.K. Cairncross ([1953] 2015, p. 180).

3 Hobson didn't use the term "neo-colonial" and concentrated the bulk of his inquires on formal territorial annexation. But nineteenth-century British penetration within Latin America gave his formal theory additional credence.

4 These concerns took up a good deal of Hobson's inquiries. He was convinced that the resources of the world should be available to the whole world and developed by those best able to develop them. But the lack of markets—or, more exactly, markets utilizing money—in the vast bulk of the world begged the entire question of their development. The view that imperialism was absolutely necessary for the development of non-market societies was commonly espoused by the powerful. (See quotes of Cecil Rhodes and Joseph Chamberlin, in Dutt, 1949, p. 22).

5 Keynes did not refer specifically to any of Hobson's later works in the critique. *The Physiology of Industry* was the only one of Hobson's work in Keynes's library at his death.

6 Hobson was on his deathbed when Keynes and he were engaged in their last correspondence. Hobson was quite pleased that Keynes's *General Theory* was now being read by

a new generation. But even in this last correspondence, Hobson did not refer to his inquiries into the industrial structure and how they might have enhanced Keynes's theoretical understanding of over-saving (Medlen, 2012, pp. 791–793).

7 In his later *The Engineers and the Price System* ([1921] 1990), Veblen ruminated on the possibility of engineers directing production, "on the initiative and under the direction of the country's technicians, taking action in common and on a concerted plan." The "Vested Interests" would move over, not by "forcible dispossession" but "involuntarily after the industrial situation gets quite beyond their control" (Veblen, [1921] 1990, p. 132). This new order would put industry in the service of human welfare, not business. Veblen, however, was never so optimistic to see this new order as other than a low-probability outcome.

8 This turn to manufacturing predominance, however, did not extend to the export market. Hobson himself noted that U.S. agricultural exports were over double that of manufacturing from 1890 to 1900 (Hobson, [1902] 1965, p. 79).

9 In 1875, fixed capital in British manufacturing was less than railway capital, but by this time "most of the main-line railways were already in being, and from then on railway-building normally absorbed smaller amounts of capital and, what was more important, a smaller proportion of new capital" (Cairncross, [1953] 2015, p. 8).

References

Baran, Paul A. and Paul M. Sweezy, *Monopoly Capital: An Essay on the American Economic and Social Order*, Monthly Review Press, New York, 1966.

Beaud, Michel, *A History of Capitalism: 1500–2000*, Monthly Review Press, New York, [1981] 2001.

Cain, Peter, "Introduction" (written in 1999) to J.A. Hobson's, *Democracy After the War*, Routledge/Thoemmes Press, London, 2013 edition.

Cairncross, A. K., *Home and Foreign Investment 1870–1913: Studies in Capital Accumulation*, Cambridge University Press, Cambridge, UK, [1953] 2015.

Dutt, R. Palme, *Britain's Crisis of Empire*, Lawrence & Wishart, London, 1949.

Hobson, J.A., *The Evolution of Modern Capitalism: A Study of Machine Production*, George Allen and Unwin Ltd., London, 1894.

Hobson, J.A., *The Problem of the Unemployed*, Methuen & Co., London, 1896.

Hobson, J.A., *Imperialism: A Study*, Ann Arbor Paperbacks, University of Michigan Press; George Allen and Unwin Ltd., London, [1902] 1965.

Hobson, J.A., *The Industrial System*, 2nd edition. Longmans Green, London, 1910.

Hobson, J.A., *An Economic Interpretation of Investment*, Strong and Sons, Ltd., East Street, Bromley, Kent, 1911.

Hobson, J.A., *Work and Wealth*, New York: Macmillan and Co., 1914a

Hobson, J.A., *The Export of Capital*, Thesis approved for the Degree of Doctor of Science, (Economics) in the University of London, [1914b] 2012.

Hobson, J.A., *Democracy After the War*, Routledge/Thoemmes Press, London, [1917] 2013.

Hobson, J.A. and A.F. Mummery, *The Physiology of Industry*, Kelly & Millman, Inc., New York, [1889] 1956.

Kalecki, Michal, *Selected Essays on the Dynamics of the Capitalist Economy 1933–1970*, Cambridge University Press, Cambridge, UK, [1933] 1971.

Kenwood, A.G. and A.L. Lougheed, *The Growth of the International Economy 1820–2000*, Routledge, Taylor and Francis Group, London and New York, 2001.

Keynes, John Maynard, *The Economic Consequences of the Peace*, Penguin Books, Harmondsworth, [1920] 1988.

Keynes, John Maynard, "Am I a Liberal?": An address to the Liberal Summer School at Cambridge, in *Essays in Persuasion*, W.W. Norton & Co. New York and London, [1925] 1963.

Keynes, John Maynard, *The General Theory of Employment, Interest and Money*, Harcourt, Brace Jovanovich, New York, [1936] 1964.

Landes, David S., *The Wealth and Poverty of Nations*, W. W. Norton & Company, New York, 1998.

Lenin, V.I., *Imperialism: The Highest Stage of Capitalism, A Popular Outline*, Martino Publishing, Mansfield Centre, CT, [1917] 2011.

Medlen, Craig, "A Historiographical Exhumation of J.A. Hobson's Over-Saving Thesis: General Theory versus Historiography," *European Journal of the History of Economic Thought*, October 2012.

Nelson, Ralph L., *Merger Movements in American Industry 1895–1956*, National Bureau of Economic Research, Princeton University Press, New York, 1959.

Porter, Bernard, *Critics of Empire, British Radicals and the Imperial Challenge*, I.B. Tauris, London and New York, 2008.

Rostow, Walter, *World Economy: History and Prospect*, University of Texas Press, Austin and London, 1978.

Smith, Adam, *The Wealth of Nations*, Liberty Fund, Indianapolis, IN, [1776] 1981.

Strachey, John, *The End of Empire*, Random House, New York, 1960.

Sweezy, Paul, "Obstacles to Economic Development," in *Socialism, Capitalism and Economic Growth*, edited by C.H. Feinstein, Cambridge University Press, New York, 1969.

Tiberi, Mario, *The Accounts of the British Empire: Capital Flows from 1799 to 1914*, Ashgate Publishing, Aldershot, England, and Burlington, VT, 2005.

Veblen, Thorstein, *The Theory of Business Enterprise*, Reprint, Transaction Books, New Brunswick, NJ, [1904] 1978.

Veblen, Thorstein, *The Engineers and the Price System*, Transaction Publishers, New Brunswick, NJ and London, [1921] 1990.

4 Free cash and the stock bubble of the 1920s

The 1920s stock boom is most often associated with the profitable activity tied to the 5–6 percent growth during the decade.[1] A large part of this growth was linked to the coming of the internal combustion engine and mass production. The 1920s brought in a new automobile age, with its accompanying suburbs, electrical and gas systems, and municipal, state and federal outlays for roads and highways, as well as a boom in various industries linked to modern communications, entertainment and household appliances. The internal combustion engine also drove major advances in agricultural productivity such as the tractor and other agricultural instruments that moved people off the farms, cheapened food, and provided a larger industrial workforce that migrated to industrial cities. Cheapened food allowed for an enlargement of mass markets that expanded profits and stock prices. The enormous jump in World War I's positive trade balance receded to more normal levels in the 1920s, and became more and more tilted to industry as industrial production rose relative to that of agriculture. This tilt to industry also furthered manufacturing, which in turn expanded profits and stock values in the export trade. In contrast to the pre-War capital imports that helped develop the expansion of U.S. rail systems and other industrial undertakings, U.S. banks and multinational firms now exported capital, both to a war-devastated Europe and Latin America.

Along with a description of the manic behavior associated with stock psychology, economic historians generally use an expanded version of the above to explain the stock bubble of the late 1920s. In this chapter, I stress another aspect, related to the new oligopolistic character of the industrial structure. The boom of the 1920s *was the first major boom superimposed upon monopoly-oligopoly foundations.* I maintain that these monopoly foundations were a key component to understanding the speculative overindulgence of the decade that led up to the stock market crash of the 1930s. Monopoly pricing allowed a restriction of output driving abnormally high gross profits that spilled into the stock market. Given the large expansion of markets, this "restriction" has to be understood in a relative sense. Expanded markets drove increased production, and released some large part of the braking power that monopoly power entailed. But given the general reduction in per unit costs resulting from the assembly lines, scientific management and the new technological advances of the 1920s, one might have expected significant price reductions across the board. Apart from specific instances like autos, no general price reductions accompanied the rapid technological advances of the 1920s. Administered prices, attained through oligopoly pricing, restricted demand and output even in the face of significant underutilized capacity in the latter part of the decade. Restriction of output meant a relative restriction of investment, which, in the context of expanded profits, allowed the generation of free cash.

Free cash was dispensed to stockholders in the form of dividends and merger receipts. Such an outpouring of cash directed to stockholders not only funneled new monies into the hands of the rich but encouraged stock buying directly. Merger acquisition premiums expanded stock values at the same time dividends provided the wherewithal for additional purchases. Just as important, the self-financing of corporations drove banks into speculative loans. As George Soule once noted, "big business was financing itself to such an extent that the need for commercial credit was reduced. This policy left bank resources free to extend a large volume of collateral loans, which helped to finance speculation" (Soule, [1947] 1975, p. 279).

As a partial resultant of monopoly power, the stock bubble of the late 1920s should be understood as a crescendo point of the preceding decades when monopoly pricing power became general. Front-seat observers, like Thorstein Veblen, noticed the slowdown of investment that accompanied the first trustification of industry, beginning roughly in the mid-1870s. This trustification was a direct result of the price competition ushered in with the coming of national markets. By 1914, the installation of railtrack mileage was equivalent to almost ten times around the globe. This new national market put into competition previously insulated firms. Firms had to scale up quickly to enjoy this enormous expansion of markets. The main problem of the nineteenth-century firm was generating sufficient financial wherewithal to take advantage. The steady decline in prices from after the Civil War to the turn of the twentieth century reflected not just the new industrialization of cost cutting but the price cutting that reflected the transition from an era of intense price competition to that of monopoly. Initially, trusts, pools and syndications were notoriously unsuccessful as the prospects of price cheating were inherent in the separation of ownership claims. But this was soon to change.

By cutting into profits, price competition not only undercut internal finance, but put banks at undue risk when sponsoring individual firms that might well fail. Price competition thus undermined *both* internal and external financing. Understanding this dilemma is key to understanding the Giant Merger Wave of 1895–1904 and why the great investment banks were also its main promoters. Consolidations put numerous firms under one pricing umbrella that eliminated the very possibility of firms cheating on one another in regard to price. The wave was thus at once a counter-reaction to the ruinous competition of the late nineteenth century and a movement towards an industrial structure populated by dominant firms (Stigler, 1950). Trusts, pools and other monopolistically oriented efforts became transformed into unified entities, leaving second-tier firms at the pricing discretion of larger firms. Cutting any giant's price by a secondary outsider subjected the outsider to discretionary retaliation that advantaged the larger firm.

Free cash, mergers and speculation

The Great Merger Wave (1895–1904) involved consolidations encompassing over three hundred industries. Shaw Livermore (1935, pp. 68–96) surmises that perhaps half of the consolidations generated a significant degree of monopoly power in their industries, as gauged by their "success" over the next two decades, where "success" indicated survival. This is probably a conservative estimate if we recognize that any dominant firm or small collection of such firms can enforce price maintenance by threat of retaliation. According to Naomi R. Lamoreaux (1985), "more than half of the consolidations absorbed over 40 percent of their industries, and nearly a third absorbed in excess of 70 percent" (p. 2).

Monopoly profits would justify and allow fabulous fees for the investment bankers that arranged the mergers, as well as provide the wherewithal to service the debt obligations that financed the consolidations. Financial institutions, comprised mainly of investment and commercial banks, extended into manufacturing the equity-based fee arrangements that had earlier been developed in the consolidation of the rail systems after 1870 (Carosso, 1970, pp. 29–50). Consequently, financiers became an integral part of the new industrial order. Apart from taking equity stakes, this intrusion of finance into industry encompassed a variety of other forms, documented most completely in the reports emanating from the Pujo Committee hearings (1912): voting trusts; scores of interlocking directorships between the largest investment banks, largest commercial banks, insurance companies and industrial firms; horizontal and vertical cross-ownership between firms and, perhaps most importantly, a commonality of business dealings where the same large financial firms repeatedly participated in the joint offerings of securities.

Paradoxically, as the Great Merger Wave interfused the personnel of high finance and industry, it also transformed large-scale manufacturing firms into self-financing entities. So while investment banks might still play a major role in mergers and acquisitions and commercial banks a major role in rediscounting various types of paper, these financial institutions became less and less important in financing large-scale internal investment projects. During the most intense period of merger activity, towards the turn into the twentieth century, external finance was critical. But starting almost immediately, internal cash generation became predominant, so that in the period from 1900 to 1910, "70.4 percent of the new funds in manufacturing came from internal sources" (Kolko, 1963, p. 145).

This self-financing continued into the 1920s where dominant firms and oligopolies generated free cash. Using data from the National Bureau of Economic Research prepared under the supervision of Simon Kuznets (1937), we can construct estimates of free cash. In Table 4.1, Column (3) below portrays the difference between Cash (Profits after tax plus Depreciation) and new investment after dividends have been subtracted out. Dividends, however, are subject to the discretionary actions of management. In consequence, free cash should include dividends. Columns (1) and (2) portray two possibilities for defining free cash: a narrow conception defined as Cash inclusive of Dividends (Profits after tax plus Depreciation)—new investment Column (2), and a wider one that adds all security payouts to equity holders (Cash + interest – new investment), Column (1).

The payout of dividends suggests that the expected return to internal investment prospects dipped below the cost of capital for that portion of cash paid out. Otherwise shareholders would have been better off had management reinvested the dividend payout. The narrow "definition" of free cash (Cash – new investment) would no doubt correspond to management's understanding of "free cash," as the definition focuses on funds that are available to management over and above monies devoted to internal investment. From a manager's standpoint, the wider definition (Cash + Interest – new investment) might possibly be ruled out as interest is a committed obligation. The wide definition of free cash is perhaps misnamed. But for understanding speculation and mergers, I believe the widest definition of free cash is the most revealing, for it shows the difference between the total cash generated from operations and new investment. The wide definition includes discretionary funds that might well be utilized for mergers and acquisitions. It also includes payouts to security holders, who, by their demonstrated investment proclivities, tend to drive up security prices. If we add up the annual totals of wide free cash shown in Table 4.1 and divide by total new investment over the decade, we find that the free cash generated in the 1920s was 60 percent of new investment. Kuznets and his team were handicapped by an unspecified "lack of a number of sources for years before 1929,"[2] so it is probably hazardous to compare this free cash to investment ratio to subsequent booms. Nevertheless, this wide free cash/new investment ratio of the 1920s indicates that the boom of the 1920s might well have been at the high end of the cash flow-new investment spectrum when compared to subsequent booms of the twentieth century. Kuznet's data for the 1920s pertains to all business enterprises, not just corporations. Data limitations prevent a direct comparison of free cash ratios of all business enterprises across decades. But analogous *corporate* free cash ratios for the post-WWII booms were 51 percent for the 1960s, 38 percent for the 1980s, 44 percent for the 1990s, and roughly 50 percent from 2000 through 2017.[3]

By facilitating the merger wave of the 1920s, free cash was also instrumental in driving up the share prices of targeted companies. Indeed, the 1920s can be understood as the first example of the free cash theory of mergers, a theory elaborated by Dennis Mueller (1969) for the 1960s and by Michael Jensen (1986) for the 1980s.[4] In the pursuit of growth, managers have only two ways to acquire physical assets: through new investment or mergers and acquisitions. When new investment prospects peter out, or at least are meager in reference to newly generated cash, mergers become attractive for growth-minded managers.

In his famous commentary coming immediately on the heels of the wave, Willard L. Thorp (1931) noted a series of reasons that would account for the wave, including the necessity in modern times for large-scale merchandising and production, and the enhanced profitability consequent on the elimination of competitors. He noted also—as if to advance a contrary argument to the Q theory of investment and mergers–that during prosperity, "it is quicker and simpler to buy an existing plant" than it is to build a new one. But above all, Thorp stressed the ease of financing mergers during booms, even when the "owners . . . see little technical advantage to be gained from the new organization" (p. 86). In addition to utilizing

Table 4.1 Free cash in the 1920s

	(1)	(2)	(3)
	Wide free cash ([Cash + interest] – I)	*Narrow free cash (Cash – I)*	*Cash – (dividends + new investment) (Cash – div. – I)*
	(Billions of dollars)		
1919	4.29	2.67	–.13
1920	–.59	–2.58	–5.70
1921	6.80	4.67	1.83
1922	3.99	1.71	–1.21
1923	3.04	.54	–3.15
1924	6.80	4.09	.44
1925	5.40	2.39	–1.83
1926	7.43	4.26	–.34
1927	6.41	2.97	–1.92
1928	8.53	4.77	–.44
1929	5.13	1.14	–4.67
1930	6.74	2.65	–3.06
1931	5.55	.08	–4.19

Figures from Simon Kuznets, *National Income and Capital Formation 1919–1935: A Preliminary Report*, National Bureau of Economic Research, New York, 1937. Retaining Earnings, designated as "net saving" taken from line 11, Table 6, p. 24, uncorrected for gains and sales on the sale of capital assets prior to 1929; dividends, line 7, Table 6, p. 24; depreciation, line I.1, Table 13, p. 48; business investment; line 2, Table 10, p. 40; interest, line 8, Table 6, p. 24 minus interest payments from all levels of government. The latter interpolated from the virtually constant outlays of 1922, 1927 and 1933 (Historical Statistics of the United States: Colonial Times to 1970, Part 2, Series Y522–532).

free cash as a means of acquisition, large amounts of securities could be floated, particularly when collateralized, implicitly or explicitly, by large cash reserves.

Severe data limitations prevent any exact estimation of the direct contributory impact of mergers and acquisitions to the stock bubble of the 1920s.[5] Nevertheless, the very large amounts of book assets absorbed over a wide swath of industry[6] suggest that the acquisition wave must have driven stock prices up considerably, particularly in the latter part of the decade (1928–1929) when mergers picked up to the point where merged asset values in manufacturing grew to over 70 percent of new plant and equipment expenditures. This ratio was *almost double* the very high ratio of 37–38 percent that was registered from 1923 to 1927 (Eis, [1968] 1978, p. 118), and *almost double* the 1968 ratio recorded four decades later at the height of the conglomerate merger wave.[7] Carl Eis and Willard Thorp would characterize merger activity at the end of the decade as "merger frenzy" (Eis) and a state of merger "hysteria" (Thorp).[8]

Moreover, the *indirect* effects of the merger wave on stock prices pushed in the same direction as the direct effects. During a merger wave, stocks increasingly resemble lottery tickets and are valued as such. The lucky winners in the 1920s were the owners of targeted firms. And they were numerous. Unlike the Great Merger Wave of 1895–1904 that often consolidated firms into dominant status, the wave of the 1920s typically saw larger firms pick up smaller firms or saw "second-tier" firms consolidate to challenge the giants left over from the first merger wave.[9] In consequence, the second merger wave encompassed many more firms than the first. From 1925 to 1931, there were twice as many mergers than during the Great Merger wave (Reid, 1976, p. 68) with total disappearances totaling over 4,580 firms in manufacturing and mining alone (Thorp, 1931, p. 78) and another 2,927 in the public utility sector (Soule, [1947] 1975, p. 142). While we have no acquisition premium series for the 1920s, there is no reason to suspect that acquisition premiums were any less than in recent decades when such premiums routinely have averaged more than 35 percent and have sometimes hovered over 50 percent.[10] Figure 4.1 shows the Thorp series on firm disappearances in manufacturing and mining and how the series moved upwards in the 1920s in broad association with the expansion of free cash. Under a finance-based theory of mergers, this association is what we would expect. Not only did the acquisition premiums lead to a lottery-type atmosphere where stocks were valued as tickets, but the stock inflation eased security-based financing of mergers as more and more issues could be floated profitably.

In regard to security holders, payouts between 1925 and 1929 were $49 billion against equity expansion on the New York Stock Exchange of around $40 billion (Soule, [1947] 1975, p. 295). So in reference to both mergers and monies paid out to security holders, the free cash generation of the 1920s should be understood as one of the important *initiating* factors in the stock bubble of the 1920s.

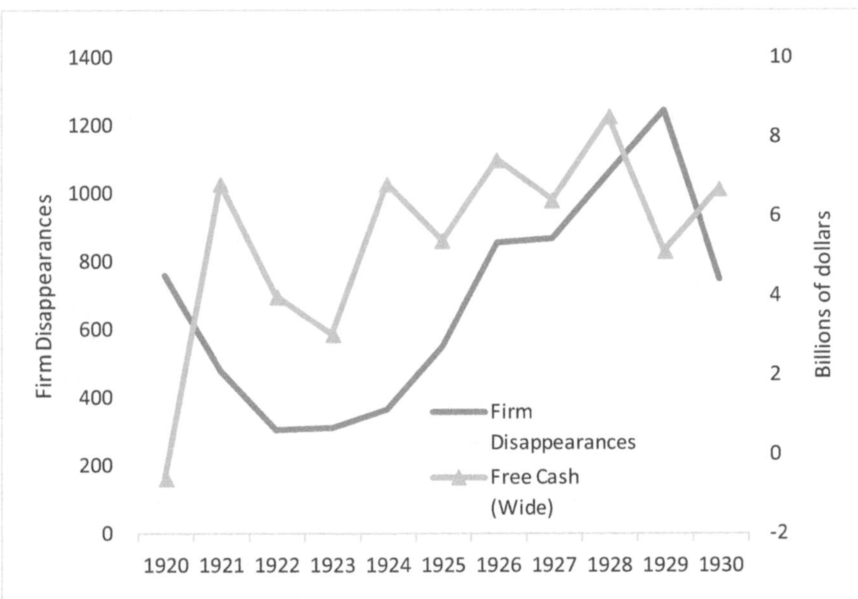

Figure 4.1 Wide free cash and mergers

The disconnection of finance from industry

> The *extraordinary absorption of funds* in speculative loans, which has characterized the credit movement during the past year or more, in the judgment of the Federal Reserve board, deserves particular attention lest it become a decisive factor working towards a still further firming of money rates to the prejudice of the country's commercial interests.
>
> (Board of Governors, February 2, 1928; reprinted in Reed, 1930, p. 154; emphasis added)

The speculative run-up of stocks of the late 1920s has often been understood as a zero-sum game—monies flowing into speculation constituted monies that were not available for commerce and industry, or would raise interest rates so as to stifle industry and commerce.

Understanding the magnitude of "free cash generation" in the 1920s gives an entirely different view of the matter. The Board's assertion that the "firming of money rates to the prejudice of the country's commercial interests" might well apply to the interest-sensitive housing market and to the credit-dependent agricultural sector. That said, the plethora of cash relative to new investment raises the issue of how corporate commerce might have used more cash through whatever source, credit markets or otherwise. Given that the plethora of excess cash was disgorged into mergers or into the hands of the wealthy,[11] who typically have a very high propensity to save, it appears that this excess found its way back into speculative activity and security purchases. In the case of bonds, such purchases lowered interest rates under the levels that would have otherwise occurred. In the case of equity, expansion of stock values lowered the real cost of capital across the board. Corporations took advantage of this through new stock issues. From 1922 to 1929, monthly averages for corporate stock issues expanded over ten-fold, with the expansion from 1928 to 1929 almost doubling (Reed, 1930, p. 175).

Understanding the generation of free cash allows us to understand the almost complete unhinging of finance from industry and the redirection of finance into speculation. This redirection has been anecdotally documented by Senate Hearings in the 1930s.[12] That industrial corporations, including giants like General Foods, International Nickel, Standard Oil of New Jersey, Electric Bond and Share, were funding the market rather than vice versa demonstrated the existence of a 1920s version of a "shadow banking system" predicated on the backflow of free cash (Lundberg, 1937, p. 221). A couple of stylized facts gives a sense of the almost complete disconnect of finance and industry: "Loans to brokers 'for the account of others' rose in 1929 to become the majority of total loans outstanding in New York City banks" (Reed, 1930, p. 165). Yet, brokers' loans issued by industrial firms, wealthy individuals and investment banks rose to the point that the New York City banks that stood at the heart of the call market had less than 13 percent of total broker loans outstanding in October, 1929 (Chandler, 1958, p. 426).

Free cash and the Federal Reserve

The large volume of free cash gives substance to Elmus R. Wicker's claim that actions by the monetary authorities to control stock market speculation were actually "increasing, not decreasing the supply of funds feeding the stock market" (Wicker, 1966, p. 129). Wicker's claim might well be too strong, but the monetary policies geared towards the speculative bubble certainly lacked effect. The "direct pressure" policy advocated by prominent Board members such as Miller, Hamlin, James and Cunningham was designed to cut back on speculative lending while holding interest rates down. Yet any such restriction on the part of banks was easily circumvented by the expansion of non-bank sources of monies. Wicker notes: "The volume of new funds flowing to the stock marketed amounted to about $2.6 billion between January, 1928, and September, 1929. The stream was continuous without any signs of letup in its rate of increase" (p. 129). Governor Harrison of the New York Federal Reserve preferred a policy of allowing interest rates to rise, noting that the policy of "direct pressure" inhibited banks from borrowing from the discount window for any purpose (p. 139). Moreover, the fungible nature of money meant that loans specified for trade might well be redirected to speculative endeavors, negating any arbitrary "direct pressure" directive.

Direct pressure failed to halt the increase in rates, and, indeed, a good number of the Board members came to agree with interest rate increases. But the effect on speculation could only remain uncertain. Depending on the interest-sensitivity of investment, a policy of increasing interest rates might tend to draw monies out of industry and other non-bank sources and into speculation, but not necessarily. Early on, Harold L. Reed (1930) noted that a

> good part of the funds dispatched to the street by "others" did not represent an equivalent withdrawal from industrial financial resources. The high rates in the street induced many corporations to draw down bank balances and place the funds on call. Such call loans were considered as the equivalent of deposits in bank(s).
>
> (p. 149)

Still, to the extent that the interest rate hikes in the latter part of the 1920s did expand speculative monies, monetary policy operated at counter-purposes to the authorities' intentions to dampen speculation.

The large volume of free cash helps explain the seemingly muddled and confused response of the Board and the New York Federal Reserve. Prominent monetarists maintain that the authorities should have loosened the money stock towards the end of the decade even in the face of the gargantuan bubble. Allan H. Meltzer (2003) contends that had the authorities loosened the money supply in the late 1920s, they "would have ameliorated or possibly prevented the 1929 recession" (p. 265). Along much the same lines, Milton Friedman and Anna J. Schwartz ([1963] 1993) have suggested that the authorities might well have broken the stock speculation earlier in 1927 and 1928. But, according to them, such action would have stymied economic growth. In their view, the monetary authorities "followed a policy which was too easy to break the speculative boom, yet too tight to promote healthy economic growth." On ignoring the stock boom, Friedman and Schwartz are explicit: "In our view, the Board should not have made itself an 'arbiter of security values' and should have paid no direct attention to the stock market boom" (pp. 291–292). The monetarists' position concerning the expansion of the money supply is tantamount to saying that even had an expanded bubble popped, such an outcome would have been of relative unimportance. In the absence of any possibility of historical experiment, Meltzer's and Friedman and Schwartz's assessment of unimportance can only remain conjectural. For these monetarists, the speculative boom appears as just that: a phenomenon without reference or causal connection to the industrial order. In neglecting the self-financing of industry, the monetarists are able to claim that a looser monetary policy would have allowed "healthy economic growth" (Friedman and Schwartz, [1963] 1993) and "possibly have prevented the 'recession' of 1929" (Meltzer, 2003, p. 265). But the real question is how a looser monetary policy could have funded additional economic activity when industry was overflowing with cash.[13]

Understood in light of the free cash generation of the 1920s and the build-up of speculative loans, the opposition of the New York Federal Reserve to qualitative restrictions on credit takes on a wider dimension than a simple argument concerning the fungible nature of money. The existence of large amounts of free cash begged the question of how banks could expand their commercial loans sufficiently to maintain profits. The existence of free cash explains why an increasing amount of speculative loans were being undertaken during the decade and why a good number of bank Governors like Harrison would oppose qualitative restrictions on credit. In 1923, "loans on securities" were roughly half of the loans that the Federal Reserve labeled "largely commercial"; by 1928, "loans on securities" were roughly two-thirds of commercial loans.[14] While the famous February directive of 1929 brought about a cutback on brokers' loans for the banks' own account and for out-of-town banks (Wicker, 1966, p. 137) the portfolios of the New York banks were by that time overloaded with speculative issues. Like other corporations, the health of banks depended on a continual expansion of markets and in the latter part of the 1920s, this expansion could only be accommodated by security loans and other non-industrial credits.

Understanding the free cash generation of the 1920s makes the conflict between the Board and the New York Federal Reserve at least partially understandable. The uncoupling of finance from industry, begun at the turn into the twentieth century, had expanded the problems of speculation in the late 1920s to the point where there were no remedies available. As speculative loans in the late 1920s became a larger component of banks' assets, neither the Board nor the officials of the Federal Reserve Banks could have directly controlled speculation without damaging the banks. The Board certainly understood this. In the Board's famous February warning against the use of the discount facility for speculative purposes, it explicitly noted that the "board has no disposition to assume authority to *interfere with the loan practices* of member banks, so long as they do not involve the Federal Reserve banks" (emphasis added).[15]

Having veto power over discount rates, but reluctant to take any direct control over portfolios, the Board exercised its public obligation in the only formal way that it could: by expressing concern over an alleged misuse of the discount facility. Officials of the Federal Reserve Banks, understanding the fungible nature of money and committed both to countering the stock mania and maintaining the financial health of the banking industry, had only one option: expanding interest rates. In neither case could these policy alternatives offset the speculative channels cut from the decade's free cash generation.

The 1920s and Michal Kalecki's free cash model

Data limitations disallow a full account of the factors underlying the free cash generation of the decade. But it is possible to focus on probable causes. State and local expenditures and revenues were in balance, but the federal balance registered surpluses during the decade averaging roughly three-quarters of a billion dollars.[16] So this factor must be ruled out as a cause of the decade's free cash. The current account made a modest contribution to the generation of free cash, particularly in the early post-War period when the average balance in 1920 and 1921 was over $2½ billion a year and towards the end of the decade when the balance was over $1⅓ billion.[17]

The net of the fiscal and current account balances varied considerably over the decade but the average could not possibly account for the large free cash aggregates displayed in Table 4.1 above and displayed in Figure 4.1. Accordingly, we can surmise that the largest causal part of the free cash generation was derived from capitalists' consumption. The large discrepancy between the wide cash figure of Column (1) and the after-dividend cash of Column (3) testifies to the large amounts of security payouts. Such payouts were available for high-level consumption. The spectacular capital gains of the decade and rents no doubt also contributed their weight to the new higher standard of living among the rich, particularly the new rich.

That capitalists' consumption was the main factor behind the generation of free cash is also supported by statistics relating to the distribution of income during the decade. Wages made very modest gains but the income gains of the top 10 percent of income recipients rose during the decade from roughly 40 percent to 45 percent of total income If one includes capital gains in income, the top 10 percent received even more (Piketty, 2014, p. 291).

Underlying Kalecki's model is the assumption that workers spend what they get. This is a first approximation. Certainly the average wage gains per hour during the decade were quite modest, expanding in nominal terms by 8 percent from 1923 to 1929 (Soule, [1947] 1975, p. 321). But consumer and mortgage debt did expand during the 1920s with the arrival of the automobile and the accompanying suburbanization. Workers were certainly a part of this. The annual change in consumer and mortgage debt moved upwards from around $1 billion a year just after the war to over $3 billion in 1928 before the bottom dropped out.[18] In Chapter 6, I show that consumer deficit spending of all varieties has an analogous effect to government deficit spending in creating free cash. The expansion of such debt during the 1920s certainly added its contribution to the expansion of free cash.

Notes

1 "From the end of the recession in July 1921 to the economic peak in August 1929 that preceded the Great Depression, economic output growth averaged 5.95 per year" (Hall and Ferguson, 2001, p. 17).

2 Kuznets, 1937, p. 76. Appendix B of the report includes a comparison between the estimates of the Department of Commerce and the NBER study for 1929 to 1935 on aggregate income payments, national income and net savings of enterprises. As the Department of Commerce began its data tabulations in 1929, the comparison dates completely miss the decade of the 1920s. Moreover, none of the comparisons are directly pertinent to comparing free cash divergences. Unlike the estimates of net savings of enterprises constructed by the Department of Commerce, the net savings of enterprises in the Kuznets study included "savings of government" so direct comparisons are impossible. The Kuznets study also charges depreciation at "original cost" rather than at current market prices, but this should not affect the comparisons of cash as an increase (or decrease) in depreciation would lessen (or expand) profit by an equivalent amount. Differences in price indices also generated significant differences in inventory changes.

3 Corporate profits, taxes, depreciation and net interest from the U.S. Department of Commerce, Table 1.14; Fixed corporate business investment and inventory change from the Flow of Funds Division, Federal Reserve, Table F.6.

4 Mueller, 1969, pp. 643–659; Jensen, 1986, pp. 322–329.

5 What capitalization figures on mergers we have are by book value in manufacturing and mining only and there is no acquisition premium series for the 1920s. Nor, apart from rough estimates, are there universe stock capitalization totals.

6 Of 16 industries tabulated by Carl Eis, merged asset values constituted 19 percent of the total value of assets in those industries and in some industries, notably petroleum refining and metal products, the percentage was over 30 percent: Eis, 1969, p. 278.

7 Federal Trade Commission, *Statistical Report on Mergers and Acquisitions*, Bureau of Economics, November 1979, Table 24, p. 111.

8 Eis, 1968, p. 119.

9 Eis, 1968, p. 93.

10 *Mergerstat Review*, various issues, Table 2–14.

11 G. Soule estimates that in 1929 there were only about 9 million shareholders, or about 7.4 percent of the total population. ([1947] 1975), p. 294.

12 Senate Report No. 1455, "Stock Market Practices," Banking and Currency Committee, Seventy-third Congress, second session, 1934.

13 In reference to Friedman and Schwartz's description of the Depression, Peter Temin has pointed out, that there is an "almost complete indifference to income determination." Temin's critique is open-ended and is not employed to buttress the free cash argument presented here. But his critique fits: Temin, 1976, p. 26.

14 *Federal Reserve Bulletin*, October 1928, p. 694.

15 In Galbraith, [1954] 1961, p. 38.
16 Series Y 335–338, p. 1104 Part 2, *Historical Statistics of the United States, Colonial Times to 1970.*
17 Series U 1–25, p. 864, Part 2, *Historical Statistics of the United States, Colonial Times to 1970.*
18 Series N 262–272, p.648 and Series N 273–277, p. 649, Part 2 in *Historical Statistics of the United States, Colonial Times to 1970.*

References

Carosso, Vincent P., *Investment Banking in America: A History*, Harvard University Press, Cambridge, MA, 1970.

Chandler, Lester V., *Benjamin Strong: Central Banker*, Washington, DC, Brookings, 1958.

Eis, Carl, "The 1919–1930 Merger Movement in American History," *Journal of Law and Economics*, Vol. 12, No. 2, October 1969, pp. 267–296.

Eis, Carl, *The 1919–1930 Merger Movement in American History*, Ph.D. Thesis, Arno Press, New York, [1968] 1978.

Friedman, Milton and Anna Jacobson Schwartz, *A Monetary History of the United States, 1857–1960*, National Bureau of Economic Research, Princeton University Press, Princeton, NJ, [1963] 1993.

Galbraith, John Kenneth, *The Great Crash*, Houghton Mifflin Company, Boston, MA, [1954] 1961.

Hall, Thomas E. and J. David Ferguson, *The Great Depression: An International Disaster of Perverse Economic Policies*, University of Michigan Press, Ann Arbor, 2001.

Jensen, Michael, "Agency Costs of Free Cash Flow, Corporate Finance, and Takeovers," American Economic Review: Papers and Proceedings, 1986, pp. 322–329.

Kolko, Gabriel, *The Triumph of Conservatism, A Reinterpretation of American History, 1900–1916*, Quadrangle Books, Chicago, IL, 1963.

Kuznets, Simon, *National Income and Capital Formation 1919–1935: A Preliminary Report*, National Bureau of Economic Research, New York, 1937.

Lamoreaux, Naomi, R., *The Great Merger Movement in American Business, 1895–1904*, Cambridge University Press, New York, 1985.

Livermore, Shaw, "The Success of Industrial Mergers," *Quarterly Journal of Economics*, Vol. 50, No. 1, November 1935, pp. 68–96.

Lundberg, Ferdinand, *America's 60 Families*, The Vanguard Press, New York, 1937.

Meltzer, Allan H., *A History of the Federal Reserve, Vol. 1 1913–1951*, University of Chicago Press, Chicago, IL and London, 2003.

Mueller, Dennis, "A Theory of Conglomerate Mergers," *Quarterly Journal of Economics*, Vol. LXXXIII, No. 4, November 1969, pp. 643–659.

Piketty, Thomas, *Capital in the Twenty-First Century*, Belknap Press of Harvard University Press, Cambridge, London, 2014.

Reed, Harold L., *Federal Reserve Policy 1921–1930*, McGraw Hill Company Inc., New York, 1930.

Reid, Samuel Richardson, *The New Industrial Order, Concentration, Regulation and Public Policy*, McGraw Hill Co., New York, 1976.

Soule, George, *The Prosperity Decade: From War to Depression 1917–1929*, M.E. Sharpe, Inc., New York, [1947] 1975.

Stigler, George J., "Monopoly and Oligopoly by Merger," *The American Economic Review: Papers and Proceedings*, May 1950, Vol. XL, No. 2, pp. 23–34.

Temin, Peter, *Did Monetary Forces Cause the Great Depression?* W.W. Norton & Co., New York, 1976.

Thorp, Willard L., "The Persistence of the Merger Movement," *The American Economic Review: Papers and Proceedings of the Forty-third Annual Meeting*, Vol. XXI, No. 1, March 1931, pp. 74–89.

Wicker, Elmus, *Federal Reserve Monetary Policy 1917–1933*, Random House, New York, 1966.

5 Veblen's Q-Tobin's Q and relative valuation

During the trustification and consolidation wave in the latter part of the nineteenth century, companies acquired new valuations that often dwarfed their net assets. Stocks reflected capital values assessed on the basis of earning capacity, theoretically expressed by Irving Fisher as the value of firms' present and discounted expected future profitability.[1]

For Thorstein Veblen, these new capital valuations reflected the new monopoly pricing power of dominant firms that arose as an inevitable result of a previous competitive phase. Competitive firms under the whip hand of price competition and continual technological change required additional investment in order to lower costs and survive. Financing this investment was a problem, as internal funds were short. But in addition, increased capital expenditures, placed in the most up-to-date equipment, would in turn disappear through a never-ending cycle of obsolescence. Not to invest under the competitive pressures of the late nineteenth century was to lose out in the competitive race for low-cost production. Yet to "win out" under the "cut-throat" competition that Veblen discussed could only be a short-term victory. The decline in capital valuation due to obsolescence was so rapid that any new investment could be anticipated to fall shortly into the same category. This impasse was most pronounced in the capital goods industry that drove the obsolescence factor to new heights. At the crest of the Giant Merger Wave, Veblen wrote:[2]

> The cheapening of capital goods has overtaken the lowered capitalization of investments before the shock-effect of the liquidation has worn off. Hence *depression is normal* to the industrial situation under the consummate regime of the machine, so long as competition is unchecked and no deus ex machine interposed.
>
> (Veblen, [1904] 1978, p. 255; emphasis added)

In another passage, Veblen explained:

> the competitive management of industry becomes incompatible with continued prosperity so soon as the machine process has been developed to its fuller efficiency. Further *technological advance must act to heighten the impracticability of competitive business*. As it is sometimes expressed, the tendency to consolidation is irresistible.
>
> (Veblen [1904] 1978, p. 266; emphasis added)

Under monopoly, obsolescence could be partially controlled, as new investment could be introduced in a timely sequence to minimize obsolescence. But control of investment also meant stagnant investment growth and a tendency to deep economic decline. In short, the competitive phase of expanded national markets in the nineteenth century was an unstable configuration that led into the monopoly phase of restricted investment.

Monopoly also meant speculative excess. High stock prices mirrored a general restriction of production in the service of heightened profitability and controlled obsolescence. In this regard, Veblen was certainly prescient in sketching out factors instrumental in bringing about the Great Depression. Veblen was also prescient in understanding the volatility in capital valuations when capital was measured by stock values. This volatility was due to the uncertain prospects of future earnings. Under the competitive order, prices of firms tended to approximate costs of reproducing them. However uncertain the technologically induced levels of obsolescence, the determinate reproductive costs of firms constrained the volatility of capital valuations. Not so under monopoly. Profitability rather than costs dictated capital valuations. And profitability was anything but certain.

The "total value of the material assets," was, for Veblen, a sub-current of valuation inherited from the competitive past. In his *Theory of Business Enterprise*, Veblen wrote that "for economic theory of a hundred years ago," capital was the "capitalized (aggregated) cost of the industrial equipment" (Veblen, [1904] 1978, p. 136). The new stock valuations of firms represented the monopolized restriction of output brought about in the quest for higher profits. According to Veblen, such valuations represented the monopolistic "sabotage" (Veblen's term) of industry. Veblen never fully listed the various "intangibles" and "immaterial wealth" that signified "assets [that] are not serviceable to the community, but only to their owners" (p. 139), but he repeatedly suggested that the new monopolistic forms of industry undercut the material welfare of the underlying population. In one of his later writings, he wrote that "The question is not whether this traffic in privation is humane, but whether the underlying population will put up with a sufficient degree of privation for a sufficiently long time" (Veblen, [1923] 1964, p. 307). Veblen sardonically answered his own question that the underlying population probably would, as it "is notoriously tolerant as regards all those things that are done in the name of business" (p. 221). In a somewhat earlier work, he noted that the augmented valuations of "property rights [have] come to exceed the aggregate wealth of the community." According to Veblen's normative conception of serviceability, the summation of the aggregate capitalized value of wealth was a "spurious summation" (Veblen, [1908] 1998, p. 156).

This uncertainty of capital valuations as measured by equity had repercussions in the debt market as well. Stock valuation represented the collateral base upon which corporate debt rested. The use of equity as collateral for bond subscriptions melded promises and imagination into one unbreakable totality whereby the explicit promises of bond returns rested upon "putative" expectations and imagined futures. The term "putative" is generally understood as "supposed." Veblen, however, often used the term "putative" in the anthropological sense of optimistic belief. This should be expected, for optimistic assessments allowed more stock and debt subscriptions than would otherwise obtain. Moreover, Veblen held that optimistic belief went beyond an efficacious force for generating cash. In religion and in other aspects of life, Veblen maintained that people would fill in knowledge vacuums with "putative" ascriptions that would assign some kind of "make-believe" outcome to the unknowable or assign some kind of causal dimension that would explain the unknowable. In Veblen's words, "The Imponderable is an article of make-believe that has become axiomatic by way of settled habit" (Veblen, [1919] 2002, p. 6). Veblen understood that optimistic assessments were often self-fulfilling. But apart from gains derived from optimistic expectations, Veblen also understood "make-believe" as a mental outlet affording comfort and a source of legitimacy surrounding the social order.

The industrial structure and the New Deal

Veblen never lived to see the "putative" capital gains of the New York Stock Market fall into the abyss of the 1930s. He died just before the onslaught of the Great Depression. But the presence of dominant oligopoly structures in the context of quasi-competitive industries gave Veblen's stage theory of capitalist development a type of statist configuration. This dual nature of the industrial structure also provided a good deal of New Deal angst. This was particularly true in reference to the widespread observation that in many dominant industries, "administered prices" failed to fall to what might have been expected under earlier competitive conditions.[3] Businesses preferred to restrict production rather than lower prices. In the view of many, price declines might have resuscitated demand—or, at least in part. Unlike the relatively competitive industries of lumber, dyestuffs, cotton textiles and agricultural products, oligopolistic industries such as steel, aluminum, copper, electrical manufacturing, paper and glass maintained prices at the expense of output. In the face of massive idle capacity, new investment fell to abysmally low levels.

In line with what Hobson and Veblen had earlier discussed, the observed price maintenance and restricted output suggested not just that recuperative measures were lacking but a monopoly explanation for the Depression itself. The dualism of competitive industries and oligopoly structures also encapsulated what Veblen understood as the insoluble problems of modern industrial structures. On the one hand, competition led to price declines, bankruptcies and instability. Monopoly power configurations, however, whether established through trusts, pools, combinations, or simple oligopoly arrangements, led to the restriction of output. In the context of the Depression, problems endemic to both types of industrial structures became accentuated and, in the absence of sufficient aggregate demand, made recovery impossible. The lack of aggregate demand was particularly acute as a result of the farm problem where price declines hit the rural areas with particular devastation. Rexford G. Tugwell, one of Roosevelt's original "Brain Trust," noted that

> farm people . . . made up nearly half the population . . . counting owners, tenants, sharecroppers, laborers and small villagers . . . [If they] could not sell, they could not buy; and if they could not buy, no one need supply the goods and services they would like. Thus, closed factories, unemployment, general paralysis!
>
> (Tugwell, 1977, p. 32)

The New Deal response to the crisis was mixed. Ellis W. Hawley (1966) divides New Deal planners into business advocates wishing to avoid price declines and the eruption of deleterious competition in the face of disaster and those who wished for a return to the price flexibility associated with a previous age (dubbed by Hawley "neo-Brandeisians"). There were others such as Rex Tugwell, Mordecai Ezekiel and Gardiner Means who accepted the new industrial order but envisioned a new type of government-directed planning whereby investment and employment would be expanded. The National Industrial Recovery Act of 1933–35 brought these various contenders into debate. For the most part, the economic and political clout of the business elite allowed them to come out on top, solidifying "scarcity profits" and government-sanctioned cartelization. As Mordecai Ezekiel characterized it, the NIRA "was largely captured by business groups and diverted to their own special interests rather than used for the general welfare" (Ezekiel, 1939, Preface, p. x). The trade associations of the 1920s and the memory of the War Industries Board provided precedents for price maintenance and coordinated business arrangements that carried over into the NIRA period. But during the 1930s, these arrangements existed without the national planning that was part of the War.[4] Over 700 "codes" were established with enforcement possibilities largely varying by the degree of underlying competitive conditions. "Ethical" concerns that understood price cutting as "chiseling" were also part of the mix. Oligopolies, with few firms in each industry, had an easy time in solidifying price maintenance through price leadership. In more competitive fields, the codes existed without effect. It should be noted, however, that in light of the ever-present threat of national planning, government-sanctioned cartels were not universally endorsed by business. In consequence, the Supreme Court, in ruling the Act unconstitutional, gave at least some psychological relief to business. This relief extended even to those executives of industries that benefited from the codes.

In the wake of the downturn of 1937, the Temporary National Economic Committee (TNEC) was set up to inquire into the industrial practices that restricted production. Led by Thurman Arnold who had earlier disparaged the Antitrust laws,[5] the Justice Department went after a host of industries, including the motion picture industry and assorted others: tobacco, sleeping cars, aluminum, auto-finance and a group of industries like oil, steel, and chemical and electrical manufacturing whose prosecution was cut short by World War II. Informed by a view that a "true" competitive capitalism of old was undermined by monopolistic practices, the prescribed remedy was a return to an industrial structure of a previous era. The monographs consisted of many volumes. The last report came out in

1941. But, as John Kenneth Galbraith explains, the collection "attracted no notice and was lost in the urgent concerns of wartime" (Galbraith, 1987, p. 243).[6]

Lost too was the possibility of major change in the industrial structure. This was partially due to the courts' reluctance to order divestiture, even when monopolistic practices were uncovered. But it was also due to the political influence of big business and a general hesitancy to experiment in the face of uncertainty. Not discounting the significant government projects associated with the Public Works Administration and the Works Progress Administration, private capital flows still provided the larger portion of funds sustaining investment throughout the Depression.[7] In a paradoxical twist most easily explained by the political power of large firms, the failure of the NIRA experiment to extend planning beyond the auspices of self-governed industrial groups was largely due to the failure of the self-governed industrial groups themselves. The logic seemed to be that if planning on an industrial scale did not work, national planning would certainly not work. This unwillingness to challenge big business extended also to tax policy. The Revenue Act of 1936 did impose a graduated undistributed corporate profits tax, as undistributed profits often resided in sterile idle money balances. But the Act limited the range to a modest 12.5–15 percent. In addition, the tax imposed on intercorporate dividends, initially imposed to limit the attractiveness of holding companies, was lowered. Ellis W. Hawley summarizes the ongoing tax war as a defeat for the anti-monopolists who had hoped for "a breakthrough into the central bastion of concentrated economic power. But as it turned out, the attack never reached much beyond the outer picket lines" (Hawley, 1966, p. 359).[8]

This is not to say that New Deal reforms accomplished nothing of industrial substance. The elaborate public utility holding company structures of the 1920s were largely simplified after the 1935 Public Utility Holding Company Act. The Security Acts of 1933–34 and the Federal Reserve Act of 1935 provided for and reinforced information disclosure, the divorce of commercial and investment banking, and quasi-public control over the money supply.[9] The establishment of the Federal Deposit Insurance Company was fashioned to prevent the reoccurrence of bank runs. Extended relief and retirement programs were established to help the unemployed, destitute and elderly while bolstering purchasing power.[10] Agriculture was supported by numerous financial subsidy programs, government buying schemes and the rationing of production. Combined with various programs to alleviate hunger, such rationing allowed prices to stabilize and "kept a floor under farm income . . . [maintaining] . . . the buying power of the country" (Ezekiel, 1939, Preface, p. x). This maintenance of buying power was particularly important in stabilizing the economy after the downturn of 1938.

But the basic industrial structure of oligopoly that characterized the late 1920s remained intact throughout the 1930s. The best evidence is contained in the 1935–37 tabulations of industrial output presented in the TNEC hearings. In over 52 industries, ranging from structural steel, to various types of building materials, elevators, plumbing equipment, electrical supplies and equipment, air conditioning, rails, sanitary ware, range boilers, the average production of the top four comprised over half of the total, with some industries having the top four produce over 80 percent.[11] Other tabulations across the 1930s showed a similar oligopoly pattern in whiskey, tobacco, oil, lubricants, copper pipelines, insurance and investment banking. Across various oligopolies, there was a wide variation in concentration ratios. The oligopolistic pattern, however, was pervasive. No longer was the trust, pool and combination necessary. The limitation of price competition due to pervasive concentration allowed for "a gentleman's world of 'live and let live' [that could] . . . be effectuated without formality, without overt evidence of collusion and without fear of prosecution" (Lynch, 1946, p. 142).

Tobin's Q

In the prosperity of the post-WWII period, Veblen's understanding of differing capital valuations as reflective of industrial stages was largely lost to history. Veblen's critical assessment that high stock prices reflected the monopolistic restriction of output and speculative excesses was replaced by an optimistic prognosis relating stock market booms to expanded levels of investment. This prognosis put the discrepancy in valuations examined by Veblen in the form of the ratio Q—the stock valuation of companies divided by their replacement costs, or in Veblen's taxonomy, the stock valuation accorded to firms through monopoly power divided by costs reflecting entry costs under an earlier competitive phase.

Q theory maintains that replacement costs continue to function in the modern oligopoly system. It maintains that a wide discrepancy between stock valuations and replacement costs will encourage investment. In abbreviated form, Q theory asserts that stock market booms drive new investment through the comparative pricing of building new firms (investment), as compared to buying firms on the stock market through mergers and acquisitions. Sometimes, Q theory is shortened to the epigram, "Build or Buy," reflecting the choice applicable to firms in their acquisition of additional capital assets.

Q theory was first popularized by W.C. Brainard and James Tobin (1977), but it was Keynes's brief remarks in the *General Theory* that first sketched out the logic:

> the daily revaluations of the Stock Exchange, though they are primarily made to facilitate transfers of old investments between one individual and another, *inevitably exert a decisive influence on the rate of current investment.* For there is no sense in building up a new enterprise at a cost greater than that at which a similar existing enterprise can be purchased; whilst there is an inducement to spend on a new project what may seem an extravagant sum, if it can be floated off on the Stock Exchange at an immediate profit.
>
> (Keynes, [1936] 1953, p. 151; emphasis added)

Without explicitly saying so, modern Q theory implies that speculation is good for the economy. A high valuation of Q brings forth new capital, in particular when the market value of firms exceeds their replacement costs, "i.e. when [Q] exceeds one" (Tobin, [1985] 1996, p. 14).

Tobin and Brainard's argument makes sense in terms of start-up corporations. Optimistic assessments in the stock market permit new ventures to be sold off quickly. It makes sense too when there is a prevalence of free entry and price competition. Indeed, Tobin and Brainard's assessment that the critical value of Q is one, is an implicit admission that competition and free entry are the prevailing conditions for the theory to operate unimpeded. With price competition, an increase in Q above one would call forth new entry. The increased level of production would drive prices down. Presumably profits and stock prices would follow and, in time, readjust Q downward. Moreover, an increase in Q above one would drive up the *additional* stock valuation of competitive firms consequent upon *additiona*l investments—what is called "marginal Q"—and drive up both investment and production. In time, this increased production would operate also to readjust Q downward.

A test of Tobin's Q theory is a partial test of whether the entry conditions germane to price competition operate in the modern industrial order of oligopolistic competition. I emphasize "partial test." Horizontal mergers and acquisitions are often consummated quite independently of any differential cost considerations as to "Build or Buy." Such mergers eliminate competition and expand the market share of the acquirers. Nevertheless, if Tobin's Q theory operates, high Qs should involve the entry of new firms. A converse tendency towards consolidation through mergers and acquisitions during booms when Qs are high would refute the theory. It should be emphasized again that Tobin's Q theory operates through assessing the cost differential of capital acquisitions. Apart from start-ups, the choice of "Build or Buy" refers to the comparative costs of capital expansion.

Q theory implies not just expanded new investment in stock booms—an implication that borders on tautology as new investment creates profits and booms—but the additional implication that in booms the Merger/New investment ratio should decline. Stock booms make mergers and acquisitions expensive. Conversely, downturns should raise the Merger/New Investment ratio, as acquisitions through mergers become cheap. Surprisingly, Tobin and Brainard never undertook a study of mergers in reference to their Q ratio or engaged in other than peripheral remarks concerning the relationship of Q to takeovers. But Tobin and Brainard's infrequent comments are intriguing. In explaining the common sense of Q as a comparison of the pricing of new and used capital assets, Tobin and Brainard explain that corporations bring into being combinations of capital items that make up a totality that goes beyond the separate listing of particular capital assets. Nevertheless, those used capital items are acquired by firms "either by buying [other firms'] assets or acquired their stock" (Brainard and Tobin, 1977, p. 37). At one point, Tobin (1984) ruminated on a decade-long undervaluation of equity prices and indicated that "takeover mania" was "motivated by egregious under-valuations" in reference to "the fundamental value of the underlying assets" (pp. 6–7). One year later, Tobin noted that

> It is common sense that the incentive to make new capital investments is high when the securities giving title to their future earnings can be sold for more than the investments cost . . . We see the reverse in takeovers of companies whose [Qs] are less than one; it is cheaper to buy their productive assets by acquiring their shares than to construct comparable facilities from scratch.
>
> (Tobin, [1985] 1996, p. 14)

In summary, there are two implications of Q theory: (1) investment should expand during stock market booms and (2) the Merger/New Investment ratio should fall off during stock market booms and rise during stock market declines. Given the quasi-tautological nature of the first implication, only the second is subject to test.

Up until recently, a test could not have been given as data on merger considerations and new investment were not available. Ralph Nelson's famous and invaluable compilation of merger data on manufacturing and mining firms from 1895 up through the mid-1950s valued acquisitions "based on a mixture of measures of firm size, on the assumption that all the measures were roughly equivalent" (Nelson, 1959, p. 18). Nelson noted, however, that these measures included such varied components as "gross assets, capitalization or purchase price" (p. 18). However indicative of main trends, a summation or compilation of these disparate measures would hardly qualify for an accurate measure of monies flowing into merger and acquisition activity. Moreover, there was (and is now) no series available on new corporate investment until 1945.

The data on merger activity in the post-WWII period is contained in two series readily available to the public.[12] The first is the FTC Large Merger Series that began in 1948 and ended in 1979. The series is confined to the manufacturing and mining sectors of the economy and is based on assets acquired (valued at book) rather than actual monies flowing into merger activity. The second is contained in the *Mergerstat Review*, initially established by the W.T. Grimm Co., and has merger considerations for all industries beginning in 1968. The aggregate data represent all dollar expenditures on mergers and acquisitions on all announced transactions reporting a purchase price. Numerous mergers do not report a purchase price, but the bigger ones typically do. Accordingly, the series should be understood as an underreported proxy variable.[13] The series does, however, allow a comparison of monies flowing into merger activity relative to new corporate fixed investment.

Figure 5.1 plots two Merger/New corporate Investment series against Q1, as calculated by the Department of Commerce.[14] The larger series is inclusive of both divestitures and foreign acquisitions, whereas the smaller series excludes these items. As shown in the figure, Tobin's Q theory fails a basic test. In contrast to the implication of Q theory, that Q should move counter to the Merger/New Investment ratio, Q and the Merger/New Investment ratios move almost in virtual lockstep. In terms of the relative costs of acquiring capital assets the co-movement of Q and the Merger/New Investment ratio appears anomalous and counter-intuitive. Yet, there is no denying it. Despite Q logic, mergers have come in waves coincident with stock market booms. This fact transcends one hundred years.

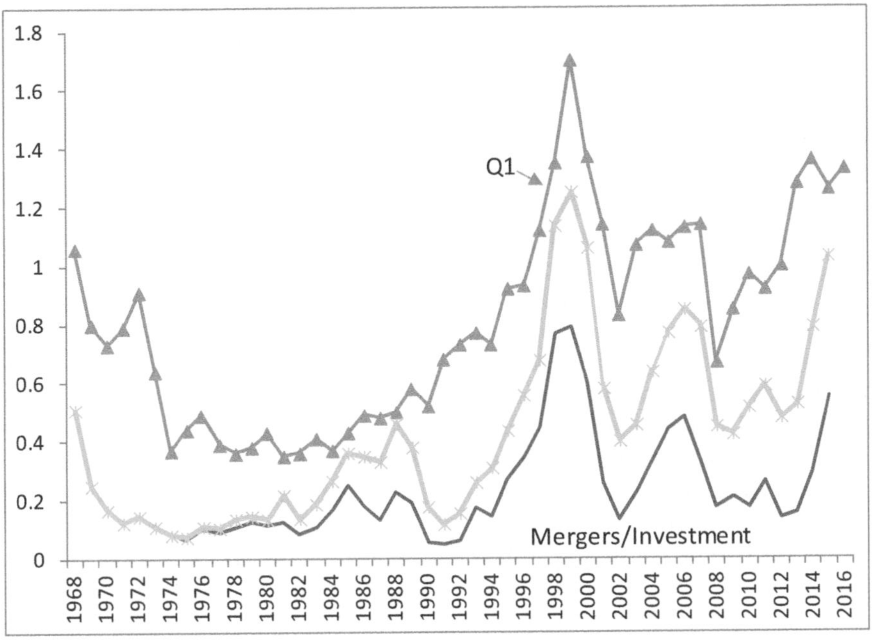

Figure 5.1 Tobin's Q

Sources: *Survey of Current Business*, December 2016; *Mergerstat Review* (various issues); corporate investment, Flow of Funds, Federal Reserve, Table F.2, addition of lines 10, 12,15.

Explanations are varied. One explanation surrounds a finance explanation that stresses the role of investment-banker promoters (Du Boff and Herman, 1989) and the role of overvalued acquirers using their stock as collateral or currency for takeovers (Shleifer and Vishny, 2003). Michael Gort (1969, p. 628) and Shleifer and Vishny (2003, p. 297) also argue that booms create a wider divergence of capital valuations that encourage mergers. But as Dennis Mueller (1977, p. 318) and Bart Lambrecht (2004, p. 42) have argued, it is far from certain that booms drive diverse valuations any more than downturns. Indeed, stock market contractions typically are far more severe over a shorter period of time than expansions of equity during booms.

Apart from the fact that mergers have been coincident with a heightened expense surrounding their consummation, the other anomalous fact about mergers surrounds their unprofitable nature. This fact begs the question: why are mergers carried out? Theories that encompass efficiencies surrounding shifts in corporate governance (Jensen, 1986) find at least some evidence in the early 1980s for increased profitability, although by the late 1980s a third of the leveraged buyouts defaulted (Holmstrom and Kaplan, 2001, p. 128). Theories that rely on industry shocks, such as the recent deregulation surrounding telecommunications and financial services, point to a tendency of merger actors to cluster around particular industrial settings (Mitchell and Mulherin, 1996). Such theorizing understands mergers largely on an ad hoc basis, with particular historical periods giving rise to distinct merger characteristics—conglomeration in the 1960s, leveraged buyouts in the 1980s, New Economy acquisitions in the 1990s. The lack of demonstrated profitability of these acquisitions, however, still begs the question: why are they carried out? Some like Roll (1986) and Morack, Shleifer and Vishny (1990) suggest that empire building and hubris play a role, but such theorizing ignores the possibility that empires might well be built through internal investment.

This lack of evidence of profitability extends over eighty years. In summarizing numerous studies from the 1920s to the late 1960s, T.F. Hogarty (1970) said that the one major difference in the studies surrounds the question of "whether mergers have a neutral or negative impact on profitability" (p. 389). This characterization largely summarizes the studies since 1970 as well. In one large study encompassing a sample of 12,023 acquisitions by public firms from 1980 to 2001, the researchers found "the average dollar change in the wealth of acquiring firm shareholders when acquisition announcements are made" was negative (Moeller, Schlingemann and Stulz, 2004, p. 202). Other studies are, at best, inconclusive.[15]

This lack of demonstrated profitability *is the most important piece of evidence surrounding the limited investment prospects of acquiring firms*. For if acquirers could expand their firms profitably through internal investment, certainly they would choose this route, even if such building required more time. This focus on the limited investment opportunities of acquirers has motivated a host of merger studies since Thorp's (1931) merger inquiry of the 1920s referred to above.[16] In recent years, these investment limitations have also been apparent in the new global economy, particularly in manufacturing. For a variety of firms, it has simply been more profitable to offshore production, or to import product and use existing distribution outlets. Cash acquired through profitable use of offshore facilities can be diverted from unneeded domestic investment towards mergers and acquisitions.

Relative valuation and distributive shares

Q theory assesses the relative choice of "Build or Buy" by costs of acquisition. The theory fails. In what follows I suggest a theory of the "Build or Buy" choice based not on costs but on the *relative* cash-generating power of the alternatives. The theory of relative valuation is analogous to the changing valuations involved in bond finance. Bond prices vary *inversely* with interest rates. Changing rates on new financial instruments provide an ever-changing set of measuring rods that revalue older investments. Older financial instruments are revalued *relative* to new financial instruments.

I propose a new *relativistic* measure of the existing capital stock, calculated in an analogous way to the valuation of bonds. In pursuing cash-rich growth, firms assess the relative cash-generating power of existing capital as measured by the cash-augmenting prospects of new investment. Unlike traditional measures of the capital stock that assesses the capital stock's valuation by expenditures, or replacement costs, my proposed relativistic measure varies as the prospective cash-generating power of new investment changes through time.

The existing capital stock constitutes what Keynes termed "old" investments (Keynes, [1936] 1953, p. 151) that could be acquired on the stock exchange. A relativistic measure of the existing capital stock thus implicates the relative value of acquiring "old" investments through merger as opposed to expansion through new investment.

A simple example illustrates: a firm ascertains that its best investment prospect over a given time horizon is to install new investment (**I**) of $100 million. Lacking the new investment, the firm would expect to generate a certain amount of money (**Z** dollars) attributable to the existing capital stock, designated as **K.** But with the new $100 million investment added, the firm expects to earn **C** dollars on the old capital plus the new investment (**K** + **I**). So the additional cash expected to result from the new investment is (**C** – **Z**). Assume further that this new expected cash is equal to 10 percent of (**C**) so that the cash attributable to the older capital stock **K** constitutes 90 percent of the total cash generated. Thus, for the time period considered, the cash-generating value of the older capital stock (**K**) is in *relativistic* terms worth nine times the value of the new investment of $100 million, or $900 million. If the cash-generating power of the new investment were to shrink to 5 percent of (**C**), then **K**'s value would expand to $1,900 million, over double the $900 million figure.

By a relativistic valuation of **K**,

$$(1) \quad \frac{K+I}{I} \equiv \frac{C}{C-Z} \text{ or } \mathbf{K} \equiv \left[\frac{C}{C-Z} - 1\right] * \mathbf{I}$$

Where (**C** – **Z**) = cash attributable to New Investment over a specified time horizon

Z = cash attributable to the existing capital stock **K** over a specified time horizon

Notice that each firm will have a different measuring rod for growth, depending on its own investment prospects. In assessing the value of the capital stock of others, managers will apply their own measuring rod as designated by **(1)** to value the relative worth of other firms. So, for example, if the prospective cash flow of a potential target is equal to (**p**) dollars over the given time horizon, the potential acquirer will substitute (**p**) dollars for (**z**) in the numerator of **(1)** above to calculate the *relative* value of the target. Under relative valuation, firms with low internal investment prospects will value the cash flow of others at a higher relative rate than firms with more internal investment opportunities. Relative valuation helps explain why firms with low internal growth prospects are often acquirers (Jensen, 1986; Lang, Stulz and Walkling, 1989).

New investment can expand cash generation in a variety of ways. But apart from the important case of new product areas, new investment acts primarily through operating on output—either through the expansion of capacity (potential revenues), or through reducing input costs per unit of output. These cases, of course, often operate in combination. But it is analytically convenient to separate them. In the capacity case, I assume—along with Evsey Domar (1957)—that a given level of new investment will expand the capital stock so as to expand *potential* revenues by a proportion of the prospective output (and revenues) that would otherwise occur. To be clear, I am not assuming the firm naively believes that potential revenues will always be achieved without interruption. Rather, in the face of uncertainty, the firm assumes a certain proportional gain as a crude approximation. With a given interest rate, capital costs would also be proportional to the given expansion of capital (**I**) and output. Assuming per unit variable costs and price as givens, cash generation, net of capital costs, will rise by a proportion of output consequent on the new investment. Allow **H** to designate the proportionality constant relating the expanded level of cash to the expanded level of output (see Appendix 1 for a detailed derivation of **H**). In summary,

$$(2)\quad \mathbf{C} - \mathbf{Z} = \mathbf{H}\ \mathbf{y}$$

Where: **y** = value of gross output over the specified time horizon

H = the proportionality constant relating the additional cash due to the new investment to **y**.

In the efficiency case, I assume—as did Joan Robinson (1953–54, pp. 81–106)—a certain rigidity in input-output relationships corresponding to various vintages of the capital stock. With given input prices, a reduction in inputs will reduce per unit costs by a certain proportion of what would otherwise occur. Accordingly, the efficiency case takes the same form as **(2)**, with a different proportionality constant, which we will term λ. (Again, see Appendix 1 for more detail.)

If we aggregate across all firms and allow "**h**" to be a weighted amalgam of **H** and **λ** (weights apportioned by the fraction of output of each firm), these proportionality relationships allow us to write

$$(3)\quad \mathbf{C} - \mathbf{Z} = \mathbf{hy}$$

Substituting **(3)** into **(1)**, we obtain the condition that the *relative* valuation of **K** varies inversely with **h** and positively with the *cash flow/output* ratio:

$$(4)\quad \frac{K}{I} = \frac{1}{h} c / y - 1$$

At the level of the firm, cash returns relative to output (**c/y**) constitute a cash-flow analogue of the profit/sales ratio. (All figures below depict cash as profits after tax plus depreciation.) But at the level of the system taken as a whole, firms' cash receipts and payables cancel out to that the cash flow/output ratio (**c/y**) constitutes the share of output accruing to capital, with the remainder of output accruing to labor. Thus **(4)** relates relative valuation to distributive shares with the relative value of older capital rising along with the share of corporate income.

The linkage of distributive shares to relative capital valuation is fully in line with the observed facts concerning the use of capital vintages over the business cycle. During downturns, the cash flow/output ratio falls off and drives up the relative value of newer vintages of capital as demonstrated by the shutdown of older vintages of capital. The obverse is true in cash-rich booms when "capacity" of previously obsolete vintages of capital is somehow resuscitated. All of this is in line too, with the correlation of merger activity and cash-rich booms. Mergers and acquisition constitute the purchase of older capital and follow in near-lockstep with firms' purchase of used capital equipment (Jovanovic and Rousseau, 2002, p. 198).

The specification in **(4)** is for a given time horizon and magnitude of new investment, but the expression can be completely generalized over a time spectrum in which new levels of investment in subsequent time periods provide new measuring rods for evaluating previous levels of investment that have become embedded in the existing capital stock. In that older capital vintages decay and become obsolete over time, we should expect that the shorter the time period considered, the greater the relative valuation of the given capital stock. The main point, however, is that *whatever time period is considered, the theory predicts that the existing capital stock will expand with capital's share.*

Figure 5.2 plots the Merger/New Investment ratios from the FTC Large Merger Series (discontinued in 1979)[17] and the *Mergerstat Review* series referred to above against capital's share (profits after tax plus depreciation/corporate output). The *Mergerstat* series includes divestitures and foreign acquisitions. I include divestitures and foreign acquisitions because such acquirers certainly

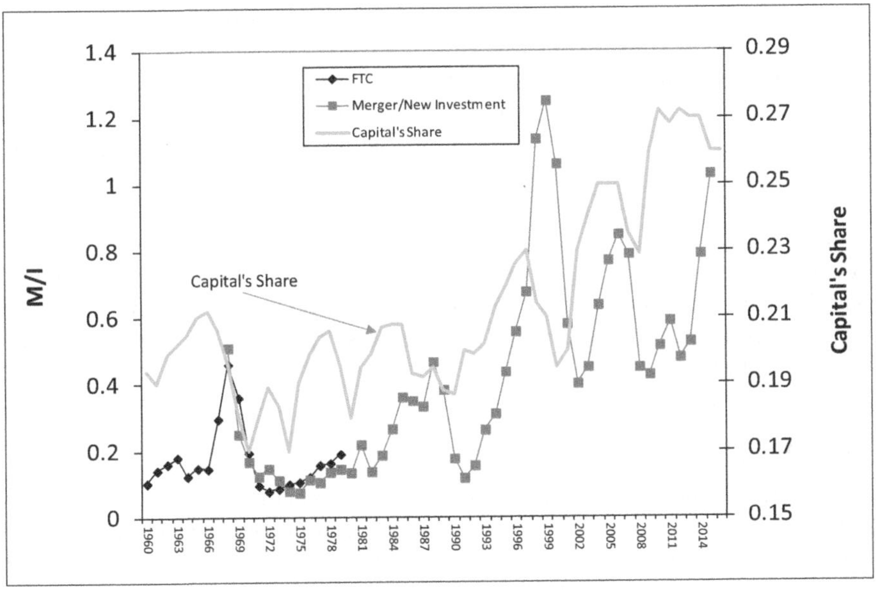

Figure 5.2 Capital's share and the Merger/New Investment ratio

Sources: Federal Trade Commission, Large Merger Series; *Mergerstat Review*, various issues. Department of Commerce, Table 1.14.

assess the cash-generating power of targets relative to their own internal investment possibilities. As predicted by the relative capital valuation measure in **(4)**, the Merger/New Investment ratios move upward with capital's share. Moreover, as theory would predict, capital's share tends to lead movements in the Merger/New Investment ratios.

Relative capital valuation and the confirming evidence as indicated in Figure 5.2 give a ready explanation of why Q theory fails in its prediction that the Merger/New Investment ratio would move counter-cyclically. The long booms of the post-WWII period have raised capital's share and have thereby expanded the relative valuation of the older capital stock. Moreover, the theory gives a ready explanation for the recent expansion of stock repurchases as well. Stock repurchases, like mergers and acquisitions, constitute the purchase of existing capital. Although Standard and Poor's does provide stock repurchase data for the top 500 corporations, there is no universal total for all firms. But Robert Brenner shows that in the 1980s, equity retirements due to stock repurchases in the non-financial sector were over 50 percent of equity retirements due to mergers and acquisitions and roughly 100 percent in the 1990s (Brenner, 2002, p. 149). As will be shown in Chapter 8, stock repurchases for the Standard and Poor's 500 have continued their upward march in recent years in accordance with the steady rise in capital's share.

Relative capital valuation makes sense of the often-noted lack of synergistic returns accruing to acquirers. Stymied by an inability to move forward through new investment, but replete with cash and a heightened stock market, acquirers will tend to overpay in the pursuit of growth. Some time ago, Sanford Grossman and Oliver Hart showed that whatever synergistic gains takeovers generate will tend to accrue to target shareholders, not those of the acquirer. This result occurs because existing shareholders of the target can "free ride." If "a shareholder thinks that the raid will succeed and that the raider will improve the firm, he will not tender his shares, but will instead retain them, because he anticipates a profit from their price appreciation" (Grossman and Hart, 1980, p. 43). Consequently, the acquisition premium will tend to expand to absorb whatever profit the raider initially anticipated. This insight may explain why acquisition premiums are often so high (over the last several decades, running about 40 percent on average), but raises the question of why acquirers would pay them. In the context of low internal growth prospects, relative valuation comprehends this apparent anomaly—there is simply no other way to grow but to pay a high price.

Marginal Q

As the ratio of stock valuation to replacement costs, Q utilizes measures pertaining to blocks of capital, not additional stock valuation consequent on additional capital (investment). In understanding how firms make investment decisions, however, Tobin and Brainard maintain that it is *marginal* Q, rather than Q, that is the motivating variable (Brainard and Tobin, 1977, p. 243). Marginal Q is defined as the expected *additional* stock valuation divided by the new investment that presumably accounts for the additional stock valuation. Brainard and Tobin never attempted to measure marginal Q perhaps because of their belief that "for short-run variations of aggregate demand, we can expect that the same factors which raise or lower [Q] on the margin likewise raise or lower [Q] on average" (Brainard and Tobin, 1977, p. 243). But this correspondence is far from certain. An explanation of why marginal Q might decline during stock market booms or at least be subject to dampening forces could account for the fact that mergers become relatively more attractive than new investment during those same booms. But if such an explanation were available, Q theory would have to be turned on its head: the theory would then predict that stock market booms may inhibit new investment over and above the levels that would otherwise obtain. In other than the rarified case of pure competition, where under certain conditions marginal Q reduces to average Q (Hayashi, 1982), or in the similarly rarified case that assumes homogeneity of capital and disembodied change (Able and Blanchard, 1986), marginal Q has defied estimation.

Unlike Q, marginal Q is an elusive variable as the change in stock valuation resulting from new investment is unobservable. To observe marginal Q, one would have to know what the stock valuation would have been in the absence of new investment so as to calculate the difference. Nevertheless, if we assume that changes in stock valuation reflect the anticipated rate of return on new investment we can, with the aid of relative valuation, sketch out the general movement of marginal Q. As will be demonstrated, this general movement has declined over time, even when average Q has expanded. I argue below that such a decline helps us to understand the general decline in rates of corporate investment growth at least since the late 1960s.

Assume marginal Q to be a monotonic function of the expected rate of return on new investment:

(5) $\frac{\Delta sv}{I} = \mathrm{F}\left[\frac{C-Z}{I}\right]$ where: ΔSV = the change in stock value due to new investment

Then from **(3)** above, marginal $\mathrm{Q} = \mathrm{F}\left[h\frac{Y}{I}\right]$ and should expand (contract) in accordance with the output/investment ratio.

This pared-down form allows a straightforward test of investment growth. An expansion (contraction) of the investment growth rate should expand (contract) with the movement of the output/investment ratio.

But additional insight into marginal Q can be gleaned if the theory is placed in the context of relative valuations whereby the choice of "Build or Buy" is explicitly formulated. By **(1)** above, **(5)** is equivalent to defining marginal Q as a function of the total cash generated over the time period divided by the total capital stock inclusive of the new investment. In accordance with relative valuation, the older capital stock is valued *relative* to the new investment:

(6) $$\text{Marginal Q} = \mathrm{F}\left[\frac{h*Y}{I}\right] = \mathrm{F}\left[\frac{C}{K+I}\right] = \mathrm{F}\left[\frac{C/I}{\frac{K}{I}+1}\right] = \mathbf{F}\left[\frac{\boldsymbol{h*C/I}}{\boldsymbol{C/Y}}\right]$$

The cash/investment ratio—as contained in the numerator of **(5)**—is just *another way to express free cash.*[18] So marginal Q is a race between free cash and capital's share. As shown by **(6)**, an expansion of capital's share tends to *reduce investment incentives on the margin.* By raising the relative value of existing capital in relation to new investment, an expansion of capital's share raises the relative "benchmark" of cash generation by which the cash-generating power of new investment is to be assessed. In accordance with the marginal Q specification above, an increase of investment growth would be justified only if the cash-investment ratio rises faster than capital's share. Of course, such assessment assumes that (**h**) remains relatively constant over the short-term time horizon through which investment decisions are made. Over time, efficiency gains per unit of output and capacity utilization might well change and alter the marginal Q specification above. For example, a build-up of excess capacity would no doubt lower (**h**) over time and present an additional obstacle in motivating new investment.

One might assume that because investment becomes ever more "efficient," the output/investment ratio would necessarily increase through time. But as Figure 5.3 shows, for the aggregate corporate sector, the exact opposite has been the rule with output per unit of fixed investment in recent decades being almost 20 percent below the decade following World War II. The biggest drop-off occurred in the mid-1960s through the late 1970s—a period coincident with the end of what Stephen A. Marglin and Juliet B. Schor (1991) have termed the "Golden Age"—a period of very rapid investment growth that evolved after the War.

The decline in the output/investment ratio appears paradoxical. But in view of **(5)** above, one recognizes that the decline in the ratio might well be explained by *social and institutional* aspects pertaining to the class division of income (c/y), the

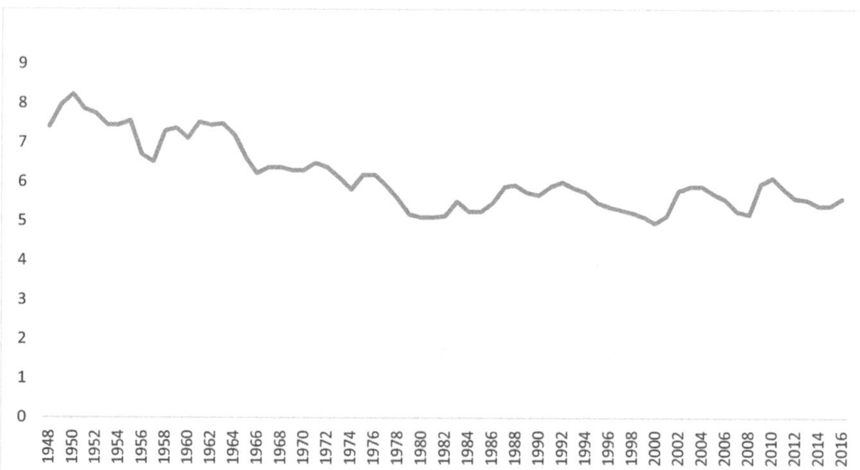

Figure 5.3 Corporate output/corporate fixed investment

Sources: Department of Commerce, Table 1.14; Flow of Funds Federal Reserve, Table F.2, lines 10, 12, 15.

corporate generation of free cash (c/I), and the more rapid rise of the former over the last thirty-some years.

Figure 5.4 displays the post-WWII race between c/I (free cash) and c/y. Both begin their strong upward ascent in the mid-1970s after the "Golden Age." The right-hand Y axis of Figure 5.4 records the corporate division of income in the post-WWII period. After a decade and a half of modern increases beginning in the 1950s, capital share eroded from the mid-1960s until the mid-1970s, at which point it started to climb to historical heights.

Compared to the three-decade-long increase in capital's share of corporate output, the decline dating from the mid-1960s period seems quite mild. Nevertheless, this short-term fall-off gave rise to an extensive literature surrounding this "profit-squeeze."[19] Although riddled with some controversy, profit-rate theorists explained this "squeeze" in terms of increased foreign competition in concert with a breakdown of a *tacit and limited* social compact between capital, labor and government.[20] This social compact accorded high priority to demand management through high wages, high employment and low cost of job loss, due to various entitlement programs and prospects of renewed employment. Forged during the Depression-WWII era, the social compact implicitly understood that high employment meant for high demand, so there was no necessary trade-off between wage growth and profit. The onslaught of foreign competition, however, made such a compact unworkable. The period of "relative isolation" (Bluestone and Harrison, 1988, pp. 22–23) in which managers could simply mark up costs

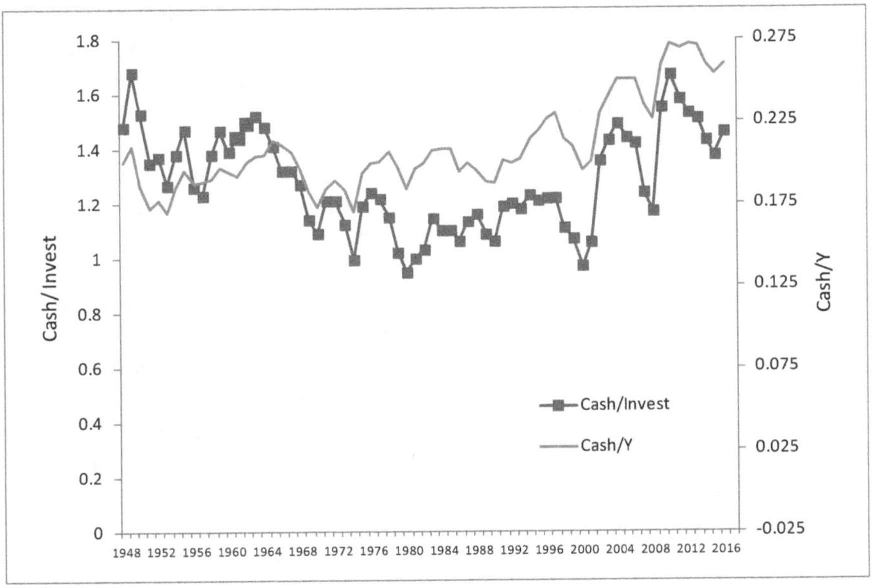

Figure 5.4 Cash/I; Cash/Y

Sources: Dept. of Commerce, Table 1.14, Federal Funds, Federal Reserve, Table F.22. lines 10, 12, 15.

came to an end when "prices . . . were . . . imposed [on] the world market by . . . leading competitors," particularly in the late 1960s (Brenner, 2006, p. 109). This imposition of world prices was aided enormously by the high dollar regime of Bretton Woods that allowed foreign competitors an export advantage. U.S. managers responded in part by expanding the automation of production, but not entirely. Brenner maintains that in understanding existing capital as "sunk costs," managers continued using increasingly obsolete plant and equipment as a rational but short-term response to the pricing power of foreign competition. Accordingly, the profit rate, calculated on total capital, declined and set off a corresponding decline in the "rate of capital accumulation" (investment relative to the capital stock). These declines in the profit rate and rate of accumulation were exacerbated by more militant strike activity, particularly in the manufacturing sector (Brenner, 2006, p. 114). Higher wage gains eroded profit (Bowles and Gintis, 1987, p. 60); Bowles, Gordon and Weisskopt, 1990, pp. 70–71).

Profit rate theorists have generally maintained that investment follows the profit rate on capital.[21] This profit-rate conception is theoretically flawed because it does not distinguish between returns to new investment and returns attributable to the total capital stock. Linking investment to the rate of profits on total capital completely misses investment incentives *on the margin.* The driving force behind new investment should not be the profit rate on all capital, but rather the additional prospective cash consequent on new investment, a variable that marginal Q attempts to measure.

It is also important to emphasize that the rate of profit involves a conception of what capital actually is. Measuring capital by sunk expenditures minus depreciation not only begs the measurement problems associated with depreciation,[22] but does not address the valuation of capital in reference to its current and future cash-generating potential. No correction can be made. To value existing capital by its returns, i.e. having the value of capital move up and down with profits, is to completely abandon the conception of a profit rate. Relative valuation, however, values capital not as an absolute figure but as the benchmark by which to measure the cash-generating power of new investment and *vice versa.* I say vice versa because the cash-generating power of new investment dictates the relative valuation of existing capital.

In understanding the profit-rate squeeze of the late 1960s as the multiplicative result of capital's share and the output/capital ratio, profit-rate theorists understand the erosion of capital's share as overpowering the rise in the capital/output ratio (Armstrong, Glyn and Harrison, 1991, p. 121). Under relative valuation theory, however, any decline in capital's share needs to be assessed relative to free cash as expressed by the cash/investment ratio. In contrast to a "profit-rate" interpretation of investment incentives, relative capital valuation maintains that a decline in capital's share *increases* investment incentives on the margin. This is because such a decline expands the relative valuation of new investment as measured by the lowered benchmark cash-generating power of existing capital (see **(5)** above). All is dependent on the movement in the cash/investment ratio. In the latter part of the 1960s when the output/capital ratio increased, the cash/investment ratio fell off precipitously, declining at a faster rate than capital's share. Under the supposition that marginal Q follows the output/investment ratio, marginal Q fell off in the latter part of the 1960s, not because capital's share fell, but because free cash fell off faster. This decline precipitated the end of the "Golden Age."

Given that the bulk of gross saving is either cash or derives from it through security payouts, Kaleckian-Keynesian theory tells us that there should be a tight short-term relationship between cash (or profit) and investment. This is an abbreviated version of Michael Kalecki's understanding that "capitalists earn what they spend" (Feiwel, 1975, p. 89). Variations in the ratio of cash (or profit) to investment should be bounded. Profit -rate theorists have been remiss in not making this point explicit. In showing that the rate of capital accumulation (investment/capital stock) follows the rate of profit (profit/capital stock, profit-rate theorists simply replicate the short-term profit-investment linkage.

This is not to say that over the long haul, the cash/new investment ratio has not varied considerably (see Figure 5.4). The rapid fall-off of the ratio beginning in the mid-1960s and its subsequent rise since the mid-1970s begs the question of how the simple Kaleckian-Keynesian lockstep of cash (or profit) and investment could be violated over significant periods of time. The short answer is debt. The longer answer is debt plus corporate responses to shifts in the foreign balance. Cash can be realized even under conditions of lackluster investment if aggregate demand is sufficiently propped up through debt. A Kaleckian account recognizes that free cash can be realized when fiscal deficits act like an "export surplus."

A full account of free cash generation and debt expansion will be presented in the next chapter. The rise of capital's share is now the topic at hand.

The Golden Age, the subsequent "zapping of labor" and class shares

Figure 5.4 shows the rapid turnaround in capital's share since the late 1970s. Thirty years ago, Barry Bluestone and Bennett Harrison termed this reversal "The Great U-Turn" in 1988. It has not turned back. From the mid-1970s to 2017, capital's after-tax share of corporate output expanded almost 50 percent.[23]

Among profit-rate theorists, there has been a variety of contributing explanations for the U-turn. Stung by the profits squeeze of the late 1960s (Marglin and Bhaduri, 1991, pp. 153–154) and stung again by the OPEC price increases of the 1970s (Glyn et al., 1991, pp. 107–110; Brenner, 2006, p. 145), managers engaged in an extended effort to cut costs. In response to the exogenous oil shocks, foreign competition and high wage employment of the late 1960s, U.S. mega-corporations outsourced production while attempting to stabilize domestic market shares. They also cut back on labor costs through part-time employment, a two-tiered wage structure that retained higher wages for "legacy" employees and a lower one for recent hires and automation. According to Bluestone and Harrison (1988), this corporate restructuring involved

> more than anything else the abrogation of the social contract that labor, management and government had slowly but surely constructed in the course of nearly fifty years of union struggle, collective bargaining and government regulation of the age-old battle over the disposition of the nation's total output.
>
> (p. 5)

By the middle of the 1980s, the

> assault on the cost of labor . . . could be summarized in the globalization of production, the hollowing out of the firm, outright union busting, and revised labor-management relationship that included demands for the lowering of wages, the proliferation of part-time work schedules (in opposition to the workers' expressed preference for full-time employment), and the increased subcontracting of work. Together, these developments added up to a realization of the objective—publicly enunciated by a conservative government back at the very beginning of the 1970s—of "zapping labor."
>
> (p. 51)

Part of the explanation of capital's share up to the present can be understood as a simple extension of the factors making up the initial "assault" on labor. But, following Brenner's interpretation of history (2006), some other part has to be understood in terms of successive waves of imports—first from Germany and Japan, then from the newly industrializing countries (NICs) of Asia—Korea, Taiwan, Singapore, Hong Kong, South East Asia and now, China (pp. 262–264). The negative effect on wages in "trade"-related work as well as services associated with such work has been particularly pronounced (Tyson and Spence, 2017, p. 171). The list of NICs enumerated here could be extended. But the main point is that labor forces around the world put U.S. workers in competition with overseas counterparts, while firms lowered the investment rate, undercutting employment possibilities.

The coming of a new digital age has involved a new digital "zapping" of labor that has crossed large swaths of the labor market, particularly focused around routine work that machines can perform or can be performed offshore. The new digitized world has allowed all types and combinations of supply chains to coordinate across geographical boundaries to affect product placement and production. Such supply chains have allowed an expansion of labor arbitrage, placing the working class of developed nations in competition with working people—often arriving from peasant villages—used to working under poverty conditions and now working for a small fraction of working-class wages in the developed world.[24] The resulting insecurity and downsizing among the working class of advanced nations is reflected in the long recovery times after U.S. recessions, the decline of male labor force participation, the growth of self-employed contracting, temporary employment and a myriad of other forms of "flexible" work engagement.

In reference to the new high-tech world, the McKinsey Global Institute points to a new "Digital America," which it characterizes as a "Tale of the Haves and Have-Mores" (McKinsey Global Institute, 2015). The study might well have been entitled a "Tale of the Haves and Those Who Have Recently Lost." The rise of high technology and its multiple uses have made obsolete a large number of previous skills permeating not just manufacturing but all types of services and middle-management positions. The skill set associated with engineering the new digital workplace has put a premium on individuals who have adapted to the new digital requirements, whether such requirements have entailed programming skills, cognitive initiative, adaptability to the new digitization of health, education, legal and other services, flexible attitudes towards complex changes in the work environment, or some combination thereof. Although skill sets associated with the new digital economy have been widely absorbed—particularly in geographical areas associated with innovation hubs—large numbers of working people have been left behind.

The successive downturns of 1973–75, 1981–82, 1990–91, 2001 and the one begun in late 2007 disciplined labor repeatedly, holding wages down and allowing capital's share to rise to historical heights. The significance of this meteoric rise is made more pronounced when consideration if given to the expanded "labor" compensation of high-tech labor, health workers, financiers, legal advisors and assorted managerial workers reporting to other professionals and top-level management, who themselves constitute part of the recorded labor force. James Galbraith (2000) finds that the disparity of wage earnings largely followed the changing mix of technological advance, with industries with higher value added per worker (computers, missiles and aircraft, chemicals, medical) showing the highest wage growth (p. 111). The growth in inequality in the wage structures was particularly pronounced from the late 1960s to around 1980, when it leveled out into the early 1990s (p. 148). However, this leveling came in the face of an actual decline in production workers' real wages across all industries. Average production workers' real compensation at the end of 2014 was actually below that of 1973 (Leopold, 2015, p. 23).

Joined by an increased precariousness of employment, such disparity in the wage structure has intensified labor's lack of collective identity. This lack of labor solidarity, of course, is nothing new. But recent developments surrounding the massive decline in union membership, the forty-year-long cutting-loose of labor's New Deal affiliation with the Democratic Party, and the widening disparity in compensation driven by the new high-tech artisan fields have deepened traditional splits among the laboring class based on ethnicity, race, gender, geographical location and immigrant status.[25] In focusing on the "other [i.e. bottom] 99 percent," David H. Autor (2014) documents that "about two-thirds of the overall rise of earnings dispersion between 1980 and 2005 is proximately accounted for by the increased premium associated with schooling in general and postsecondary in particular" (p. 843). Autor also documents a deceleration in the growth rate of U.S. college graduates from 1982, at the very same time that the demand for cognitive skills increased dramatically. Among advanced nations, this disparity in the demand and supply of cognitive ability—coined the "education race"—has put the U.S. at the extreme end of the dollar-denominated skill premium spectrum

(p. 846). Unlike the First Industrial Revolution whereby artisan skills dissolved before the onslaught of factory work powered by steam engines, the new "Second Machine Age" has required skill sets associated with a new adaptability and aptitude honed towards constant learning, and the ability to take on a corresponding educational expense. The First Industrial Revolution tended to unify labor by forming an industrial proletariat. The Second Machine Age has not. The large numbers of workers falling outside the "education" race are increasingly directed towards low-paid retail, wholesale and service employments of all types.

The fractured nature of the working class and its consequent inability to fight for a larger piece of the economic pie explains a large part of the rise in capital's share.

It should also be noted that the actual expansion of capital's share is considerably larger than the recorded rise. Executive compensation should be included in capital's share. But it is not. By including executive compensation in labor's share, the statistical record is significantly distorted. On the executive front, the globalized presence of automation, supply chains and markets have allowed such "employees" to extend their reach and expand their "super-status" in garnering increasingly exorbitant pay packages. The top receivers of such packages are often involved in the digital world of low marginal costs associated with production and distribution. In such a world, "winner takes all" economics dictates outcomes. When market areas are huge, even a small premium associated with increased service over a rival, or an entrenched position like that of Microsoft, can generate super-compensation premiums to the commanders of such outreach. Thus from 1980 to 2003, there was a six-fold expansion of top executives' compensation (Gabaix and Landier, 2008, p. 49). Compensation of such "employees" across a broad spectrum of firms rose from around 20 times the "typical" worker in 1970 to around 300 times in recent years (Mishel, Gould and Bivens, 2015, p. 9). This ratio seems modest if one compares the very top executive earners to production workers. In 1970, the "wage gap" of the average top 200 chief executive officers to the compensation of the average non-supervisory production worker was 38 to one; by 2013, the gap had expanded to 587 to one (Leopold, 2015, p. 25). Cozy arrangements between top CEOs and CEO-selected Board members have long been part of U.S. corporate culture. The outsized CEO compensation of late suggests that such coziness might well have expanded along with the compensation.

The decline of marginal Q, investment slowdown and underutilization

The historical and institutional literature explaining the increase in capital's share is quite developed and no quick summary can capture its full dimensions. But in terms of profit-rate investment theory, such an increase should have expanded returns and investment. Yet, however volatile during short periods, the profit rate calculated on fixed capital (measured by accumulated net investments) was relatively trendless after the Golden Age, implicating a 47-year increase in the capital/output ratio of roughly 19 percent from 1968 to 2016.[26] Given the increased efficiency of capital, this increase has been somewhat difficult to explain. Brenner (2006) holds that firms' ownership of intangible assets and their inability to exist and to enter new lines contributed to over-accumulation (p. 155). Armstrong and colleagues (1991) indicate that the capital stock might well be overstated to the extent that "scrapping" takes place at a faster rate than depreciation schedules specify (p. 181). They also suggest that a slow-up of labor productivity and a decreasing use of capital utilization might also explain the rise in the capital/output ratio (p. 182).

Underutilization does help explain the long-term increase in the recorded capital/output ratio and consequently the decline in the rate of accumulation. Does underutilization also explain the decline in the rate of investment growth? Figure 5.5 plots normalized data on the rate of investment growth, the rate of growth of corporate output and capacity utilization. (I use normalized data so as to use the same Y axis to compare variables with different units.) There is a close correspondence between all three variables. The rate of investment growth, however, leads capacity utilization, suggesting that the causal sequence runs from investment growth to utilization. In that a decline in marginal Q can explain the fall-off of investment growth, a decline in marginal Q can also partially explain underutilization. That said, the long-term correspondence of the two variables no doubt indicates mutual influence.

Figure 5.5 also shows the close correspondence between the secular stagnation in corporate output and corporate investment. Not surprisingly, this general correspondence correlates with the general decline in growth rates across the entire economy. Comparison of decade average growth rates of income since the 1960s show that while the1960s demonstrated a roughly 4 percent growth rate, rates of growth have fallen over time into the 2 percent rate of the first decade of the twenty-first century (Foster and McChesney, 2010, p. 5).

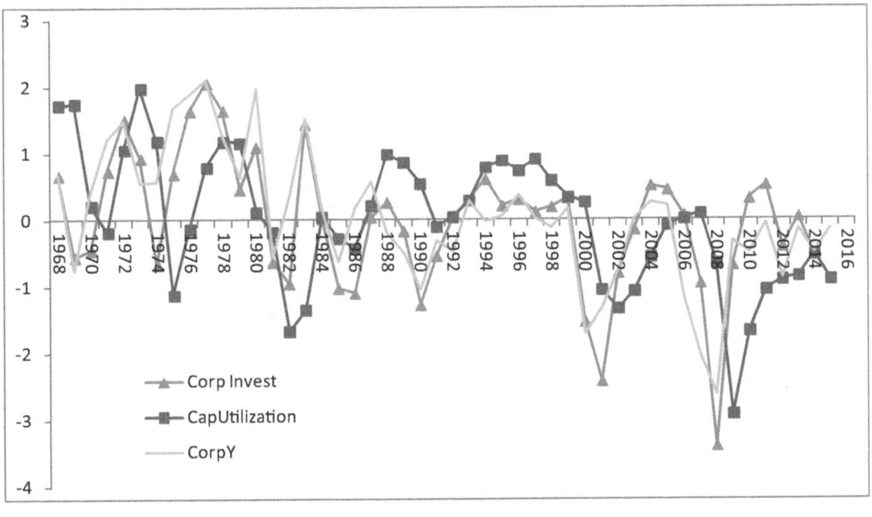

Figure 5.5 Corporate investment and income growth rates

Sources: Flow of Funds, Federal Reserve, Table F.2, lines 10,12,15; Federal Reserve St. Louis for Total Industry capacity utilization.

The evidence for relative valuation

I argued above that in utilizing (sunk) expenditures and arbitrary depreciation schedules, the recorded valuation of capital is devoid of operational meaning in understanding how new investment responds to *marginal* profit incentives. I argued that the correlation between the recorded "rate of capital accumulation" and the profit rate simply replicates the Kaleckian-Keynesian lockstep of profit (or cash) and investment.

A simple inversion of **(4)** above produces a relative valuation analogue of the "rate of capital accumulation" (i.e. I/K). Unlike movements in the traditional measure of the rate of capital accumulation, however, movements in the *relative* rate of capital accumulation act as direction signals, with a decline in I/K directing firms to give less weight to expansion through new investment. Given financial constraints and an inability of firms to pursue all avenues of growth with equal intensity, new investment growth should fall off with an increase in capital's share of output. There should therefore be a correlative relationship between investment growth and the *inverse* of capital's share (i.e. the output/cash ratio).

A stronger test involves the output/investment ratio—the derived result of the race between free cash and capital's share—depicting the movement in marginal Q. We should expect a lowering of investment growth with the long-term fall-off of the output/investment ratio portrayed in Figure 5.3.

Figure 5.6 compares normalized data on the output/cash and output/investment ratios with the corporate investment growth rate. (As before, I use normalized

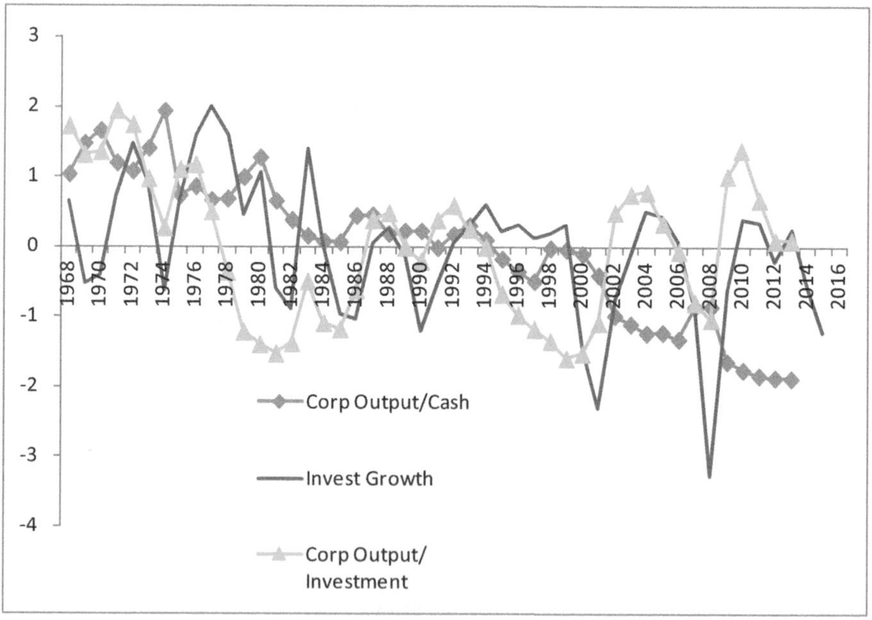

Figure 5.6 Investment stagnation and marginal Q proxies

Sources: Department of Commerce, Table 1.14; Flow of Funds, Federal Reserve, Table F.2, lines 10, 12, 15

data so as to place variables with different units on the same Y axis.) The highly volatile investment rate falls along with the inverse of capital's share and the output/investment ratio underpinning marginal Q. As predicted by relative valuation theory, the marginal Q proxy (the ratio of corporate output to investment) leads corporate investment growth. I take this as evidence that marginal Q does indeed help explain the volatile investment growth rate.

Summary and conclusions regarding Q theory and relative valuations

As traditionally formulated, Q theory has been unduly abstract. Q theorists have universally abstained from placing the theory in an institutional or historical context. In accordance with the long secular rise in Q over the bulk of the last thirty-some years, Q theory would have predicted both an upward movement in the rate of investment growth and a decline in merger activity relative to new investment. Q theory has been wrong on both counts. In this chapter, I have integrated a reformulated marginal Q theory based on relative capital valuation with an explanation concerning the recent rise in capital's share. The literature pertaining to the latter is quite rich and any brief synopsis like the present one cannot possibly do it justice. But however inclusive and historically rich, the literature would be better informed were it to utilize class-share theory to illuminate investment decisions on the margin—a project that marginal Q theory at least recognizes. Unlike profit-rate theory that specifies a unidirectional relationship between capital's share, the profit rate and investment, relative capital valuations show that an expansion of capital's share actually reduces investment incentives by lowering marginal Q. Marginal Q and investment growth declined as a result of *the inability of debt-fueled free cash (the cash/investment ratio) to overpower the rise in capital's share.* As has been noted above, this conclusion rests on an underlying assumption that the unobservable "**h**" (the proportionality coefficient relating expected augmented cash flows to new investment) has remained relatively constant or at least has not risen appreciably. In light of the secular trend of capacity utilization, it is highly likely that "**h**" actually fell.

A long-term decline in marginal Q, even in the face of the long-term expansion of average Q, would certain explain Q theory's weakness in predicting new investment expenditures and the long-term secular decline in the corporate rate of investment growth.

Notes

1 Fisher applied the present value analysis of bond financing to that of virtually every capital asset, inclusive of stock equity. But such extended application was not without problems. Bond financing harbored the uncertainties associated with the possibility of bankruptcy and interest rate risk. But at least in the case of bonds, the promised future returns were explicitly stated. In contrast, returns to equity approximated a guessing game where expectations of the future could be manipulated or, as Thorstein Veblen frequently mentioned, could be "imputed" on the basis of "make-believe" projections. This imagination element broke the symmetrical appearance of discounted earnings streams being but a simple transposition of bond finance to that of equity and brought

psychology squarely into the economics of finance. Imagination could apparently expand beyond any reasonable limit. As Veblen noted, these imputations could run to "several times the total value of the material assets which underlie them" (Veblen, [1919] 2002, p. 78). In a response to Thorstein Veblen's critique that Fisher conflated serviceable with pecuniary valuation, Fisher contended the "principles of capitalizing income are *immutable* principles of relationship . . . entirely independent of particular valuations of applications" (Fisher 1909, p. 511; emphasis added). In a footnote in *The Nature of Capital and Interest* (1906), Fisher was to make his preference for generality explicit, saying "It is well known that in science the most general conceptions are the most fruitful" (Fisher [1906] 2012, p. 65).

2 Veblen was relying on J.A. Hobson's analysis in *The Problem of the Unemployed* (1896).

3 *The Structure of the American Economy* (1939) prepared under the direction of Gardiner C. Means was the most complete study of the administered price phenomena. Over a hundred industries were examined in reference to price sensitivity. The study showed a general correlation between industry concentration and price stickiness (Means, 1939, p. 143).

4 Here again, Ezekiel, in contrasting the possibilities of national planning during the war with the supposed impossibility of fighting hunger, unemployment and destitution during peace. During depression, "It is better, we are told, that they stay 'ill-housed, ill-clad, ill-nourished' than that the business community be shocked by having to learn new ways of doing things." But during war, "as long as all that we produce is to be blown into the air, then it is recognized as both proper and fitting that we should plan" (Ezekiel, 1939, p. 3).

5 In Arnold's *Folklore of Capitalism* ([1937] 1959, pp. 207–229).

6 Galbraith himself, along with Henry Sturgis Dennison, wrote a book entitled *Modern Competition and Business Policy*, which advanced the monopoly-restrictionist thesis. But his own doubts about the argument led him to omit it from his list of published writings (Galbraith, 1994, p. 86).

7 In reference to construction, however, public works construction was roughly 40–50 percent of the total (Galbraith, 1940, pp. 17–18).

8 For a fuller discussion, see Hawley (1966, pp. 347–359).

9 I say "quasi" because while the twelve-member Open Market Committee included seven officials from the Board of Governors, who are publicly appointed officials, the Committee also included five presidents of the twelve privately owned and managed Federal Reserve Banks.

10 One might add to this short list of reforms the extension of loans through the Reconstruction Finance Corporation, the subsidies of the Export-Import Bank, the efforts of the Federal Housing Administration, Rural Electrification Administration, Civil Aeronautics Authority and Maritime Commission and other assorted agencies and commissions that acted to support the economy. In reference to these agencies and commissions, Charles Beard and George Smith (1940) tally "about fifty in all" (p. 221).

11 For example, plumbing products of various types; asphalted felt-base floor coverings—all figures from Lynch (1946, pp. 139–140).

12 I omit the Thompson series as it is proprietary and not readily available in most libraries.

13 For two other reasons, the series is less than ideal. The series omits the separate tabulation of divestitures and foreign acquisitions for the earliest years (divestitures earlier than 1981) and foreign acquisitions earlier than 1975. For the subject at hand, one might subtract out divestitures as they do not represent net acquisition activity. On the other hand, divestitures do drive up stock prices and are hence partially reflected in Q. These arguments also apply to the inclusion or exclusion of foreign acquisitions.

14 Three different definitions of Q and their corresponding figures are calculated by those affiliated with the Department of Commerce. I have taken as representative what they term Q1—defined as the "market value of outstanding equity" to the "net stock of produced assets" (Osborne and Retus, 2016, p. 5).

15 Some studies (Rau and Vermaelen, 1998; Loughran and Vijh, 1997) showed some positive returns accruing to acquirers on tender offers, but Mitchell and Stafford (2000) and Andrade, Mitchell and Stafford (2001) noted that these merger observations were not statistically independent. They present evidence that long-term gains to acquirers were actually insignificant. Jensen and Ruback (1983) summarized six studies showing "negative results" in the year after takeover. In the "negative return" category are studies by Asquith (1983), Agrawal, Jaffe and Mandeler (1992), and Loderer and Martin (1992). In the "no significant result" category are studies by Langetieg (1978) and Franks, Harris and Titman (1991).

16 For example, the merger theory of Dennis Mueller concerning the 1960s conglomerate wave; that of Michael Jensen in reference to the 1980s; also, the limited investment opportunities surrounding industries subject to "shock" such as those, like telecommunications, energy and finance subject to deregulation. See Mitchell and Mulherin (1996); Andrade, Mitchell and Stafford (2001).

17 As noted above, the FTC series deals with manufacturing and mining only. Plant and equipment is the proxy for new investment.

18 When **C/I** is greater than one, free cash appears.

19 See, for example, Bowles and Gintis, 19867; Bluestone and Harrison, 1988; Bowles, Gordon and Weisskopt, 1990; Bhaduri and Marglin, 1991, pp. 153–186; Armstrong, Glyn and Harrison, 1991; Glyn, 2006, and Brenner, 2006.

20 In his *Global Turbulence* (2006), Robert Brenner sees the "supply-side" profit thesis as being fundamentally misplaced when applied to the period after the "Golden Age" and even during the "Golden Age" (p. 102). He also takes issue with the social compact interpretation that was supposed to gird capital, labor and state in a common understanding in the immediate post-WWII period. To substantiate his case, he brings up various assaults on labor during the so-called "Golden Age" (pp. 62–63).

21 Bowles, Gordon and Weisskopt, 1990, pp. 45–46; Glyn et al., 1991, pp. 83–86; Marglin and Bhaduri, 1991, pp. 160–162; Armstrong, Glyn and Harrison, 1991, pp. 251–256; Brenner, 2006, p. 180; Glyn, 2006, pp. 134–136.

22 Measuring capital's return by cash (profits after tax plus depreciation) puts the focus on the amount of internally generated monies that management either dispenses or has available for expansion purposes. Cash also avoids the pitfalls of trying to arbitrarily discern which part of cash is "true" depreciation and which is profit—a distinction that has not been worked out even on a theoretical level.

23 Corporate returns measured by profits after tax plus depreciation: Table 1.14, National Income and Product Accounts, Department of Commerce.

24 "The share of workers globally making two dollars a day or less stood at 25 percent in 2014. Precariousness is particularly high, however, in the developing world, where the working poor (making four dollars or less per day) make up more than half the workers. Nearly 60 percent of wage workers globally are part-time or in some form of temporary employment" (Foster and Jonna, 2016, pp. 16–17). Figures in the Foster and Jonna article are from the International Labor Organization.

25 A good introduction to the wide disparities in wages, poverty and the segmentation of the labor force is to be found in Bluestone and Harrison's *Growing Prosperity* (2001).

26 Department of Commerce: Fixed corporate capital, historical cost net stock, Table 4.3; corporate output (value added), Table 1.14.

References

Able, A.B. and O.J. Blanchard, "The Present Value of Profits and Cyclical Movements in Investments," *Econometrica*, March 1986, Vol. 54, No. 2, pp. 249–273.

Agrawal, A., J.F. Jaffe and G.N. Mandeler, "The Post-Merger Performance of Acquiring Firms: A Re-Examination of an Anomaly," *Journal of Finance*, Vol. 47, 1992, pp. 1605–1621.

Andrade, Gregor, Mark Mitchell and Erik Stafford, "New Evidence and Perspectives on Mergers," *Journal of Economic Perspectives*, Vol. 15, No. 2, Spring 2001, pp. 103–120.

Armstrong, Philip, Andrew Glyn and John Harrison, *Capitalism Since 1945*, Basil Blackwell, Oxford, 1991.

Arnold, Thurman, *The Folklore of Capitalism*, Yale University Press, New Haven, CT, [1937] 1959.

Asquith, P., "Merger Bids, Uncertainty, and Stockholder Returns," *Journal of Financial Economics*, Vol. 11, 1983, pp. 51–53.

Autor, David, "Skills, Education, and the Rise of the Earnings Inequality Among the 'Other 99 Percent,'" *Science*, Vol. 344, Issue 6186, May 23, 2014.

Beard, Charles A. and George H.E. Smith, *The Old Deal and The New*, Macmillan Company, New York, 1940.

Bluestone, Barry and Bennett Harrison, *The Great U Turn*, Basic Books, Inc., New York, 1988.

Bluestone, Barry and Bennett Harrison, *Growing Prosperity: The Battle for Growth with Equity in the 21st Century*, Century Foundation Book, University of California Press, Berkeley, Los Angeles and London, 2001.

Bowles, Samuel and Herbert Gintis, *Democracy and Capitalism*, Basic Books, Inc., New York, 1987.

Bowles, Samuel, David M. Gordon and Thomas E. Weisskopt, *After the Waste Land*, M.E. Sharpe, Inc., Armonk, NY, 1990.

Brainard, W.C. and J. Tobin, "Asset Markets and the Cost of Capital," in *Economic Progress, Private Values and Public Policy: Essays in Honor of William Fellner*, edited by R. Nelson and B. Balassa, North-Holland, Amsterdam, 1977, pp. 235–262.

Brenner, Robert, *The Boom and the Bubble: The U.S. in the World Economy*, Verso Press, New York, 2002.

Brenner, Robert, *The Economics of Global Turbulence*, Verso, London and New York, 2006.

Dennison, Henry Sturgis and John Kenneth Galbraith, *Modern Competition and Business Policy*, Oxford University Press, New York, 1938.

Domar, Evsey, *Essays in the Theory of Economic Growth*, Oxford, Oxford University Press, 1957.

Du Boff, Richard B. and Edward S. Herman, "The Promotional-Financial Dynamic of Merger Movements," *Journal of Economic Issues*, Vol. 23, No. 1, March 1989.

Ezekiel, Mordecai, *Jobs for All*, Alfred A. Knopf, New York, London, 1939.

Feiwel, George R., *The Intellectual Capital of Michal Kalecki*, University of Tennessee Press, Nashville, 1975.

Fisher, Irving, *The Nature of Capital and Income*, London: Forgotten Books, [1906] 2012.

Fisher, Irving, "A Reply to Critics," *Quarterly Journal of Economics*, 1909, Vol. 23, No. 3, pp. 536–541.

Foster, John Bellamy and R. Jamil Jonna, "Marx's Theory of Working-Class Precariousness," *Monthly Review*, Vol. 69, No. 11, April 2016, pp. 1–19.

Foster, John Bellamy and Robert W. McChesney, "Capitalism, the Absurd System," *Monthly Review*, Vol. 62, No. 2, June 2010, pp. 1–16.

Franks, J., R. Harris and S. Titman, "The Postmerger Share-Price Performance of Acquiring Firms," *Journal of Financial Economics*, Vol. 29, 1991, pp. 81–96.

Gabaix, Xavier and Augustin Landier, "Why Has CEO Pay Increased So Much?," *Quarterly Journal of Economics*, Vol. CXXII, No. 1, February 2008, pp. 49–100.

Galbraith, James, K., *Created Unequal*, University of Chicago Press, Chicago, IL, 2000.

Galbraith, John Kenneth, *Economics in Perspective*, Houghton Mifflin Company, Boston, MA, 1987.

Galbraith, John Kenneth, *A Journey Through Economic Time: A Firsthand View*, Houghton Mifflin Company, Boston, MA and New York, 1994.

Galbraith, John Kenneth and Gove Griffith Johnson, *The Economic Effects of the Federal Public Works Expenditures*, National Resources Planning Board, Washington, DC, 1940.

Glyn, Andrew, *Capitalism Unleashed*, Oxford University Press, Oxford, 2006.

Glyn, Andrew, Alan Hughes, Alain Lipietz, Ajit Singh, "Rise and Fall of the Golden Age," in *The Golden Age of Capitalism*, edited by Stephen A. Marglin and Juliet B. Schor, Clarendon Paperbacks, Oxford, 1991.

Gort, Michael, "An Economic Disturbance Theory of Mergers," *Quarterly Journal of Economics*, Vol. 83, 1969, pp. 624–642.

Grossman, S. and O. Hart, "Takeover Bids, the Free Rider Problem, and the Theory of the Corporation," *Bell Journal of Economics*, Vol. 11, No. 1, Spring 1980, pp. 42–64.

Hawley, Ellis W., *The New Deal and the Problem of Monopoly*, Princeton University Press, Princeton, NJ, 1966.

Hayashi, F., "Tobin's Marginal Q and Average q: A Neoclassical Interpretation," *Econometrica*, January 1982, Vol. 50, No. 1, pp. 213–224.

Hobson, J.A., *The Problem of the Unemployed*, Methuen & Co., London, 1896.

Hogarty, T.F., "Profits from Mergers: The Evidence of Fifty Years," *St. John's Law Review* special edition, Vol. 44, Spring 1970, pp. 378–391.

Holmstrom, Bengt, and Steven N. Kaplan, "Corporate Governance and Merger Activity in the United States: Making Sense of the 1980s and 1990s," *Journal of Economic Perspectives*, Vol. 15, No. 2, Spring 2001, pp. 121–141.

Jensen, Michael, "Agency Costs of Free Cash Flow, Corporate Finance and Takeovers," *American Economic Review, Papers and Proceedings*, 1986, pp. 322–329.

Jensen, Michael and Richard S. Ruback, "The Market for Corporate Control: The Scientific Evidence," *Journal of Financial Economics*, Vol. 11, 1983, pp. 5–50.

Jovanovic, Boyan and Peter L. Rousseau, "The Q Theory of Mergers," *American Economic Review, Paper and Proceedings*, January 4–6, 2002, pp. 198–204.

Keynes, John Maynard, *The General Theory of Employment, Interest and Money*, Harvest/HBJ Book, Harcourt Brace Jovanovich, San Diego, CA, New York and London, [1936] 1953.

Lambrecht, Bart M., "The Timing and Terms of Mergers Motivated by Economies of Scale," *Journal of Financial Economics*, Vol. 72, 2004, pp. 41–62.

Lang, Larry H.P., Rene M. Stulz and Ralph A. Walkling, "Managerial Performance, Tobin's Q and the Gains from Successful Tender Offers," *Journal of Financial Economics*, Vol. 24, 1989, pp. 137–154.

Langetieg, T.C., "An Application of a Three-Factor Performance Index to Measure Stockholder Gains from Merger," *Journal of Financial Economics*, Vol. 6, 1978, pp. 365–383.

Leopold, Les, *Runaway Inequality*, Labor Institute Press, New York, 2015.

Loderer, C. and K. Martin, "Postacquisition Performance of Acquiring Firms," *Financial Management*, Vol. 19, 1992, pp. 69–79.

Loughran, T. and A. Vijh, "Do Long-Term Shareholders Benefit from Corporate Acquisitions," *Journal of Finance*, Vol. 52, 1997, pp. 1765–1790.

Lynch, David, *The Concentration of Economic Power*, Columbia University Press, New York, 1946.

Marglin, Stephen A. and Amit Bhaduri, "Profit Squeeze the Keynesian Theory," in *The Golden Age of Capitalism, Reinterpreting the Postwar Experience*, edited Stephen A. Marglin and Juliet B. Schor, Clarendon Paperbacks, Oxford, 1991.

Marglin, Stephen A. and Juliet B. Schor, eds., *The Golder Age of Capitalism: Reinterpreting the Postwar Experience*, Clarendon Press, Oxford, 1991.

McKinsey Global Institute, *Digital American: A Tale of the Haves and Have-Mores*, December 2015.

Means, Gardiner C., *The Structure of the American Economy: A Report Prepared by the Industrial Section Under the Direction of Gardiner C. Means*, National Resources Committee, United States Government Printing Office, Washington, DC, June 1939.

Mishel, Lawrence, Elise Gould and Josh Bivens, "Wage Stagnation in Nine Charts," *Economic Policy Institute*, January 6, 2015.

Mitchell, M. and J. Harold Mulherin, "The Impact of Industry Shocks on Takeover and Restructuring Activity," *Journal of Financial Economics*, Vol. 41, 1996, pp. 193–229.

Mitchell, M. and E. Stafford, "Managerial Decisions and Long Term Stock Price Performance," *Journal of Business*, Vol. 73, 2000, pp. 287–329.

Moeller, Sara B., Frederik P. Schlingemann and Rene M. Stulz, "Firm Size and the Gains from Acquisitions," *Journal of Financial Economics*, Vol. 73, 2004, pp. 201–228.

Morak, Randall, Andrei Shleifer and Robert W. Vishny, "Do Managerial Objectives Drive Bad Acquisitions," *Journal of Financial Economics*, Vol. XLV, No. 1, March 1990, pp. 31–48.

Mueller, Dennis, "A Theory of Conglomerate Mergers," *Quarterly Journal of Economics*, Vol. LXXXIII, No. 4, November 1969, pp. 643–659.

Mueller, Dennis, "The Effects of Conglomerate Mergers: A Survey of the Empirical Literature," *Journal of Banking and Finance*, 1977, pp. 315–347.

Nelson, Ralph, *Merger Movements in American Industry*, National Bureau of Economic Research, Princeton University Press, Princeton, NJ, 1959.

Osborne, Sarah and Bonnie A. Retus, "Returns for Domestic Nonfinancial Business," *Survey of Current Business*, December 2016.

Rau, P. Raghavendra and Theo Vermaelen, "Glamor, Value, and the Post-Acquisition Performance of Acquiring Firms," *Journal of Financial Economics*, Vol. 49, 1998, pp. 249–251.

Robinson, Joan, "The Production Function and the Theory of Capital," *Review of Economic Studies*, Vol. 21, No. 2, 1953–54, pp. 81–106.

Roll, Richard, "The Hubris Hypothesis of Corporate Takeover," *Journal of Business*, Vol. 59, 1986, pp. 197–216.

Shleifer, Andrei and Robert W. Vishny, "Stock Market Driven Acquisitions," *Journal of Financial Economics*, Vol. 70, 2003, pp. 295–311.

Thorp, Willard L., "The Persistence of the Merger Movement," *The American Economic Review: Papers and Proceedings of the Forty-third Annual Meeting*, Vol. XXI, No. 1, March 1931, pp. 74–89.

Tobin, J., "On the Efficiency of the Financial System," *Lloyd's Bank Review*, July 1984, Vol. 153, pp. 6–7.

Tobin, J., Remarks in a lecture at Trinity University, San Antonio, Texas, April 30, 1985, printed in *Essays in Economics: National and International*, MIT Press, Cambridge, MA, [1985] 1996.

Tugwell, Rexford G., *Roosevelt's Revolution*, Macmillan Publishing Co., Inc., New York, 1977.

Tyson, Laura and Michael Spence, "Exploring the Effects of Technology on Income and Wealth Inequality," in *After Piketty: The Agenda for Economics and Inequality*, edited by Heather Boushey, J. Bradford DeLong and Marshall Steinbaum, Harvard University Press, Cambridge, MA and London, 2017.

Veblen, Thorstein, *The Theory of Business Enterprise*, New Brunswick, NJ: Transaction Books, [1904] 1978.

Veblen, Thorstein, "Fisher's Capital and Income," *Political Science Quarterly*, Vol. XXIII, reprinted in *Essays in Our Changing Order*, Transaction Publishers, New Brunswick, NJ and London, [1908] 1998.

Veblen, Thorstein, *The Vested Interests*, New Brunswick, NJ: Transaction Publishers, [1919] 2002.

Veblen, Thorstein, *Absentee Ownership*, New York: Sentry Press, [1923] 1964.

Appendix 1

Expansion of cash through new investment

Capacity Case

Assume a "tacit" joint profit-maximizing oligopoly situation where in the short run price (P) is determined by a "tacit" agreement of the industry. Allow the expected revenues that could be produced by the existing capital stock (K) to be Px, where x is the profit-maximizing output that is constrained by existing capacity. New investment (I) enlarges capacity so as to permit a larger amount of revenues PX = vPx + Px where (v) is a proportionality constant that reflects the expansion in revenues net of capital costs. À la Evsey Domar, capacity varies proportionately with the capital stock. So changes in capacity (and crudely output and revenues) will vary proportionately with changes in the capital stock (i.e. I). With a given interest rate, capital costs will therefore vary proportionately with output.

Given a per unit variable cost (u) and a given markup (m = P/u), the net increase in cash consequent upon the new investment (i.e. c – z) is:

$$c - z = vx(P - u)$$

or: $$c - z = [(1 - 1/m/(1/v + 1)]^{*}\ PX$$

$$\mathbf{c - z = HY^{*}}, \text{ where } Y^{*} = \text{value of output} = PX$$

Efficiency Case

For a given level of output (x), new investment will reduce one or more of the physical inputs per unit of production over and above the input levels that would otherwise obtain. For a given price structure of inputs, the new investment will reduce per unit input costs by a particular fraction (a) of what would otherwise occur. The savings (additions to cash) are therefore (au), whereas in the Capacity Case, u is the per unit variable cost prior to the introduction of the new technology. As in the Capacity Case, these savings are net of capital costs. Accordingly,

$$c - z = (au/P)^{*}Px$$

or: $$c - z = \lambda Px$$

$$\mathbf{c - z = \lambda Y}$$

6 Stagnation and free cash

A neo-Kaleckian model

Relative valuation Q theory does a tolerable job in tracking the nearly five-decade-long decline in growth rates of investment and the economy, and the correlation of this creeping stagnation with capital's rising share. Tracking such declines, however, does not explain the general movement towards stagnation.

Falling growth rates over nearly half a century should have elicited alarm bells among economists. Yet, apart from a long-term dialogue in the *Monthly Review*, and isolated comments from a variety of persons, economists largely neglected the topic. This changed with the Great Recession of 2008–09. Among mainstream economists, the opening salvo was initiated by Lawrence Summers. In his Keynote Address delivered to the National Association for Business Economics (2014), Summers maintained that stagnation is now upon us; that the "preoccupation" in "the use of monetary policy to reduce the already small amplitude of fluctuations around a trend has given way to a new concern about the trend itself" (Summers, 2014, pp. 65–66). In the face of very low interest rates, Summers questioned whether monetary policy could counter the main obstacle which he identified as low investment levels and growth. Although not referring to Kalecki, he noted that the lopsided income distribution tended to expand saving rather than spending and called for an enlarged role for public investment. In an oblique reference to Keynes's critique of Say's Law, Summers indicated that in recent years, "We are seeing very powerfully a kind of inverse Say's Law . . . [where] . . . lack of demand creates its own lack of supply" (p. 71).[1]

Historical references to Say's Law and a Keynesian "inverse" suggest the possibility that the recent stagnation might be tied to history in a larger way than just being a mild analogue of the 1930s. But typifying the short period stance of modern macroeconomics, Summers's remarks were enclosed within the post-WWII experience.[2] This period experienced numerous recessions, the rise of finance and services relative to manufacturing and the increasing use of monetary policy as the main tool of stabilization. In a paper written with Oliver Blanchard subsequent to his NABE address, Summers mentioned that many economists subscribed to the view that monetary policy had been largely successful in bringing about the "Great Moderation" that began around the mid-1980s (Blanchard and Summers, 2017, p. 4). For Blanchard and Summers, the Great Recession brought this optimistic appraisal to an end.

Blanchard and Summers questioned whether the destabilizing factors associated with finance undercut the reputed self-correcting properties of a modern economy (pp. 20–21). This alleged lack of self-correcting properties might have directed inquiry into longer-term forces involving not only finance but the larger industrial structure. But this was not to be. Despite Blanchard and Summers's comparison of the lackluster recoveries of the Great Recession and the Great Depression (p. 5), they avoided any analysis of stagnation forces. In their view, fiscal spending and monetary policy needed to be readjusted to move "aggressively [against] adverse shocks" so as to reduce "risks" (p. 21). Short-term policy prescription replaced long-term analysis.

A wide-angle view over the course of the last 120 years, however, opens the possibility that the most recent stagnation is a modern resurgence of long-term forces related to the industrial structure. The restrictionist tendencies associated with monopoly power—highlighted first by Thorstein Veblen and J.A. Hobson at the turn into the twentieth century—are ever present in a modern industrial structure comprised of oligopolistic formations. In *Monopoly Capital* (1966), Paul Baran and Paul Sweezy have likened these restrictionist tendencies to the force of gravity on an airplane (p. 218). In their view, the restrictionist forces of monopoly and oligopoly have been countered by "epoch-making" inventions, such as the railroad and the automobile, hot and cold war expenditures, an enlarged government involvement in the economy and an expanded sales effort devoted to market enlargement. But, according to Baran and Sweezy, the force of oligopolistic gravity remains, threatening downturn whenever simulative forces fail or subside. In this understanding, the slow growth of the economy between the Crash of 1907 and World War I and the subsequent Great Depression are understood not as anomalies, but as the ultimate result of an industrial structure whose inherent tendency is to sink to rock bottom.[3]

From this perspective, the major question of growth is not how growth is accomplished, but what prevents the system from collapsing under its own weight. Earlier scholarly endeavors, inclusive of the writings of Thorstein Veblen,[4] provided the foundation for Baran and Sweezy's work. Perhaps the most important of these earlier endeavors was Josef Steindl's *Maturity and Stagnation in American Capitalism* ([1952] 1976). Steindl examined how oligopoly structures, approximating monopoly-pricing arrangements, utilized excess capacity to ward off competition, maintaining low levels of investment demand, while garnering in a disproportionate amount of profit. Steindl held that this cash-garnering ability allowed the stronger firms to expand disproportionately within their own industries (p. 48). This relative ability of the dominant firms to expand faster than their competitive brethren might be taken to mean that the expanded profitability accorded to monopoly would mean a faster rate of growth for the economy. But Steindl's insight was fashioned around a longer view. The rapid expansion of dominant firms ultimately meant that monopoly power increasingly gripped the whole economy and led inexorably to investment stagnation. Steindl garnered statistics that showed an uninterrupted long-term slow-down in the growth of capital accumulation dating from the late nineteenth century and from which even the

"Roaring Twenties" was not exempt. The growth of "total reproducible wealth" in the 1920s was below the previous four decades" (p. 160). The Great Depression of the 1930s was the end-point of this long-term trend.

In addition to understanding the counter-acting forces of epoch-making inventions and wars, Baran and Sweezy (1966) also sketched out how the sales effort of oligopolies operated to maintain market growth. Building on Alvin Hansen's remarks on the rise of promotional advertising (Hansen, 1939, p. 379), Baran and Sweezy (1966) noted how marketing and production melded together under oligopolistic conditions. Unable to compete in terms of price without setting off price wars, oligopolies resorted to product differentiation in the contest for market shares. Along with advertising, such differentiation had the ancillary benefit of creating "wants" in a growing synthetic cultural web. Stagnation was put off—or at least stalled—by the constant implantation of fabricated desires (pp. 123–137). In decades subsequent to *Monopoly Capital*'s publication, others, like John Bellamy Foster and Fred Magdoff, have extended Baran and Sweezy's stagnation thesis to explain how debt-driven stimulants have added their own offsetting power in countering the forces of stagnation.[5]

The most recent contribution to understanding the stimulants underpinning U.S. economic growth is Robert Gordon's *The Rise and Fall of American Growth* (2016). Although Gordon does not relate his narrative to the oligopolistic structure of U.S. capitalism or its need for continual stimulation, he describes in some detail the foundations of post-WWII growth and its eventual petering out.

In Gordon's typology, post-WWII growth constituted a "Great Leap Forward." The Great Leap was based on a virtuous cycle: increased real wages, brought about by the unionization of labor during the New Deal, led to an increased substitution of capital for labor. Such substitution led to increased labor productivity and the opportunity for still more wage concessions and expanded markets. Mass markets were formed by higher wages that allowed "a new middle class the ability to purchase the consumer durables make possible by the Second Industrial Revolution" (p. 537). The WWII rescue from the Depression allowed for a post-war extension of education and embodied labor skills. Government projects during the New Deal and the War often involved plants and equipment that were owned outright by the government or were propped up by government contracts. Such projects enlarged the capital stock. Aircraft, ships and weapons, and the technological advances associated with government projects, filtered into private market areas. The intermixture of government research and development projects with private firms and universities helped the spread of such technological advance. The technological progress of the 1930s and 1940s, in radio, movies, appliances, health, chemicals, plastics, and oil exploration and production found a new fertile ground in the post-war period. Rounding out the list of substantial gains was the improvement of the automobile and the associated second suburbanization surrounding metropolitan areas. An extended inter-state highway system linked metropolitan centers that were themselves dotted with shopping centers, utility extensions, school systems and assorted municipal outcroppings.

Given the destruction of industrial competitors during World War II, and the sheer size of U.S. firms relative to foreign competitors, U.S. economic might extended around the world. Such might was reinforced by hundreds of military bases supplied in large part by U.S. production.[6] The Cold War provided the backdrop for government-sponsored technological advance and demand management. Demand management through "military-Keynesianism"[7] was particularly apparent. In the mid-1970s, almost two-thirds of basic research and development in the U.S. was government financed (Steindl, 1976, p. xii). Over the course of the post-WWII period, military expenditures routinely made up some half to two-thirds of that portion of the federal budget devoted to goods and services and is over half of such expenditures at the time of writing (2017).

Yet, this overall economic-political-military complex contained cracks. In addition to the rise of foreign competition, and the downsizing of manufacturing, Gordon stressed the increasingly narrow markets provided by the new technologies surrounding the computer, internet, entertainment and digitized services (Gordon, 2016, p. 567). Gordon's comparison is relative. Narrowness is understood in comparison to previous technological advances. Unlike earlier technological advances associated with rail systems, electrification of cities and industries, automobilization and the accompanying suburbanization associated with the auto, the new computerized economy did not—at least to date—provide the same enormity of market growth. Recent rates of technological growth—as measured by total factor productivity—have failed to match earlier benchmarks of expanded growth (pp. 574–580).

In consideration of the post-war boom, Robert Gordon's portrayal of the Great Leap Forward and particularly the role of government spending serves to explain how the stagnation tendencies of oligopoly capitalism could be put on hold.

But this holding pattern depended on various forms of continued stimulation that could not be maintained. In the view of oligopoly-stagnation theorists, the forces of monopoly stagnation remained intact and awaited resurgence. In the post-war period, a variety of older firms have disappeared and new industries have arisen, but the newer industrial landscape continues to reproduce itself along oligopolistic lines. John Bellamy Foster and colleagues (2011) compiled manufacturing data from 1947 through 2007 on a host of industries where the top four firms in the industry accounted for at least 50 percent of shipment value. Partly for re-classification reasons, the number of industries characterized by such concentration multiplied around four times. But the percentage of such super-concentrated industries never dipped below one-quarter over the entire time period and in the early 2000s rose to just under 40 percent (p. 4). Another recent study—based on markup pricing—suggests that monopoly power has expanded since 1980. On firm-level data, markups were relatively stable from 1950 until 1980, averaging approximately 18 percent above marginal cost, but then rose to 67 percent (De Loecker and Eeckhout, 2017).[8] Recently German Gutierrez and Thomas Philippon (2016, 2017) have confirmed that the more highly concentrated industries—and those with less entry—tend to invest less relative to their Q ratio than other firms, a fact in line with the oligopoly-stagnation thesis.

It is important to note, however, that this correlation between underinvestment and concentration does not mean an absolute decline in revenue generation for the very top firms. Mergers and acquisitions, and foreign expansion have compensated for domestic underinvestment. Buoyed by expanding revenues of both domestic and overseas markets, the very top firms—ensconced in oligopoly formations—have expanded far more rapidly than the U.S. economy. From the 1950s to 1995, the top 500 firms (ranked by revenue) grew marginally faster than the underlying economy. Since 1995, however, the growth rate of the top 500 almost doubled that of the U.S. economy (*Fortune*, June 15, 2017, p. 158).

Stagnation and stimulants

Under the optics of the oligopoly-stagnation thesis, an explanation of any protracted slowdown—like the slowdown since the late 1960s—inevitably deals with the weakening of various stimulants and the exhaustion of various counter-acting forces. Below I focus on three factors: (1) the reduction of taxes on the rich; (2) the extension of the two-earner household, and (3) the rise of household debt.

High taxes on the rich countered stagnation because they aimed at high-saving individuals and corporations whose spending propensities on investment were problematic at best and low at worst. The decline of high taxes on the rich eventually led to higher and higher government deficits, a corresponding rise in free cash and the speculative endeavors associated with free cash.

The extension of the two-earner household raised household incomes and, together with a rise of household debt, allowed markets to expand. Such debt stimulation, however, expanded the level of risk and consequently bumped up against inherent limits.

Before discussing the rising deficits of government and households, I first construct a model of free cash generation that expands upon Kalecki's original formulation. Free cash is generated not just by government deficits but by the deficits of households as well. This free cash model allows us to understand how debt stimulants countering stagnation have been intimately intertwined with the growth of speculative free cash.

An expanded Kaleckian model of free cash

The expanded national income accounting identity between saving (S), investment (I), government fiscal deficits (F.D.) and the Current Account (C.A.) is:[9]

$$(1)\quad S - I = F.D. + C.A.$$

S – I can be broken down into corporate Free Cash and a "personal" saving-investment discrepancy. This "personal" saving-investment discrepancy includes proprietors' saving and investment as well as the saving-investment discrepancy of households aimed most particularly towards residential purchase, consumer and mortgage debt.

This breakdown into a corporate free cash component and a "personal" (non-corporate) saving-investment component allows a separation out of the main corporate motor of investment from non-corporate investment. This non-corporate investment includes business investment often carried out by smaller firms and residential construction. Corporate fixed investment has expanded over the course of the post-WWII period to encompass almost two-thirds of all fixed investment in recent decades and over one-and-a-half times all non-corporate fixed investment. Running corporate cash together with the cash of proprietors' businesses would be in line with Kalecki's grouping of all "capitalists," but the intermixture of proprietors' income with personal income makes for significant difficulties in their separation.

A corporate free cash construction can be made by subtracting corporate investment from corporate cash (Profits after Tax + Depreciation). Or:

Free Cash = Profits after Tax + Depreciation – Corporate Investment

Or:

Free Cash = (Cash – I_{corp}).

Note that, like the free cash construction of Chapter 4, free cash includes dividend payouts that are discretionary payouts to stockholders. In the NIPA accounts, these dividends are contained within the category of personal income and contained (but not broken down) within the categories of personal consumption and saving. Since we have included dividends within the corporate free cash category, we must subtract out the personal saving derivable from dividend income (S Div) from "personal" saving and add in the consumption portion of dividends (C Div) to the non-corporate investment category to maintain the identity in **(1)**.

Free Cash + [(*S personal* – *S Div*) – (*I noncorp* + *C Div*)] = F.D. + C.A.

(1*) (2*) (3*)

Solving for free cash and abbreviating the italicized term 2* above as S* – I*, we obtain:

(2) Free Cash = F.D. – (S*– I*) + C.A.

In the positive space of Figure 6.1 below is the narrow free cash[10] series, together with an additive series that adds a (reversed sign) current account. *All series on the graph are expressed as a fraction of corporate fixed investment.* As **(2)** indicates, a negative current account subtracts from free cash on an *ex post* basis. Thus, the top additive series designates the maximal amount of free cash that might have been realized with a zero-current account balance. I stress "might." As will be emphasized in Chapter 7, U.S. corporations have been able to cut back on domestic investment through their use of offshore supply lines and offshore production. A negative current account is therefore not simply a one-sided subtraction from free cash. As long as there is sufficient deficit spending by the government and private non-corporate parties in the maintenance of aggregate demand, a negative current account might well be associated with an *expanded* level of free cash over and above the level that might otherwise have obtained.

The fiscal deficit and the personal saving-investment discrepancy necessary to generate existing free cash aggregates are portrayed in negative space to facilitate graphical exposition. The series on the very bottom adds these two deficits.

Noteworthy is the fact that throughout the entire post-war period, corporate free cash was in evidence, even during the 1980s when economists, such as Benjamin M. Friedman expressed concern over an alleged lack of saving. In recent years, free cash rose towards historic heights after a turnaround begun in the mid-1970s. The collective rise of government deficit spending, personal debt and that of non-corporate business climbed with virtually no interruption, reaching a crescendo with the housing bubble and the implosion of the 2008 Great Recession. The Great Recession brought on a de-leveraging of personal deficit spending but was countered by government deficits that topped over $1.5 trillion in the years 2009–11, before receding to roughly half that amount with the long and drawn -out recovery.

In the Great Recession of 2008, narrow free cash rose to over 80 percent of corporate fixed investment, while wide free cash (narrow free cash + net interest) rose to approximate corporate fixed investment. The compensating force of government deficits allowed both measures of free cash to rise in the Great Recession, the narrow (and smaller) one averaging over $800 billion a year, between 2008 and 2012, before falling into the $600 billion range in 2016.

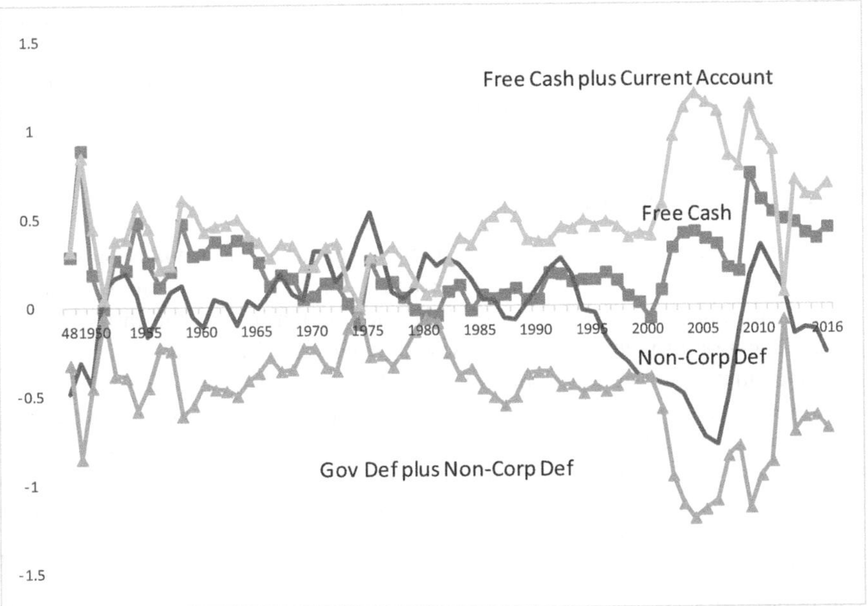

Figure 6.1 Free cash as a fraction of corporate investment

Sources: Federal Reserve Flow of Funds, Table F.2, lines 10, 12, 15; Department of Commerce Table 1.14; government accounts.

Figure 6.1 also displays the overall free cash movement in the post-WWII period. In the early post-WWII period, there were periodic government surpluses and relatively small deficits. These latter deficits were offset by a closing-off of the initial saving-investment balance of the non-corporate sector. This closing-off can be partially understood as a leveling-off of the immediate post-war housing boom (1948–60), when housing investment averaged 75 percent of corporate fixed investment. But in the course of the 1960s boom and in the early 1970s, the non-corporate saving-investment series rose to attain surplus status. Accordingly, free cash aggregates also declined somewhat to reach historic post-war lows in the early 1970s. These lows were coincident with the end of the "Golden Age." It was in the aftermath of the "Golden Age" that free cash aggregates began their secular ascent.

This ascent was no accident. The end of the "Golden Age" brought on a long-term secular slowdown of the economy that required more and more stimulation. Deficit spending—both through government and private parties—allowed for such stimulation.

On the domestic front, government deficits together with non-corporate deficits morphed into what might be called "Twin Worlds." The first world is the world of corporate free cash, available for non-productive purposes such as opulent consumption, mergers, stock repurchases and other speculative endeavors. It is a world of money in the hands of the rich available for extractive activities aimed at claiming the free cash of others. It is the world of a growing financial sector—a sector comprised of Wall Street banks, hedge fund managers, financial lobbyists, merger specialists, compensation specialists working out the details of stock options and grants. The second world is a world of working people attempting to make ends meet through consumer and mortgage debt. Together with government deficit spending, it is this second world of deficits that has allowed the first world to not only exist but to also expand.

Taxes, deficits and stimulation

Government deficits drive aggregate demand upwards. High taxes on corporations and the wealthy *in combination with government deficits* deliver a double dose of stimulants: first in the form of deficit stimulation; second in the form of tax confiscation of what would otherwise translate into free cash.

Bond financing can come directly from the printing press, allowing government purchases to raise aggregate demand without involving taxes.[11] Monetizing debt through Open Market Operations supports security prices and lowers interest rates in the service of more investment and growth. Supporting aggregate demand through the bond market, however, is most often achieved through public bond offerings. Like investors in stock, domestic bond purchasers are typically high-income receivers that have a far lower propensity to consume than the general population.[12] In the short term, procurement and spending of deficit monies obtained from the top income groups in government projects supports the economy. But along with the free cash generated, the expanded interest receipts put additional monies in the hands of the wealthy. Continual use of deficit spending raises the national debt resulting in a suction-pump effect whereby more and more monies accrue to high-income receivers.

High corporate and individual tax rates on high income recipients drain away the free cash and income that provide speculative fuel. In confiscating this fuel and directing these monies towards the general population, high taxes on the wealthy raise both consumption and aggregate demand. Such high taxes on the rich were part of the immediate post-WWII period, reflecting the back-to -back crises of the Depression and the War. These high taxes helped to keep investment and growth rates up. Over time, however, these taxes were to decline dramatically, with adverse consequences for growth.

Figure 6.2 shows the long-term fall-off in the top marginal income tax rate, the top long-term capital gains tax rate and estimates for the average effective tax rate for the top 1 percent. The very high marginal income tax rate reflected the high rates left over in the latter two years of the Depression and the need for war funds after hostilities began. The large discrepancy between the income and capital gains tax was predicated on the theory that managers, as agents for stockholders, would be more inclined to expand investment through internal funds rather than pay out dividends to high tax bracket owners. Investment would presumably make companies more valuable. Any need for cash by stockholders could be realized through the sale of stock. This theory presumed that managers had only two options rather than a third merger option and, eventually a stock-repurchase option. In the course of the next decades, the discrepancy between the income and capital gains tax rates undoubtedly encouraged mergers and consolidations over and above the levels that would have otherwise occurred.

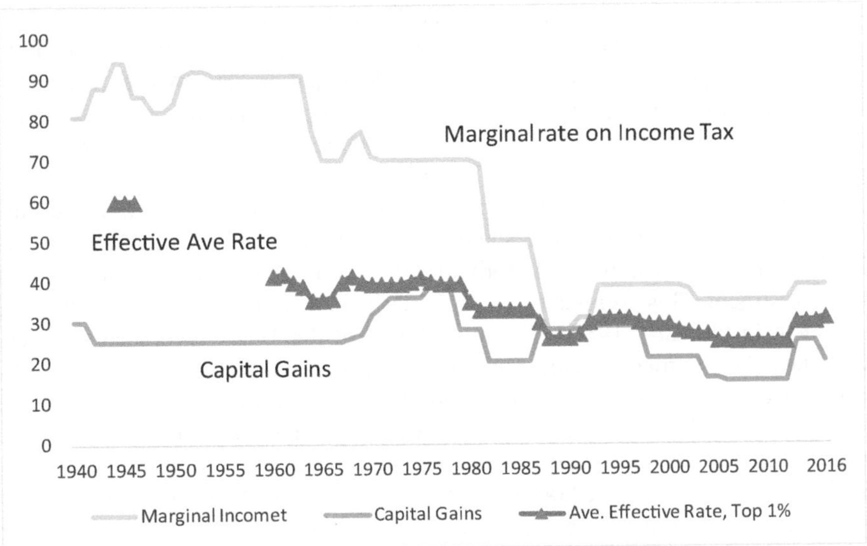

Figure 6.2 High income rates

Sources: Tax Policy Center; for effective tax rate during World War II, Brownlee, 2004, p. 115; Average effective rates since 1960, *Economic Report of the President*, January 2017, p. 176, Figure 3–9.

As marginal rates are rates that apply to additional income above statutory benchmarks, they do not capture the actual average effective rates paid. Moreover, various loopholes, such as the exemption of state and local interest payments from federal income taxes, and the very much lower capital gains tax have allowed the rich to avoid the highest nominal income tax rates. Nevertheless, the main statutory downward trend captures the overall trend of lowered taxes on the rich. "In 1944 the effective rate on the rich reached an all-time high of nearly 60 percent, or almost four times the highest level achieved during World War I" (Brownlee, 2004, p. 115). In the 1950s, the effective rate fell considerably (p. 122). The lowering of effective rates continued. As shown above in Figure 6.2, the average effective individual rates since 1960 have declined from around 40 percent to around 30 percent in recent years.

The long-term fall-off in rates can best be explained by the political clout of the upper classes in lowering their tax rates and the lack of any extended crisis since World War II. Understanding this political clout transforms the question from why taxes have fallen off to the question of why tax rates were so high during the Depression and World War II. As Mark Leff (1966, pp. 11–47) has shown, the high income tax rates during the Depression were applied only to the very top groups, with a considerable amount of federal revenues generated from consumption taxes and processing fees. Taxing consumption was to tax by increments and was politically expedient because such taxation bordered on invisibility or, in the case of alcohol and tobacco, "non-necessities." In the sponsorship of roads, the gas tax could be understood as a fee for user benefit. Broadening the tax base through direct taxation of income during the New Deal would have made extractions of taxes quite apparent and would stiffen resistance across economic classes towards the New Deal in general.

The emergency of World War II, however, brought direct taxation of both corporate and personal income into full implementation. The War extended the income tax base to the general run of the working population and greatly expanded corporate tax. Tapping sufficient monies for the War justified an extremely progressive structure.

To any explanation of the long post-WWII tax rate fall-off, one must add the constant drumbeat for lower taxes in the service of eliciting more economic activity, both in terms of individual motivation for more income and for more saving and investment. This drumbeat was particularly loud after Ronald Reagan became president in the early 1980s. The tax reforms of the 1980s embraced a variety of issues. The Earned Income Tax Credit (EITC), begun in 1975, was significantly expanded so as to encourage more work at the lower levels of the income spectrum. It had the ancillary effect of lowering wages. Employers recognized that tax credits for additional income earned allowed them to pay lower wages in the first place.[13] Reduced taxes on the rich were allegedly efficacious in eliciting more effort from high-priced labor. In arguments that prefaced those of the 1990s in support of stock option compensation, lowered rates on capital gains were supposed to entice additional managerial efforts to maximize stockholder return. Managers would be bonded to stockholders in a tighter embrace. Such arguments, of course, held the somewhat embarrassing implication that managers, unless super-compensated, would do a somewhat less than optimal job.

In eliminating a host of preferential treatments accorded to tax shelters, the term "horizontal equity" became the catch-call for general tax reform. The term "horizontal equity," masked a class-based redistribution towards high-income receivers. For working people, horizontal equity meant a continuation of more and more hikes in the regressive payroll taxes associated with Social Security. Rising from under 4 percent of labor compensation in the 1950s to around 6 percent in the mid-1960s, the combined Social Security contributions of employees and employers rose to roughly 12 percent of total labor compensation by the mid-1990s—the rough percentage today (2017).[14] In this movement towards horizontal equity across income classes, statutory rates on both corporate and individual income declined, particularly at the highest levels. In the 1981 Act, the highest marginal tax rate fell from 70 percent to 50 percent. In the 1986 Act, the highest individual marginal income tax rates fell from 50 percent to 28 percent before rising to around 39 percent in recent years.

Figure 6.3 shows the fall-off in corporate taxes actually paid expressed as a fraction of before-tax profit and before-tax narrow cash (profits plus depreciation). The decided fall-off of rates between the end of World War II and Korea was due to the on-and-off implementation of the excess profits tax. Excess profits were calculated relative to a benchmark of peacetime profits, with the excess being attributable to war. The rationale was that since government wartime spending increased profits, corporations should therefore contribute monies towards

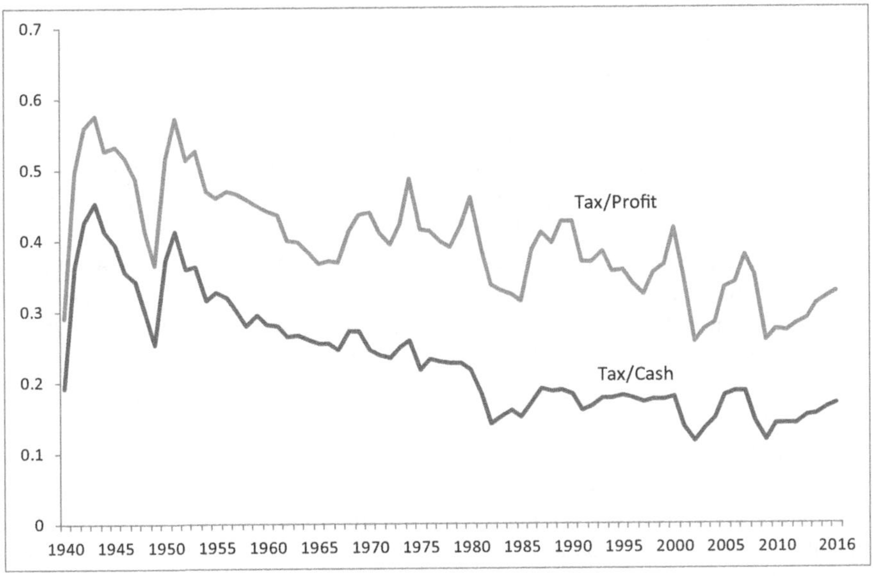

Figure 6.3 Corporate taxes as a fraction of profit and cash

Sources: Department of Commerce, Table 1.14.

the wars that made them profitable. The excess profits tax of World War II went through a variety of changes over the course of the war and was repealed at the start of January 1946. A new version was re-imposed in the summer of 1950 to help sponsor the Korean War.

Those who argue against high corporate taxes do so on the basis that high corporate taxes crimp investment. But such an argument would have to confront the high economic performance of World War II and Korea in which the excess profits tax was operational. The government imposed very high tax increases on corporations while simultaneously increasing production. This simultaneous withdrawal and re-injection of tax monies explains why the one major study on the excess profits tax during the Korean conflict failed to reveal any significant tendency to contract investment with higher corporate tax rates (Dugan and Zubrow, 1954).[15] The high-tax regimes of World War II and the Korean War show that there is no *necessary* reduction in investment with higher corporate tax rates. On the contrary: the two war episodes demonstrate that high corporate taxes and economic prosperity are quite compatible. Expenditures targeted to monetary outlays for war could just as well have involved socially beneficial projects such as infrastructure development, government medical facilities, alternative power sources, and education. There is, of course, no assurance that investment requirements surrounding socially beneficial projects would entail the same investment requirements as war. But the targeted expenditures enumerated above would certainly require high capital expenditures.

The long downward trend of corporate taxes descends from the high point in 1951 when corporate taxes as a percentage of before-tax cash reached 41 percent. After the excess profits tax of Korea was allowed to lapse in December 1953, taxes began to fall. Nevertheless, all corporate taxes—including federal, state and local taxes—were still relatively high at roughly 32 percent of (before-tax) narrow cash during 1954–56. Federal corporate taxes provided roughly 30 percent of federal receipts. Total corporate taxes accounted for about 24 percent of total government expenditures. Over the past sixty years, various assorted stimulatory policies have all driven corporate taxes to lower and lower levels. From the legalization and use of the double-declining balance and sum of years digit methods of depreciation, introduced first in 1954, to the shortening of asset lives after 1962 and modified in 1986, to the Accelerated Cost Recovery System of 1981 and its modified form in 1986, to the bonus depreciation adopted in 2002–03, to the new tax plan enacted in 2018 whereby investment can be "costed out" over the next five years, to investment tax credits introduced in 1962 and ended in 1986, to the lowering of corporate tax in a series of steps from 52 percent maintained from the early 1950s to 1962 to 35 percent—all these allowed a secular decline in corporate taxes so that in 2016, the corporate tax accounted for approximately 15 percent of cash, 13 percent of federal receipts, and 8.6 percent of total government expenditures. According to a study conducted by the Government Accountability Office (GAO) between 2006 and 2012, two-thirds of corporations paid no federal corporate tax at all.[16]

Over the long haul, on both the individual and corporate levels, tax rates on the rich have declined. On Kaleckian lines, these declines have undercut the stimulus effect of government spending. This undercutting of stimulants is particularly ironical since the rationale behind these tax declines on corporates and the rich have universally been couched in stimulative terms. Declines on individual taxes would allegedly expand productivity, saving and investment. In a similar vein, the various efforts to lower corporate taxes have been designed to encourage expanded investment. Yet the cumulative effect of reducing high income and corporate taxation over time has been to enlarge free cash aggregates and to reduce growth.

In consequence, more and more stimulatory measures have been forthcoming from government borrowing.

Figure 6.4 shows total government and publicly held federal debt expressed as a fraction of GDP since 1948. It is no accident that the U-turn into higher and higher levels of government debt relative to income began with the decline in GDP growth rates expressed on decade averages. Lower growth hampers the growth of tax receipts. Lower tax rates applied to the rich lower growth rates in the overall economy. One might have expected that lowered corporate taxes would have picked up rates of investment growth. But as shown earlier in Figures 5.5 and 5.6, the decline in corporate investment mirrored the general decline in GDP growth since the late 1960s.

Government deficits, of course, are high-powered stimulants. But, as Kalecki demonstrated decades ago, government deficits are also a main factor in generating free cash. In recent decades, this free cash has spilled into capital markets,

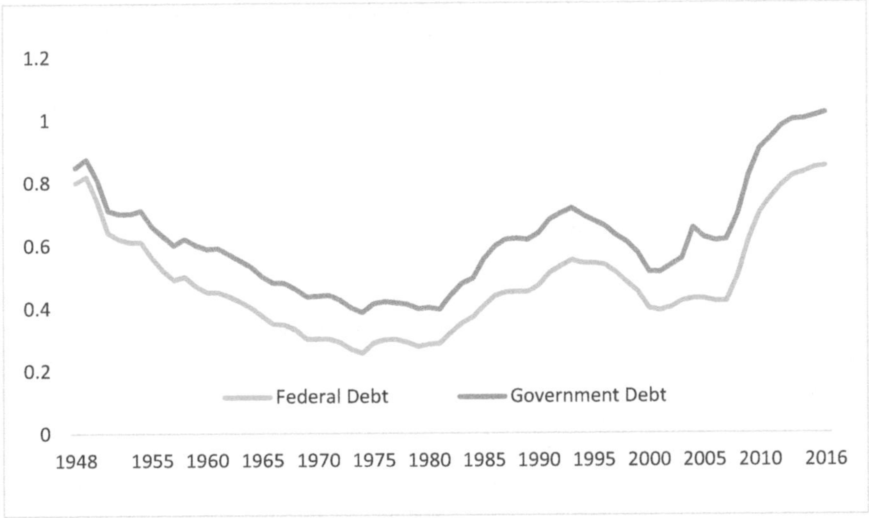

Figure 6.4 Government debt and federal debt relative to GDP

Source: Flow of Funds, Federal Reserve, Table L. 105; Table L. 106; Department of Commerce, Table 1.1.5.

raising stock prices through dividend payouts, mergers and stock repurchases. This heightened expansion of equity valuations in the face of slow growth is the hallmark of the recent tilt to finance at the expense of production and the recent ascension of a new inequality to be examined in more detail in Chapter 8.

This new heightened inequality demonstrates that government borrowings and high taxes on the rich are not simply substitute methods for stimulation. Spending monies derived from high taxes on the rich tend to dampen inequality, while sustaining the economy. In contrast, borrowings from the rich act to expand inequality. A combination of government deficits and high taxes on the rich, would, however, both stimulate the economy and dampen inequality. The historical progression, however, has been one way: more borrowings which create more inequality, less taxes on the rich.

The effects of government borrowing on income distribution have a direct impact upon government stimulation of the economy. The Keynesian multiplier depends critically upon the propensity to consume, and upon the distribution of income. Government deficit spending is most often understood as exogenous stimulation. But to the extent that such deficits tilt the income distribution towards the rich through the spillage of free cash, deficit stimulation is diminished by a reduction in the multiplier effect. Over long periods of time, such reductions in the multiplier effect undercut the efficacy of government spending in sustaining the economy.

In recent years, government deficits have raised a good deal of political alarm, particularly in the aftermath of the 2008 fall-off into the worst downturn and the worst recovery of the post-war period. Political theater surrounding debt ceilings, sequesters, government shutdowns, safety net cutbacks, proposals for extending Medicare age eligibility and limiting Medicaid, proposals for substituting chained inflation indexes for consumer price index (CPI) adjustments for social security and government pensions, limitations on federal aid to state and local governments have been the order of the day. Voluminous reports from various commissions—most notably the President's Economic Advisory Board, *The Report on Tax Reform Options: Simplification, Compliance and Corporate Taxation* (August 2010; Paul A. Volker, chairman) (Volker, 2010) and those associated with the National Commission of Fiscal Responsibility and Reform headed by Erskine Bowles and Alan K. Simpson (Bowles and Simpson, 2010, 2013)—rallied against the expansion of deficits. Yet, in neither of the reports was there any discussion, let alone any recommendation, for higher taxes on corporations or any significant tax increases on the rich. In the four "Options" on corporate taxes, contained in the presidential advisory report, not one was associated with any corporate tax increase, and three were associated with lowering corporate tax rates. In their first report, *Moment of Truth*, the main Simpson-Bowles recommendation on corporate taxes was to eliminate various corporate subsidies to various industries and to lower corporate tax rates to a single corporate tax rate, which their sequel report fixed at 28 percent.

The second report also endorsed a "Territorial Option" that would allow corporations to bring foreign profits back to the United States tax free. Such an option would clearly entice even more foreign activity and rearrangement of profits in tax havens abroad. All of the reports at least noted the difficulties associated with raising corporate taxes in the current multinational environment. Multinational operations in scores of countries entice countries to play a game of "race to the bottom," so that the low U.S. corporate tax rate looks high among the member countries of the Organization for Economic Cooperation and Development (OECD). In a study for the World Bank, Duanjie Chen and Jack Mintz (2010)

> calculated marginal effective tax rates on corporate capital for 80 countries, including subnational taxes and non-income taxes on capital such as irrecoverable sales tax on capital purchases and property taxes. For 2009, they found the United States had the highest effective corporate tax rate among OECD countries, followed by France and Japan.
>
> (Merrill, 2010, p. 624)

This high-tax relative comparison can now be marshaled to advance an argument to lower U.S. corporate taxes yet again. The high-tax relative comparison can also be used to partially explain the widespread use of tax havens abroad. Using a compilation method of enumerating tax havens, James R. Hines notes that although these havens provide just "6 percent of foreign employment of property, plant, and equipment . . . [they] account for 42 percent of foreign income" (Hines, 2010, p. 109). Foreign source income is not taxed until repatriated. A tax holiday on these foreign funds was enacted in 2004, but there is little evidence that these temporary provisions bolstered U.S. corporate investment (Krugman, 2011).

At the time of writing (January, 2018), the Trump administration, together with the Republican majority in Congress, have lowered corporate tax rates to 21 percent. The arguments were again tailored to buttress the belief that such lowering of corporate taxes would push investment ahead, both on the basis of more retained earnings and a better after-tax rate of return on new investment. The fact that free cash flows now approach or exceed new investment expenditures did not deter the first argument. The lowering of corporate taxes will demonstrate yet again that beliefs, based on long habituation and repetition, will not bend to facts. The alleged after-tax rate of return argument appeals to the microeconomics of the individual firm. But the question of macro aggregate investment growth takes on a different dimension entirely. Addressing the macro implications on how high taxes on corporations drive aggregate demand upwards requires that Kalecki's understanding be taken seriously. As Kalecki once put it, "capital taxation is perhaps the best way to stimulate business and reduce unemployment" (Kalecki, [1937] 2009, p. 325).

Households and debt

Household debt acts first as a stimulant and then as a tax. Debt allows households to spend more than they earn. Such spending drives economic activity. But in time, debt service charges and repayment act to thwart additional spending. The original stimulatory effects turn into their opposite.

The stimulatory effects of deficit spending must therefore be located historically. The Great Depression brought a general liquidation of debt predicated on thousands upon thousands of bankruptcies, foreclosures and bank closures. The post-war period was thus poised to acquire stimulatory effects from new spending based on future debt promises. The ration-induced savings of World War II helped propel a mini-boom after the War ended. But the clean slate of liquidity added its own momentum to the beginnings of new debt stimulation, particularly after the Korean War erased the depressive remnants of the 1949 recession. The spread of metropolitan areas after World War II was almost entirely debt sponsored, as suburbs grew outwards from industrial and financial hubs. Yet, the new post-war state of liquidity kept the aggregate debt totals within bounds. Despite the rapid growth of residential construction, mortgage debt in the late 1940s was less than 20 percent of personal income before taxes. The combination of mortgage and consumer debt was less than 30 percent.

Figure 6.5 shows the long upward climb of mortgage and consumer debt expressed as a fraction of personal income. The debt/income ratios seemed to hit a saturation point after the 1960s boom. But then they started to rise again after the slowdown of the 1970s. Just before the Great Recession of 2008, total debt exceeded personal income, indicating a *five-fold expansion in the total debt/income ratio over sixty years.*

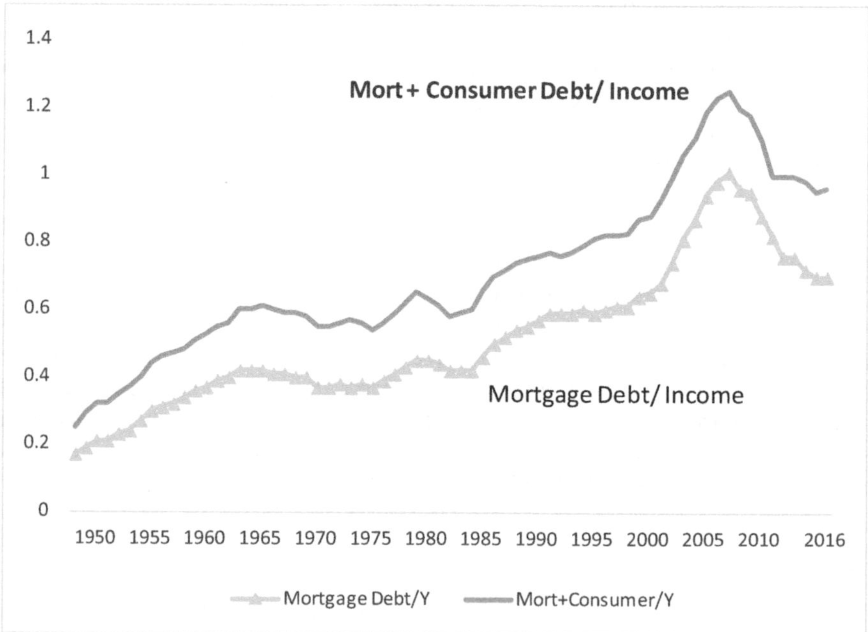

Figure 6.5 Mortgage and consumer debt/income

Sources: Federal Reserve, Flow of Funds, Table L. 101; Department of Commerce, Table 2.1.

The association of rising debt ratios with the slowdown in the economy after the 1970s was no accident. The slowing-up of economic growth hit production workers the hardest, with real average weekly earnings going flat from roughly 1973 to the present. Debt could compensate. As primarily a middle-class phenomenon (Wolff, 2010, p. 48), the rise of consumer debt allowed families to conform to rising consumption norms (Starr, 2010, p. 460) that were largely modeled by wealthier families or to compensate for income declines.

The growth of two-earner households—already steadily under way since the 1960s—was further motivated by this flattening of wage rates per worker and contributed to it. The influx of women into the workplace allowed household income to expand, but the increased supply of labor kept wages down. Although male participation in the labor force continued its downward trend from the 1950s, increased labor participation by women kept total labor participation rates up. This expansion of labor participation, however, had an outer limit as the employment of women rivaled males in recent years.[17] The rise of real median household income continued to rise but at a decidedly decreasing rate until leveling in the late 1990s. It has been flat for the last two decades (1997–2017).[18]

The rise of household median income and the dual-earner household changed the relationship between residential location and employment. Over the course of the twentieth century, the growth of suburbs made for a polycentric net of job hubs, with firms locating outwards from central city locations towards industrial burbs. The development of road systems and the automobile permitted a severance of residential location and workplace. The commute became part of the common lexicon associated with polycentric hubs associated mainly with manufacturing. Large manufacturing firms provided the largely unionized high-wage employment that allowed a plethora of other types of employment surrounding retail outlets, shopping malls, movie theatres and the like. These ancillary employments were critically dependent on the higher-wage income attributable to manufacturing. In the 1950s, roughly one-third of the workforce was employed in manufacturing, with a large part of this employment being located in the high-wage unionized sector. The long secular decline in manufacturing employment driven by automation and offshoring decimated a good many of these industrial hubs and made for migratory displacement from industrial areas such as Detroit, Cleveland, Cincinnati, Pittsburgh, Toledo and St. Louis (Moretti, 2013, p. 25).

In their place, new metropolitan areas of innovation arose populated by high-income "innovators": programmers and other IT specialists, digital artists, electrical engineers, biotech specialists, financiers fluent in global markets and other high-tech workers involved in innovation and design. Places like the Silicon Valley, San-Francisco-San Jose area, Boston, Austin, Seattle, Portland, Durham and Houston gained high-salary employment status as manufacturing employment declined. Enrico Moretti (2013) calls this re-arranged geography of high-income jobs from manufacturing to innovation the "Great Divergence." The devastation of older industrial areas stood in contrast to the development of high-end, high-income areas populated by a relatively small cadre of high-income workers. Moretti makes the case that such high-income employment made for a multiplier effect on low-end jobs far in excess of the multiplier effect of the older manufacturing centers. This is largely because high-salary jobs permit high-salary consumption that spreads expansively in the surrounding economy. It is also because high-tech companies involve themselves in clusters that amplify themselves as magnets for others. High-tech firms are attracted to areas of highly educated workers and a culture of innovation (Moretti, 2013, pp. 61–62).

Those employed in the low-end earning tier were the most susceptible to signing up for the subprime loans that imploded during the housing crisis: "The increases in home-ownership were largest in the West, for those under the age of 35, for those with below-median incomes, and for Hispanics and Blacks" (Schiller, 2008, p. 5). But the crisis crossed both the de-industrialized areas and the new innovation centers.

The rise of the two-earner household put a premium on residential location in proximity to the new job hubs. Consequently, land next to these new job centers became increasingly expensive. Those households who "got in first" in terms of home purchases experienced the greatest appreciation of home values. The race was on. Land, home prices and rents skyrocketed. In 1970, the median home value/income ratios of central cities, metropolitan suburbs and non-metropolitan areas were roughly the same at 1.72, 1.86 and 1.72 respectively.[19] At the peak of the housing bubble in and around 2006–07, similar ratios for the pricier metropolitan areas like San Francisco, Honolulu and Santa Cruz hit over 5. Adjusted for general inflation, house prices in the San Francisco metropolitan area almost doubled from 1980 until 2005; Los Angeles and New York were not far behind. In contrast, the national average experienced but a small bump in 2005–07.[20]

The two-earner household also drove land and house prices up because of co-location problems. The literature on workplace-residential location is quite extensive and it is hard to generalize any firm conclusions regarding co-location and land prices. But the documented slowdown of suburb growth from the 1970s (Muller, 1980, p. 37) and the expanded role of the two-earner family certainly contributed to expanded land and home prices in the major metropolitan areas. Two jobs reinforced residential stickiness. The loss of one job did not entail the loss of two. This meant that homes—at any given price level—would be more valued by the household as one or more of the household partners would be reluctant to move. In 1940 among young couples where both spouses had at least a four-year degree, only 20 percent of wives worked (Costa and Kahn, 2000, p. 1288). In time, however, the rise of the two-earner household increasingly became the two-career household. In the words of Dora Costa and Mathew Kahn, "dual career households are more likely to be joint decision makers, and they face the difficulty of finding two jobs commensurate with the skills of each spouse within a reasonable commute from home" (p. 1288). The spread of spaced out metropolitan areas, of course, helped in part. But the job density of new job hubs combined with co-location difficulties, made land and home expensive.

Apart from the top 1 percent of wealth holders who actually experienced debt relief between 1983 and 2007, obtaining prime residential locations meant that more typical households had to increase their debt load. The debt/equity and debt/income ratios of the top 1 percent declined from 5.9 to 2.8 in terms of equity and from 86.8 to 39.4 in terms of income. The next 19 percent of the top quintile experienced a modest increase in the debt/equity ratio, but a sizable 50 percent increase in their debt/income ratio. The biggest debt burden hit the middle class, defined as the middle three quintiles. Their debt/equity ratio went up 63 percent and their debt/income ratio jumped 134 percent. This rise of debt was driven by housing. In contrast with the top 1 percent of household wealth holders, whose principle residence constituted just over 10 percent of assets, the principle residence of the middle three quintiles accounted for 65.1 percent of assets (Wolff, 2010, p. 49).

In the face of the recovery from the Great Recession, additional problems surfaced for those earning below-median incomes and even for those earning somewhat more. In the innovation centers, low-end housing was often targeted for urban renewal as gentrification proceeded. In the San Francisco area, the long commute from the Central Valley and the increasing homelessness and quasi-homelessness of tent and RV enclaves exemplified the extreme ends of this polarization.[21] For civil servants—generally median-income employees—rents and home prices made living increasingly unaffordable. In the recovery after 2010, innovation hubs faced the problem of housing these civil servants. In one 2017 study that defined "affordability" as a household spending 31 percent of its monthly income on housing, only 0.4 percent of teachers in San Francisco could afford a house after a 20 percent down payment on a thirty-year mortgage. In Los Angeles, Honolulu, Oakland, Ventura, Denver, San Jose and Oakland, less than 20 percent of teachers could afford a home. In contrast, more than 75 percent of teachers could afford a home in Akron, Dayton, Camden, Detroit, El Paso, Syracuse and Cleveland.[22]

Free cash and the interest rate

In a vicious circle, the combined deficits and the resultant free cash portrayed in Figure 6.1 above added its own momentum to the housing bubble. All capital competes. The spillage of free cash into dividends, mergers and stock repurchases expanded stock values and reduced the cash rate of return on stocks (i.e. profits plus depreciation/stock values). Given the risk premium of stocks over bonds, any such reduction in the cash rate of return tended to lower interest rates as well. In turn, lowered rates of interest encouraged more home buying and debt expansion, which, in turn, created even more free cash.

Figure 6.6 shows the simultaneous long-term declines in the cash rate of return and Moody's long-term bond rate over the course of 35 years. As predicted by orthodox economic theory, the cash rate of return stands above the less risky rate of return on bonds. But the lockstep reduction in both rates of return corroborates the effect of free cash spillage on the interest rate.

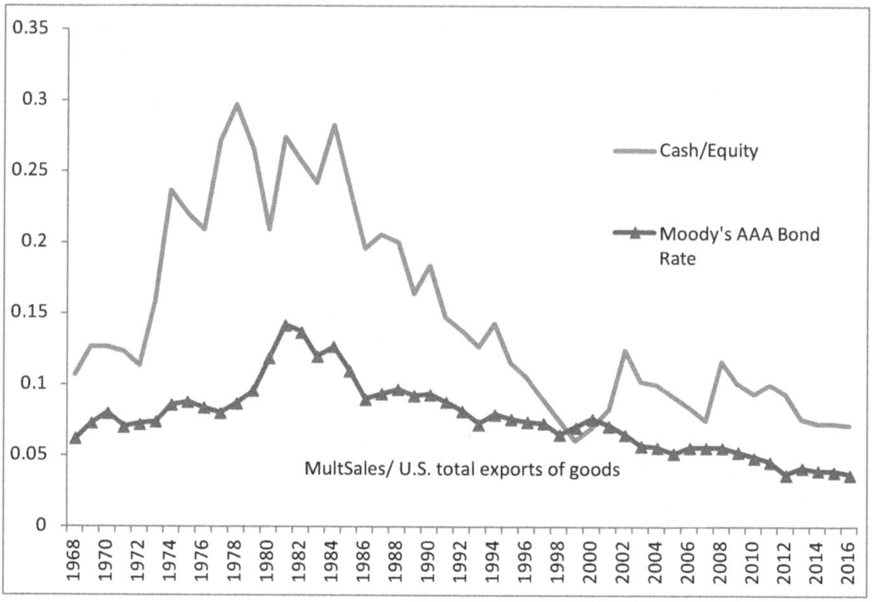

Figure 6.6 Rates of return (stocks and bonds)

Source: Department of Commerce, *Economic Report of the President*, February 2016, Table B-25, p.429.

This correlative relationship, of course, cannot be disentangled from the actions of the Federal Reserve in lowering interest rates over time and the interest-lowering capital imports from export-based nations. Nor can the long-term lowering of interest rates be disentangled from the speculative activities of bond buyers whose fortunes increased with each lowering of rates. But in any compilation of explanations, free cash spillage must be given due weight.

This last point deserves emphasis. Government deficits are often understood as saboteurs of investment, encroaching on limited amounts of savings. Allegedly, such "crowding out" raises interest rates. The free cash hypothesis advanced here reverses the arrow of causality. In showing that deficit spending of government and households generates free cash spillage and a concomitant lowering of interest rates, a free cash understanding shows that government deficits actually encourage interest rate-induced investment. The sensitivity of housing investment to interest rate changes is beyond dispute. The interest portion of a long-term mortgage takes up the largest part of monthly payments for years. Moreover, residential construction is, for the most part, carried out by relatively small firms and contractors critically dependent on outside financing. Far from crowding out interest-sensitive investment, government deficits provide the foundation for crowding in. The free cash understanding helps us to understand the institutional connection between enlarged government deficits, consumer-mortgage debt and the housing bubble.

Writing as Kalecki did in the 1930s, his prescription for high taxes on the rich was aimed exclusively at fighting the specter of unemployment. As the Depression dampened speculative enthusiasms, it was not apparent that such high taxes could also fight speculation. The high post-war taxes on the rich—by claiming free cash—also hid the relationship between free cash and deficits. In sharp contrast, the blow-ups of 1986, 1991, 2001 and the speculative excesses associated with the latest housing bubble, climaxed not only the buildup of household debt but the long-term trend of substituting high government deficits for taxes on the rich. The substitution of government deficits for taxes generated the free cash that drove speculative endeavors both through putting excess monies in the hands of the wealthy and through the lowering of interest rates.

The post-WWII taxes on the rich also mitigated the uncontrolled effects of deficits on interest rates. Claiming excess cash put control over interest rates directly in the hands of the monetary authorities. As noted above, I am not suggesting that the Federal Reserve did not play a prominent role in the thirty-some year decline in interest rates after the early 1980s; nor am I discounting the self-reinforcing dynamic of bond traders. The successive speculative crises dating from the 1980s gave rise to an extensive dialogue surrounding the salvation proclivities of the Federal Reserve and Greenspan's "put"—that is, Greenspan's injections of monetary reserves in response to the various crises during his long regime. But as Greenspan and Bernanke were the first to admit, the Federal Reserve is not omnipotent. In their estimation, the influx of foreign free cash—what Greenspan termed the saving "glut"— had its own effects on the lowering of interest rates. However, as gauged by their silence on domestic free cash, they were apparently blind not only to the derivation of free cash from deficit spending, but also to the effects of free cash spillage on interest rates.

Regulatory reform, free cash and the 2008 crisis

A virtual industry of writing and discussion has evolved around the 2008 crisis—its origin in the speculative excesses of U.S. housing, the world-wide impact of the housing bubble's implosion, the exponential growth rates of derivatives, the transference of some part of securitization from government-sponsored entities (GSEs) to Wall street banks as a consequence of the GSEs' troubled history, the concentration of Wall Street banks and their global reach, the securitization chain whereby original lenders passed on risk to intermediary Wall Street banks, which in turn constructed Collateralized Debt Obligations (CDOs) paying rating agencies to stamp subprime amalgamations with investment-grade ratings—all made for an extensive literature. The insurance directed towards the CDOs, not just by those who owned them but by speculators and Wall Street banks, also added a topic of discussion. That Wall Street banks created and sold CDOs so as to bet against them suggested that variations on financial machinations had no outer limit. The deregulatory environment and the possible regulatory capture of regulatory agencies by their respective industries and the Federal Government surrounded the historical piece with additional drama, providing copy for motion pictures and documentaries.

Any comprehensive assessment of the crisis would also have to take account of the rise of uninsured Money Market Funds that arose decades ago in solicitation of deposits. Lacking deposit insurance, these Money Market Funds—main conduits to Wall Street banks in the purchase of mortgages—would loan "overnight" so as to provide investor safety. As if to illustrate the fallacy of composition, such "safety" allowed a classic bank run of enormous proportions. As soon as the housing collateral became problematic as a result of house-price leveling and decline in 2007, the Funds failed to roll over their overnight loans that had been utilized for years as a source of long-term financing. The crisis was on. The bailout was almost immediate.

The early remarks by Federal Reserve Chairmen on the savings "glut" and its effect on interest rates were largely buried beneath efforts to reform the financial sector. Increasingly, the *cause* of the financial debacle was understood as the *absence* of an adequate financial regulatory environment and an *absence* of understanding the "fat-tail" consequences of modern bubbles. The main causal factor of the crisis was now routinely described as a developing bubble psychology operating within an inadequate financial framework encompassing inadequate capital requirements for financial institutions, inadequate insurance provisions, inadequate regulation on securitization and derivative trading, inadequate assessment of counter-party risk, inadequate regulation of credit-rating agencies and a general underpricing of risk. In a retrospective assessment of the crisis, Alan Greenspan noted, "the global demand for U.S. subprime securities by banks, hedge and pension funds supported by unrealistically positive rating designations by credit agencies was . . . the core of the problem." The "intellectual edifice" comprising the "best insights of mathematicians and finance experts" and which encompassed a "vast risk management and pricing system . . . collapsed because the data inputted in the risk management models generally covered only the past two decades, a period of euphoria" (Greenspan, 2008, p. 2).

The focus on financial reform was, of course, to be expected. But such focus sidetracked efforts to understand the structural conditions that generated recent speculative bubbles, particularly in housing but not confined to such. This neglect pertained both to the generation of free cash and the controversies surrounding the willingness of foreigners to finance current account deficits in the face of inadequate U.S. saving. This "inadequate" saving reflected not the investment requirements of business, but the new higher levels of debt-fueled consumption and housing construction. Admonitions that the United States would have to save more to offset the deficit on current account were in chronological step with a corporate world that generated savings (i.e. cash) in excess of investment at the rate of over half a trillion dollars a year and with high personal consumption (and low personal saving) maintaining aggregate demand.

The domestic saving-investment split between free cash and household deficits reflected (and reflects now) an increasingly unstable split in the distribution of income between the corporate rich and working households. Free cash constitutes monies above monies that are necessary to carry out corporate investment projects. Free cash might be assumed to dampen corporate proclivities for acquiring more debt. Such a conclusion is unwarranted. High free cash operates as implicit collateral for corporations wishing to acquire debt in pursuit of mergers, stock repurchases and dividends (cash spillage) and financial activities in general. As will be shown in Chapter 8, non-financial business debt grew along with free cash in pursuit of higher stock prices and merger consolidations. In addition, the generation of free cash also drove non-financial firms into active participation in financial markets (Crotty, 2005; Krippner, 2005). Nevertheless, recent free cash growth certainly imposed limits on the ability of traditional financial institutions—like banks—to grow markets outside of the household sector. And thus the vicious cycle: increased deficit spending by households expanded free cash that motivated banks and other financial firms to extend even more household debt. In contrast to the 1980s, when mortgage and consumer debt was about two-thirds of depository institutions' loans, the ratio jumped to over three-quarters in the years prior to the 2008 collapse.[23] Securitization of a large part of mortgage origination was underwritten by the GSEs, whose guaranteed mortgage pools expanded from virtually nothing in the early 1970s to over 50 percent of the total value of home mortgages in the early 2000s. After the collapse, such pools and consolidated trusts expanded the percentage to around 60 percent.[24]

Notoriously, more deficit spending by households encouraged the growth of a mortgage market plagued by inadequate underwriting requirements. Nevertheless, the finger wagging directed towards those associated with the subprime crisis needs to be supplemented, if not replaced, by an appreciation of why monies flowed to those who, judged by historical underwriting requirements, could not afford to purchase homes. The often-repeated answer is that under euphoric conditions, rising home prices could support higher underlying claims. Highly leveraged firms could enjoy high profits by bundling and insuring mortgage risks across a variety of prime and subprime loans through a bewildering array of structured and opaque financial instruments. Together with an examination of the securitization chain that allowed risk to be forwarded to others, this explanation goes some distance in understanding the subprime phenomenon. But the free cash hypothesis advanced here constitutes a complementary explanation: the money had nowhere else to go.

The Twin Deficit debate: a post-mortem

Since the late 1970s, the U.S. merchandise trade balance has been consistently negative. Deficits on current account were postponed until the early 1980s, when positive net income receipts failed to overpower the negative balance on the net exports of goods and services. The current account deficit then exploded over the next two and a half decades to a height of roughly 5 percent of GDP in 2006 before receding to somewhat under 3 percent in the years 2010–17.

The rapid rise of government deficit spending in the 1980s and the simultaneous rise of current account deficits gave birth to a "Twin Deficit" debate. This debate centered on whether the large government deficits of the decade translated into large current account deficits. The "logic" was that government deficits "ate" into domestic savings and in so doing attracted foreign capital to these shores.

This attraction was mirrored in the large and increasing debtor position of the U.S. and in the high U.S. interest rates of the 1980s that attracted the funds. These capital flows expanded the negative trade balance in that demand for U.S. dollars prevented a sufficient fall in the dollar to correct the trade imbalance. A balanced government budget was understood to be the corrective measure. Balancing the budget required either a hike in taxes or a reduction in government expenditures. Correction thus involved a cutback in simulative measures on both the taxation and expenditure front. Through a Keynesian analysis, these cutbacks would involve a pullback in the domestic U.S. economy. But to advocates of the Twin Deficit logic, no such pullback need occur: freeing up domestic saving through cutting government deficits would generate additional investment and prosperity.

In light of the free cash generation that government deficits create, the logic of the Twin Deficit falls on its face. High government deficits are stimulatory. To the extent that they drive the economy to higher levels of income, government deficits expand private savings. The idea that government deficits cut into the saving pool can only be maintained in the face of a full-employment, no excess-capacity economy whereby government claims on resources infringe on those already utilized for private purposes. This understanding is widely acknowledged. But a full understanding of the impact of government deficits would require a credible counter-factual story that would estimate the level of the economy and the level of savings *in the absence of government deficits.* In reference to the years between 1980 and 1991, Benjamin M. Friedman asserts that the government "absorbed nearly three-fourths of all net saving done by U.S. individuals and businesses combined" (Friedman, 1991, p. 149). He further maintains that the economy approximated "full employment" after the downturn of 1981–82. This is question-begging. Even if full employment is granted–a questionable proposition given the high level of non-participation in the labor force–the full-employment private savings of the decade was generated in part by the very government deficits that Friedman claims "absorbed" the savings!

The evidence for government deficits "crowding out" investment is nonexistent. According to the "crowding-out" explanation, the high nominal interest rates in the 1980s reflected government borrowings, which in turn sabotaged investment. But at least for the early part of the decade, a more plausible explanation is available. The early 1980s came immediately after the inflationary episode of the 1970s. With anticipated inflation, creditors raised interest rates to compensate for anticipated capital losses. The inflation of the 1970s was caused by an oil crisis and a loosening of the wide money supply by the Federal Reserve. Such expansion of the money supply came in response to the corporate debt build-up of the 1960s and the subsequent bankruptcies and near-bankruptcies of the 1970s. As exemplified by the bailouts of Lockheed, Penn Central and Chrysler, these blowouts were not confined to smaller firms.

In addition, the breakup of the Bretton Woods Gold Standard during 1971–73 drove the dollar down and raised import prices. Nor was the inflationary force confined to imports. As will be discussed in Chapter 7, U.S. export prices rose so that U.S. multinationals could avoid competition with their own offshore affiliates. In raising export prices, domestic prices rose as well.

In a now-familiar story, Paul Volker took charge of the Federal Reserve in 1979 and applied the monetary brakes. The resulting shock of the early 1980s struck at inflation through cutbacks on monetary aggregates, resulting in very high unemployment. Under non-inflationary conditions, cutbacks on the money supply would raise interest rates. But under the inflationary conditions of the time, when creditors raised nominal rates to compensate for inflation, cutbacks on the money supply brought interest rates down. In contradiction to the Twin Deficit thesis, interest rates went down significantly, even with the expansion of the Reagan deficits brought about by an expanded military budget and massive tax cuts tailored to the wealthy and the corporate rich.

In the run-up to the dot.com debacle in the spring of 2001, trade deficits continued even in the face of government surpluses. The evidence thus turned 180 degrees on the Twin Deficit thesis. The continued long-term secular fall in the dollar over nearly half a century should have arrested the trade deficits. As will be discussed in Chapter 7, their continued expansion suggested that institutional and multinational forces were at work countering the traditional argument that exchange rate depreciation leads necessarily to a reduction in trade imbalances. The rapid decline in inflation in the decades after the early 1980s, together with increased foreign inflows of capital drove a 35-year secular decline in interest rates. A large part—perhaps the largest part—of this long-term decline in interest rates can be attributable to the Federal Reserve and to Greenspan's "put." But the decline was also a reflection of the free cash spillage that resulted from expanded deficit spending by both government and private parties.

Free cash spillage extends the Keynesian-Kaleckian proposition that investment is self-funding. Deficits help create the free cash that keeps the costs of financing the deficits within bounds. The paradoxical circle: the free cash that holds down interest rates is, at the same time, reflective of government deficits that are required to maintain any investment growth at all.

Notes

1 For a similar analysis, see Krugman, 2013.

2 The short-term blotting-out of historical memory among mainstream economists is particularly striking in light of the argument relating monopoly to Depression that was advanced during the Depression itself. Monopoly meant not just a restriction of investment but an inability to recover from a downturn. Gardiner Means's thesis, that oligopoly formations engaged in administrative pricing, meant that falling demand would not necessarily result in price declines sufficient for recovery (Hawley, 1966, pp. 293–295, 383–384).

3 In *Monopoly Capital* (1966), Baran and Sweezy did not discuss the stock market collapse of 1929 that ushered in the Great Depression. Perhaps this was because of the extensive treatment accorded by others. By far the most famous and humorous is John Kenneth Galbraith's *The Great Crash* ([1954] 1961). What Baran and Sweezy emphasized was the counter-acting forces offsetting depression during the 1920s. In particular, they stressed the rise of the internal combustion engine and the growth of the suburbs. They might also have stressed, but did not, the agricultural advances in

the 1920s made by the internal combustion engine that lowered the cost of food and allowed more purchasing power for industrial growth.

4 Paul Sweezy (1958, pp. 21–29) is quite explicit about his own indebtedness to Veblen's understanding of the relationship between monopoly and the tendency to chronic depression.

5 See Foster and Magdoff (2009).

6 In 2016, there were still 800 U.S. military bases in over 70 countries with approximately 150,000 troops overseas, with over half in Germany, Japan and South Korea (*Economist*, August 13, 2016, p. 20).

7 A term often ascribed to Joan Robinson's AEA address in 1972, but apparently David Riesman got there first in designating the military dimension of growth and stability as "sub-rosa military Keynesianism" in 1958. See James M. Cypher's interesting piece on the demand-management aspects of U.S. militarism (2015, pp. 449–476.

8 This increase in markups is also confirmed in Blonigen and Pierce (2016). A wider discussion of concentration and expanded profitability is given in Zingales (2017).

9 National Production and its corresponding National Income is: (Y) = C + I + G + C.A. = C + S + T. Noting that the government gets its monies from Taxes (T) or the fiscal deficit (F.D.) and crossing out similars, we obtain **(1)** above.

10 As noted in Chapter 4, free cash can be measured in two forms: a narrow free cash measure indicated by **(2)** above that is inclusive of dividends alone and a wider version inclusive of dividends and net interest (i.e. all security payouts). As the fiscal deficit and the current account are readily available, the personal (non-corporate) saving-investment discrepancy are calculated as residuals and differ in reference to the two definitions of free cash. This is necessary as savings and consumption from dividends and total security payouts are not available. Wide free cash is, of course, larger than narrow free cash, but the two series move in tandem.

11 World War II is the exemplary instance. During the war, the Federal Reserve and the Treasury traded their debt.

12 In 2007, the top 5 percent of net worth households held more than 90 percent of bonds outside of managed asset funds and trusts (Kennickell, 2009, p. 63, Figure A3. a). In 2005, the top 5.5 percent of households, ranked by income, had a propensity to consume of after-tax income of approximately 50 percent, in contrast to the median household who had a propensity to consume of approximately 90 percent (Medlen, 2008, p. 859).

13 Rothstein (2009) estimates that per dollar spent, the Earned Income Tax Credit raises after-tax income by $.73 with the remainder reflected in lower wages.

14 As the requirements for contributions are capped at higher labor compensation rates, this figure minimizes the actual deductions from lower and average wage recipients.

15 In a survey of approximately a thousand firms in which 186 responded, 111 indicated that the excess profits tax "*had no effect upon the level of their investment expenditures on new plant and equipment*" (Dugan and Zubrow, 1954, p. 245; original emphasis). Moreover, of those that depended on internal funds for expansion, "9 out every 10 firms . . . maintained that their decisions regarding the methods of financing were independent of EPT [excess profits tax] considerations" (p. 248).

16 *Economist*, April 1, 2017, p. 21.

17 Bureau of Labor Statistics.

18 Federal Reserve Economic Data (FRED), St. Louis Federal Reserve, MEFAINUSA672N.

19 *Housing in the Seventies: A Report of the National Housing Policy Review*, HUD-0000968, November 1974.

20 Economist.co/ushouseprices.

21 In discussing the new "Recession Generation," Foroohar (2010, pp. 42–45) compares the tent cities of California in the mid-1930s to those along the American River of Sacramento that expanded during the Great Recession begun in late 2007.

22 *Trulia* study cited in the *Wall Street Journal* (April 13, 2017, A2). In a MagnifyMoney study summarized by *Fortune* (August 1, 1917, p. 15), national areas were classified by affordability in reference to a $100,000-a-year household with one child. The West and East Coasts were predictably the least affordable areas; the South with a trajectory towards the North-East was the most affordable.

23 Federal Reserve, *Flow of Funds*, Table L. 110.

24 Federal Reserve, *Flow of Funds*, Table L. 125

References

Baran, Paul and Paul Sweezy, *Monopoly Capital: An Essay on the American Economic and Social Order*, Monthly Review Press, New York, 1966.

Blanchard, Olivier and Lawrence Summers, "Rethinking Stabilization Policy. Back to the Future," Peterson Institute for International Economics, October 8, 2017.

Blonigen, Bruce A. and Justin R. Pierce, "Evidence for the Effects of Mergers on Market Power and Efficiency," Federal Reserve Board Divisions of Research & Statistics and Monetary Affairs Finance and Economics Discussion Paper 2016–082.

Bowles, E. and Simpson, A.K. (Chairmen of the National Commission on Fiscal Responsibility and Reform), *The Moment of Truth*, December 2010; http://momentoftruthproject.org/sites/default/files/TheMomentofTruth12_1_2010.pdf.

Bowles, E. and Simpson, A.K., *A Bipartisan Path Forward to Securing American's Future: Moment of Truth Project*, April 2013; http://www.momentoftruthproject.org/publications/bipartisan-path-forward-securing-americas-future-0.

Brownlee, W. Elliot, *Federal Taxation in America: A Short History*, Woodrow Wilson Center Press and Cambridge University Press, Cambridge, UK, 2004.

Costa, Dora L. and Matthew E. Kahn, "Power Couples: Changes in the Locational Choice of the College Educated, 1940–1990," *The Quarterly Journal of Economics*, Vol. 115, No. 4, November 2000, pp. 1287–1315.

Crotty, J., "The Neo-Liberal Paradox: The Impact of Destructive Product Market Competition and 'Modern' Financial Markets on Non-Financial Corporate Performance in the Neoliberal Era," in *Financialization and the World Economy*, edited by G. Epstein, Edward Elgar, London, 2005, pp. 77–110.

Cypher, James M., "The Origins and Evolution of Military Keynesianism in the United States," *Journal of Post-Keynesian Economics*, Vol. 38, pp. 449–476, 2015.

De Loecker, Jan and Jan Eeckhout, "The Rise of Market Power and the Macroeconomic Implications," NBER Working Paper No. 23687, August 2017.

Dugan, J.E. and Zubrow, R.A., "The Influence of the Excess Profits Tax on Business Decisions to Invest," *National Tax Journal*, September 1954, pp. 242–251.

Foroohar, Rana, "The Recession Generation," *Newsweek*, January 18, 2010.

Foster, John Bellamy and Fred Magdoff, *The Great Financial Crisis: Causes and Consequences*, Monthly Review Press, New York, 2009.

Foster, John Bellamy, Robert W. McChesney and R. Jamil Jonna, "Monopoly and Competition in Twenty-First Century Capitalism," *Monthly Review*, Vol. 62, No. 11, April 2011.

Friedman, Benjamin M., "U.S. Fiscal Policy in the 1980s: Consequences of Large Budget Deficits at Full Employment," in *Debt and the Twin Deficits Debate*, edited by James M. Rock, Bristlecone Books, Mayfield Publishing Company, Mountain View, CA, London and Toronto, 1991, pp. 149–172.

Galbraith, John Kenneth, *The Great Crash*, Houghton, Mifflin Company, Boston, MA, [1954] 1961.

Gordon, Robert J., *The Rise and Fall of American Growth*, Princeton University Press, Princeton, NJ and Oxford, 2016.

Greenspan, Alan, *Federal Reserve Board Semiannual Monetary Policy Report to the Congress*, Committee on Financial Services, U.S. House of Representatives, July 20, 2008; http://blogs.wsj.com/economics/2008/10/23/greenspan-testimony-on-sources-of-financial crisis.

Gutierrez, German, "Declining Competition and Investment in the U.S.," National Bureau of Economic Research Working Paper, July 2017.

Gutierrez, German and Thomas Philippon, "Investment-less Growth: An Empirical Investigation," National Bureau of Economic Research Working Paper, November 2016.

Hansen, Alvin H., "Economic Progress and Declining Population Growth," Presidential Address at the Fifty-first Annual Meeting of the American Economic Association, December 28, 1938, printed in *The American Economic Review*, Vol. XXIX, No. 1, Part 1, March 1939.

Hawley, Ellis W., *The New Deal and the Problem of Monopoly*, Princeton University Press, Princeton, NJ, 1966.

Hines, J.R., Jr., "Treasure Islands," *Journal of Economic Perspectives*, Fall 2010, Vol. 24, No. 1, pp. 103–126.

Kalecki, Michal, "A Theory of Commodity, Income and Capital Taxation," in *Collected Works of Michal Kalecki*, Vol. 1, edited by J. Osiatynsky, Oxford: Clarendon Press, [1937] 2009.

Kennickell, Arthur B., "Ponds and Streams: Wealth and Income in the U.*S.*, 1989–2007," *Board of Governors, Federal Reserve System*, January 7, 2009.

Krippner, G., "The Financialization of the American Economy," *Socio-Economic Review*, Vol. 3, 2005, pp. 173–208.

Krugman, Paul, "Corporate Cash Con." Opinion Pages, *New York Times*, July 3, 2011.

Krugman, Paul, "Secular Stagnation Coalmines, Bubbles and Larry Summers," *New York Times*, November 16, 2013.

Leff, Mark, *The Limits of Symbolic Reform: The New Deal and Taxation, 1933–1939*, Cambridge University Press, Cambridge, UK, London, New York, Melbourne and Sydney, 1966.

Medlen, Craig, "Galbraith's Preference Mappings: Needs and Wants, Evidence from the 2005 Consumer Budget Study," *Notes and Communications, Journal of Economic Issues*, Vol. XLII, No. 3, September 2008.

Merrill, P.R., "Corporate Tax Policy for the Twenty-First Century," *National Tax Journal*, Vol. 63, No. 4 (Part 1), December 2010, pp. 623–634.

Moretti, Enrico, *The New Geography of Jobs*, Mariner Books, Houghton Mifflin Harcourt, Boston, MA and New York, 2013.

Muller, Peter O., "Suburbanization in the 1970s: Interpreting Population, Socioeconomic, and Employment Trends," in *The American Metropolitan System: Present and Future*, edited by Stanley D. Brunn and James O. Wheeler, Wiley, New York, 1980, pp. 37–49.

Rothstein, Jesse, "Is the EITC Equivalent to an NIT? Conditional Cash Transfers and Tax Incidence," Working Paper 14966, National Bureau of Economic Research, May 2009.

Schiller, Robert J., *The Subprime Solution*, Princeton University Press, Princeton, NJ, 2008.

Starr, Martha A., "Debt-Financed Consumption Sprees: Regulation, Freedom and Habits of Thought," *Journal of Economic Issues*, Vol. XLIV, No. 2, June 2010, pp. 459–467.

Steindl, Joseph, *Maturity and Stagnation in American Capitalism*, Monthly Review Press, New York and London, [1952] 1976.

Summers, Lawrence H., "U.S. Economic Prospects: Secular Stagnation, Hysteresis, and the Zero Lower Bound," *Business Economics*, Vol. 49, No. 2, 2014.

Sweezy, Paul, "Veblen's Critique of the American Economy," *American Economic Association, Papers and Proceedings*, Vol. 48, 1958, pp. 21–29.

Volker, P.A. (Chairman of the President's Advisory Board), *The Report on Tax Reform Options: Simplification, Compliance and Corporate Taxation*, August 2010; https://www.treasury.gov/resource-center/tax-policy/Documents/Report-Tax-Reform-Options-2010.pdf.

Wolff, Edward N., "Recent Trends in Household Wealth in the United States: Rising Debt and the Middle-Class Squeeze—an Update to 2007," Working Paper No. 589, *Levy Economics Institute of Bard College*, March 2010.

Zingales, Luigi, "Towards a Political Theory of the Firm," *Journal of Economic Perspectives*, Vol. 31, No. 3, Summer 2017, pp. 113–130.

7 The multinational escape

In the 1930s, Michal Kalecki's understanding that export surpluses would create free cash was formulated at a time when U.S. national production was carried out almost entirely by nationally headquartered firms and when multinational production was distinctly secondary to trade. There was, of course, important multinational activity. After World War I and continuing into the 1930s, Wall St. bankers roamed Europe for suitable investments to augment U.S. investments in oil, automobiles, electrical products, and assorted other investments.[1] Moreover, U.S. investments in resource-rich areas like Latin America were involved in the production of copper, oil, tropical foodstuffs and other products dependent on geographical location. But for the most part, the U.S. economy was the economy of the U.S. firm. Export surpluses contributed to free cash streams as export earnings added to revenues in excess of import outflows.

The multinational context of modern trade requires that Kalecki's unidirectional understanding of free cash and trade balances be significantly modified. Under the current multinational order, it is far from clear that U.S. trade deficits subtract from free cash. The essential reason is that the multinational dimension of modern firms depresses domestic investment, while at the same time government and private deficits expand cash.

Multinational production and sales abroad substitute in large part for U.S. exports, allowing world profits of U.S. corporations to expand even if U.S. exports falter or recede relative to imports. As this substitution of multinational production for exports crimps domestic U.S. investment and domestic cash generation, multinational production trades off U.S. cash generation for a larger world total. Kalecki's understanding of free cash and the trade balance also needs reformulation in light of the multinational context of imports. U.S. firms' use of import supply chains allows a cutback in U.S. investment. Import supply chains, while perhaps profitable for each individual firm, undercut U.S. growth and the domestic generation of cash flow.

Cash generation, however, differs from free cash generation. As was shown in the previous chapter, countervailing forces in the form of government and household deficits have generated large amounts of cash flow in the face of declining investment growth. As long as *the deficits of the government and households are sufficiently large, deficit spending sustains the U.S. economy and generates cash, even as trade deficits crimp growth in output and investment.* In contradistinction to the Twin Deficit thesis, government deficits and trade deficits are far from "twins" whereby government deficits create trade imbalances. On the contrary. Government (and household) deficits are stimulatory deficits in the service of offsetting trade deficits based on external production and import supply chains. In summary, these deficits allow domestic cash generation despite a "hollowed-out" industrial base. In receiving large cash flows from government and consumer deficits, and in cutting back investment through diminished exports and import supply chains, enlarged amounts of free cash result.

An understanding of U.S. multinational capital and its effect on recent trade balances is best approached through an examination of multinational capital's historical growth. I propose a "stage" theory whereby the large-scale expansion of multinational capital that occurred during the Bretton Woods period (from 1944 to 1971–73) brought forth an enlarged amount of offshore production. Global firms, intent on maximizing global profits recognized (and recognize now) that this offshore production potentially competes with exports. In consequence, U.S. firms have cut back on U.S. exports. The large-scale development of import supply lines—at least in terms of their relative importance—is of more recent vintage. Many of these supply lines are now located in the manufacturing hubs and resource centers of the emerging world. This combination of offshore multinational production and import supply lines goes some distance in understanding the persistence of U.S. trade deficits, even in the face of a long near-half-century decline in the dollar. As noted, this combination has acted (and acts now) to suppress domestic investment and, in consequence, to expand free cash.

The breakup of Bretton Woods and the coming of floating rates

The last four decades have witnessed an increasing cross-border integration of Europe and a cross-border escape of Japan's largest corporations into the U.S., East Asia and Europe. Against this backdrop, it is hard to fully remember the overwhelming predominant role of U.S. corporations in foreign direct investment and worldwide sales at the time of the collapse of Bretton Woods (1971–73). In contrast to the approximate 20 percent share of outward Foreign Direct Investment (FDI) in the world that U.S. corporations have had in recent years, U.S. firms had approximately 50 percent of the total thirty years ago.[2] A comparison of world sales by the world's largest firms shows the same relative predominance, with U.S. firms having some 63 percent of worldwide sales of the top 300 industrial firms in 1971, as compared with approximately 30 percent of the top 300 firms in recent years.[3] Such predominance, of course, of course, was the legacy of the post-WWII order and the Bretton Woods system. The Bretton Woods system enshrined the dollar at the high levels corresponding to the U.S. position in world trade immediately after World War II. In subsequent decades, the export orientation of Japan and the European economies dictated that their foreign central banks support the high value of the dollar. The reason was simple: any decline in the value of the dollar would damage the exporters that stood at the heart of their economies. Understanding this one central fact allows an understanding of how the Bretton Woods system and the high dollar associated with it could be maintained for almost thirty years, even in the face of a mounting U.S. balance of payments deficit begun in the late 1950s and an enormous military presence that spread dollars all over the world. Foreign central banks, in support of their national corporations, supported the dollar.

With foreign central banks supporting the dollar, U.S. firms leveraged this advantage to buy investments and corresponding markets around the world. This was particularly true in Europe. When the Common Market was formed in the late 1950s, the U.S. fear of a common tariff and other discriminatory barriers conjoined with Europe's easing of earlier repatriation laws that hindered repatriated profits flowing back to the United States. This was a potent combination of motivations to entice and increase the presence of U.S. multinational capital in Europe. Direct investment expanded rapidly along with a corresponding European alarm. In a famous response, Jean-Jacques Servan-Schreiber described the extended U.S. presence as a "seizure of power" and an "assault on Europe" and fully recognized that no country on its own could oppose such an invasion (1969, pp. 33–40). Direct confrontation would lead U.S. investments and managerial talent to turn elsewhere to the benefit of the recipient, even as such investment competed with domestic firms. The sheer size of the U.S. giants, such as IBM, General Motors, DuPont de Nemours and General Electric, together with an industrial-academic U.S. government complex that sponsored the most advanced technological breakthroughs, put European firms at an inherent disadvantage. As if able to see the future of repeated attempts at bringing Europe together, Servan-Schreiber maintained that only an increased integration of the European Community could mount an effective response.

If there were any mystery surrounding the breakup of Bretton Woods, it concerned not its breakup, but how it could have maintained its standing for so long. Again, the export-based nature of rivals put Europe and Japan in a defensive position. To get off Bretton Woods was to lose export markets and, in the case of Europe, to maintain the Bretton Woods system was to allow U.S. capital to buy a large chunk of the world's markets on the cheap. Japan's repatriation laws, together with *keiretsu* interlocks into distribution channels kept U.S. firms—oil companies apart—from entering Japan in any large measure. But the high dollar value associated with Bretton Woods allowed the United States to obtain Japanese war supplies cheaply for both the Korean War and the Vietnam War. In 1951, 72 percent of Japan's "productive capacity was directly engaged in the manufacture of weapons" (Yanaga, 1968, p. 255). These dollars were undoubtedly welcome since Japan was in its first stages of renewed takeoff. But by the time of the Vietnam War, Japan was able to export manufactured products of high quality. The U.S. use of the printing press to command Japanese resources and labor put Japan in a position analogous to that of Europe. To make Japanese war materials expensive to the United States, the Japanese would have to get off of the Bretton Woods standard. Such an upward movement of the yen would damage the large Japanese exporters and the Japanese economy.

When the dollar started to plunge after the Bretton Woods breakup, Europe and Japan were on the defensive, trying to keep the dollar from plunging too fast. Their defense employed both exchange controls and an expansion of their monetary base. Such expansion added to the inflation of the 1970s. And, at least for continental Europe, monetary integration had to be affected in order to coordinate exchange rates so as not to compete one against another. This monetary integration went hand-in-hand with increasing cross-border affiliations and direct investment that allowed European corporations "natural" hedges when monetary coordination failed. When the monetary "snake" arrangement came apart in the 1970s,[4] a renewed attempt was established with the European Monetary Union (EMU) and progress along these lines eventually culminated in the establishment of the euro.

Multinational production, sales and the U.S. export market

The growth of U.S. direct investment in Europe was the main component shifting the relative growth of multinational capital from resource centers (often located in the developing world, which produced petroleum products, tropical foodstuffs and minerals, or in Canada, which produced food products, timber and paper) to the developed world of manufacturing and financial centers. In 1950, the Latin American republics and Canada actually had more than two-thirds of the total book value of direct foreign investment, with Canada actually having a larger chunk of manufacturing investments (32 percent) than Western Europe (24 percent). By the time of the collapse of Bretton Woods, the share of total direct investments in Western Europe had climbed from 15 percent in 1950 to 31 percent and housed 48 percent of U.S. foreign manufacturing investments.[5] In 2015, outward direct investment in Europe accounted for 50 percent of the total, with Canada having 7 percent, Latin America 17 percent and Asia and Pacific 17 percent.[6]

The rise of manufacturing investments abroad and the concomitant sales of the affiliates meant that foreigners could purchase U.S. manufactured products with their own currency and that such production abroad competed, potentially or in actuality, with U.S. exports. To avoid such competition, U.S. firms have had to arrange pricing and sales arrangements so as to be relatively immune to exchange rate changes. The statistical story on multinational sales comes in late (1957) and then only for certain broad categories in the manufacturing sector. But by this time, multinational sales were much larger than exports in virtually every major category of manufacturing examined, with the sole exception of nonelectrical machinery, where multinational sales were 60 percent of exports. In the other categories, the respective percentages were as follows: rubber, 322 percent; chemicals, 175 percent; transportation equipment, 270 percent; electrical machinery, 253 percent; and paper and allied products, 270 percent (Cutler and Pizer, 1963, p. 20). This pattern of multinational sales dwarfing exports continues to this day, and not just in manufacturing. From the first compilation of a universe total of multinational sales (beginning on a continuous basis from 1982) to 2014, multinational sales first rose from about 250 percent of the total U.S. exports of goods and services to more than

400 percent in 1977 and then sank back to more than 240 percent in 1993 and has been over 300 percent since the early 2000s.[7] Data on multinational exchange of services is not as comprehensive as that of goods, particularly in reference to the time period covered, but recent evidence shows an exponential growth in the ratio of multinational sales relative to exports. Multinational sales and U.S. exports of services were roughly equivalent from the late 1980s to the mid-1990s, but then multinational sales of services rose to 190 percent of exports in 2013 (Grimm and Krishnan, 2015, Chart 1, p. 1).

The lower line of Figure 7.1 shows the ratio of the total estimated multinational sales of goods to total U.S. exports of goods, with multinational sales being roughly triple that of exports. The upper data line shows the ratio of multinational sales to U.S. exports of goods associated with multinational enterprises, with the rapid expansion of the ratio after the late 1990s indicating that associated exports have declined relative to total exports. Multinational enterprises are generally among the largest of U.S. firms and have traditionally been the largest exporters as well. The association of multinational sales and exports traditionally led various commentators to argue that multinational outposts have actually helped sponsor U.S. exports. This was a familiar argument during and just after the Bretton Woods period when U.S. multinational capital spread out into Europe.[8] Capital goods and productive inputs, geared to U.S. production, were exported in support of U.S.-owned European facilities. Marketing facilities abroad facilitated the distribution of final products, consisting at least in part of U.S. production.[9]

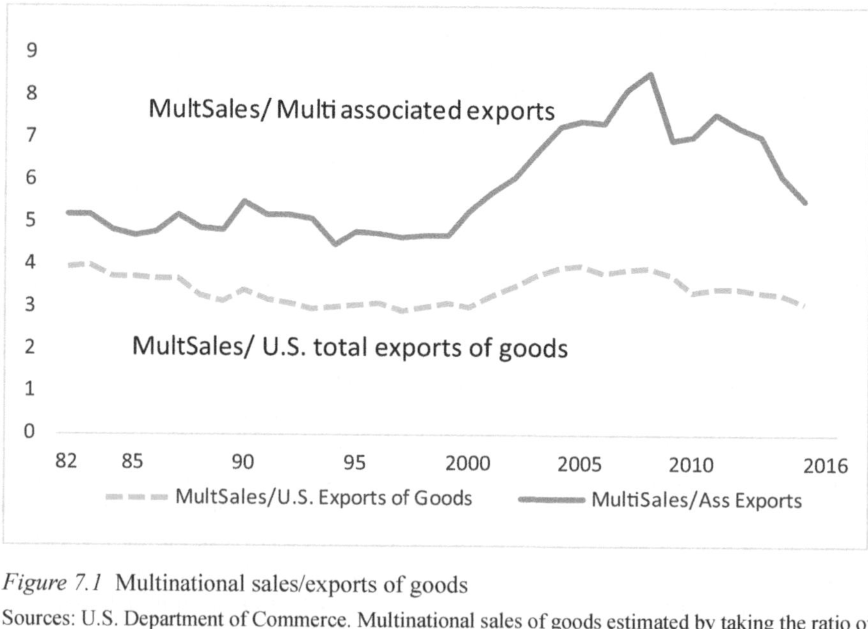

Figure 7.1 Multinational sales/exports of goods

Sources: U.S. Department of Commerce. Multinational sales of goods estimated by taking the ratio of sales of goods to services of majority-owned affiliates and applying that ratio to the aggregate sales of all affiliates.

These marketing platforms permitted sales of U.S. exports whose markets might well have been captured by others (Freeman and Frank, 1978, p. 38); Cohen, 2007, p. 221). Unlike the last two and a half decades, time slice studies conducted by the Department of Commerce showed that between 1966 and 1970, exports of multinational corporations expanded relative to the total (Barker, 1972, pp. 20–28). This relative expansion seemed to confirm the complementary nature of multinational expansion and exports and reinforced the argument that multinational expansion helped U.S. exports and the domestic U.S. economy in general.

In a tautological sense, exports (and imports) are fully complementary to multinational sales as firms choose the particular mix available to maximize global returns. But this assessment is on one side of the substitutability issue. It is often contended that in the absence of a counterfactual narrative, the question of substitutability or complementarity can be dismissed as a sterile question, or, at best an unanswerable one. In the mid-1960s, Judd Polk and colleagues maintained that

> the trade question as posed could have been recognized as unverifiable since, whatever relationship might be discovered between export growth and investment growth, there is still no way of making useful inferences as to the likely volume of exports in the absence of investment.
>
> (Polk et al., 1966, p. 18; original emphasis)

This lack of a counterfactual story is a familiar theme, taken up more recently by Stephen Cohen in asserting, that “FDI as a whole has not yet been shown to be an unequivocal cause of serious or sustained harm to aggregate exports or employment” (Cohen, 2007, p. 20). I do not believe that the question of a counternarrative addressed the main question concerning the relationship of multinational sales to exports. That history cannot be repeated as social experiment is, of course, obvious. The question is not whether firms, industries, or nations lose exports in the absence of multinational platforms abroad. Rather the question of substitutability must be located in an historical context related to a stage understanding of multinational expansion. The first large-scale intrusion of U.S. capital into Europe and beyond during the 1960s might well have expanded U.S. exports in support of overseas operations. But the larger question is what happened over time. The thesis presented here is that U.S. multinational capital, loosened from its domestic moorings, increasingly sourced inputs, talent and capital through overseas channels. Parents on the home base faced potential and unwarranted competition with their own foreign affiliates. In the interests of global returns, patents increasingly relied on production abroad so as to avoid such competition and maintain world market shares.

Post-Bretton Woods

During the Bretton Woods period, the Hobson’s choice that the U.S. offered to advanced capitalist rivals was the choice between the U.S. buying global markets, resources and talent cheaply, or the loss of rivals’ export markets. The influx of

U.S. capital abroad meant an exchange of dollars for local currencies that needed to be printed to maintain the Bretton Woods standard. Foreign central banks thus absorbed large amounted of unwanted dollars at the prevailing rates so as to maintain their exports. In order to sell electronics, automobiles and machinery, Japan was burdened by some part of the Vietnam War costs. Germany, with its traditional fear of inflation, "was unwilling to countenance inflation rates much in excess of 3 percent" (Eichengreen, 2008, p. 129). In the latter part of the 1960s and extending up until the collapse of Bretton Woods in 1971, the English pressed for gold redemption of unwanted dollars. But the French offered up the most vocal opposition. The mass strike of May 1968 seemed to confirm the view that the U.S. was importing not just capital but inflation and labor unrest. That the dollar could be conveniently printed as part of its "privilege" as the world's reserve currency added an additional dose of insult.

Added to the breakup was economic theory. Theory held that the large-scale U.S. balance of payments deficits begun in the late 1950s might well be ameliorated, if not cured, by an export-boosting decline in the dollar.

The abandonment of Bretton Woods, initiated by President Nixon in the summer of 1971, tested the efficacy of floating rates.[10] Advocates of floating rates predicted that a fall in the dollar would expand exports and limit imports enough so as to dampen and possibly arrest the dollar's decline. All would self-correct—both the deficit and the decline in the dollar. But apart from a pause in 1973, the fall continued throughout the decade of the 1970s and the trade deficit became worse. In regard to this dollar decline, Ronald I. McKinnon (2013) held that expectations and sporadic removals of capital controls acted to produce self-fulfilling cybernetics whereby prophetic visions and talking points insured "hot money" runs (p. 9). In 1978, an international consortium halted the decline (p. 9). Three years later, Paul Volker's tight money policies drove a subsequent spike in the dollar that peaked in 1985, before resuming its downward path until the mid-1990s. It is significant that the fall and subsequent spike in the dollar resulted not from self-correcting forces but from direct intervention.

McKinnon's expectations hypothesis no doubt harbors a good deal of truth. But what is noteworthy is that the trade deficit actually expanded when the dollar was at its lowest point during the 1970s. This period might be understood as exceptional, as collaborative arrangements between OPEC and the major oil firms drove both oil prices and the valuation of U.S. oil imports higher (Adelman, 1972, pp. 253–256). But these collaborative arrangements exemplify the general principle that exchange rate declines have to be understood in reference to the over-riding multinational context within which trade occurs.

The forces that held Bretton Woods together maintained potency even after the collapse of the agreement. Dependent upon exports, rival nations printed money in the 1970s and enacted exchange controls so as to minimize the dollar's fall. For U.S. multinational firms, a lower dollar presented a heightened awareness of the potential competition among U.S. parents and affiliates. Among other expedients, such as requiring customers to service products at the point of sale, U.S. firms engaged in "dollar-based" pricing systems around the world so as to ward off inter-company competition due to dollar devaluation. In other words, prices would either be lowered abroad or raised within the U.S. to avoid U.S. exports competing with affiliate production and sales abroad. Proprietary constraints as well as anti-trust concerns severely limit research on inter-company arrangement to avoid competition. However, the differential inflation between the U.S. and rivals over the course of the post-Bretton Woods period suggests that dollar-based pricing was probably extensive. In short, dollar declines were met with an expansion of U.S. inflation, based not just on expanded import prices but on domestic production as well. Dollar-based pricing systems help explain the decisive departure of the U.S. wholesale and consumer price indexes from those of U.S. export-based rivals such as Germany and Japan after 1971. These divergences continue.[11]

As noted above, the asymmetry between U.S. multinational capital and export-based rivals was certainly more apparent at the time when Bretton Woods collapsed than in recent times. But the asymmetry continues as U.S. giants have expanded their global presence. Some sense of this offshoring of production, sales and affiliate connections can be gleaned by comparing the economic variables of U.S. affiliates to those of their U.S. parents. Continuous data starts very late (1982), but in virtually all relevant variables, the majority-owned affiliate portion has risen

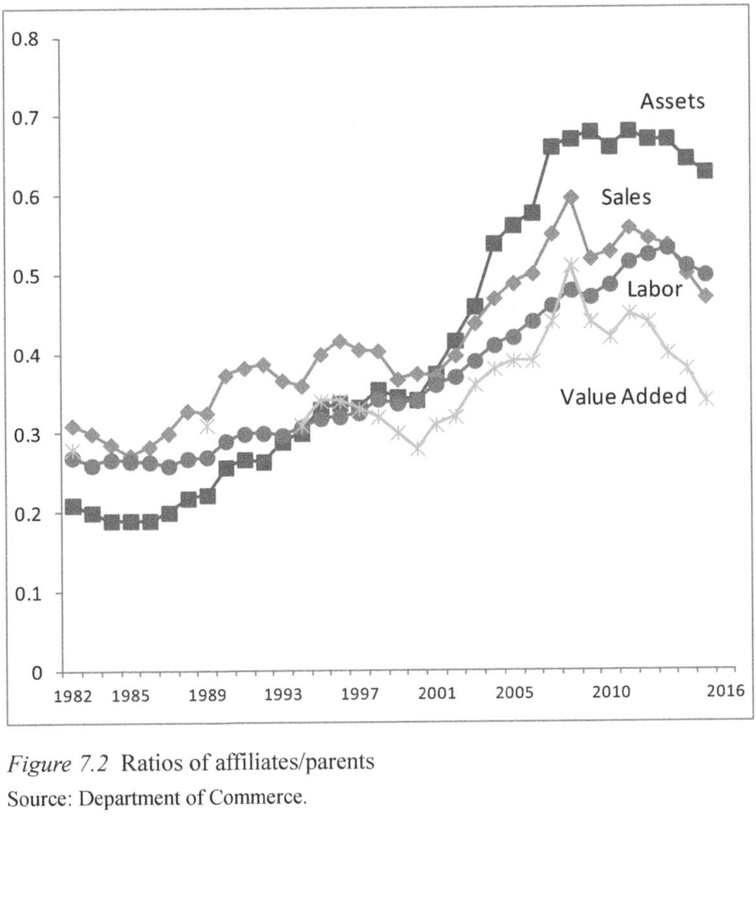

Figure 7.2 Ratios of affiliates/parents

Source: Department of Commerce.

relative to the parent. Figure 7.2 shows the relative rise of assets, sales, labor and value added, but the upward pattern can also be observed in capital expenditures and net incomes as well. The recent and rapid rise of dollar-denominated assets, sales and value reflect both the movement of U.S. capital into emerging markets[12] and the translation effects of a weaker dollar, particularly in Europe where multinational sales now constitute roughly 40–45 percent of the total. In the time span of 1999 through 2008, the euro gained almost 50 percent before beginning a rapid fall-off that continues to this day (mid-2017). Under a weaker dollar, the translations of affiliate assets, sales and income are registered as monetary gains to stockholders—rewards resulting from earlier decisions to locate abroad.

Translation effects aside, "real" exchange rate-adjusted production and employment of affiliates grew relative to parents. Existing data regarding production is limited to manufacturing and then only up through 2009 when U.S. government sequesters motivated the Department of Commerce to halt the construction of affiliate real value-added measures. Nevertheless, the overall record regarding manufacturing is relatively complete. Between 1982 and 1994, the real gross product of majority-owned affiliates in manufacturing grew, on average, at one half percentage point over their parents (Mataloni, Jr., 1997, p. 9). In the period from 1999 to 2009, the real value added of parents probably declined by 0.3 percent a year but majority-owned affiliates grew roughly 0.7 percent making the affiliate growth approximately 1 percent over that of parents (Barefoot and Mataloni, Jr., 2011, p. 32).

Over the last three decades, there has been an over-85 percent rise in the employment ratio of majority-owned affiliates to parents in all industries. Part of this increase has been due to the stagnant employment growth of the parents, which expanded about 25 percent over the 18 years beginning in 1982, before becoming almost totally stagnant after 2000. This stagnation is not surprising given the overall decline in U.S. manufacturing employment and the offshoring of manufacturing abroad (Baily and Bosworth, 2014, p. 11). In sharp contrast, affiliate employment in all industries grew 120 percent in the period 1982–2014.

This growth in affiliate employment was complemented by the growth of import supply chains emanating out of China and other developing nations. From the late 1990s to 2007, Susan Houseman and colleagues (2011) found a "dramatic shift in sourcing of intermediate goods from domestic to foreign suppliers . . . [with developing countries accounting] . . . for half of the growth in foreign material inputs" (p. 114). Multinational firms increasingly found it unnecessary to establish affiliates to take advantage of low-cost production sites. In contrast to imports from foreign affiliates, there is no data available on the geographical location of imports "associated" with multinational firms. But the fact that U.S. multinationals' "associated" imports now exceed their "associated" exports is consonant with the well-documented expansion of outsourced supply chains (Milberg, 2004; Milberg and Winkler, 2013; Timmer et al., 2014, pp. 99–118).

Foreign affiliate investment in the U.S.—continued asymmetry or convergence?

U.S. multinational firms' substitution of sales for exports provided a template for rivals, as foreign firms attained the requisite size that would allow them to challenge U.S. firms within the U.S. itself.[13] In 1959 and 1966, multinational production and manufacturing within the U.S. of firms associated with the UK, Netherlands and Switzerland was larger than their U.S. imports. But for Japan, Germany, France and "other Europe," the fraction of multinational production within the U.S. imports was miniscule (Rowthorn, [1971] 1975, p. 166). But catch-up did occur as Japanese, German, French and other European firms entered the United States, particularly after the collapse of Bretton Woods. The *continuous* story concerning the sales of goods of foreign affiliates within the U.S. begins in 1977. This story bears comparison with that of U.S. firms abroad. Figures 7.3 and 7.4 compare the estimates of U.S. multinational sales/U.S. exports to affiliates ratios in various parts of the world with the sales/U.S. import ratios of foreign-owned affiliates located inside the U.S. Imports into the foreign-owned U.S. affiliates include not just imports from parents, but from other parent-associated foreign affiliates so the data is not strictly comparable. But the data certainly captures the overall asymmetrical pattern of U.S. firms' multinational sales dwarfing exports relative to a comparable ratio of foreign firms.[14]

On a global scale, U.S. multinational sales are around 15 times that of U.S. exports to affiliates and in Europe, approximately 30 times exports. As gauged by the foreign content of production, these sales most certainly substitute for exports. The record from 1982 to 2014 shows that the foreign content of U.S. multinational sales abroad constitutes 90 percent or more, and closer to 95 percent in the last decade.[15] Given the large consumption expenditures within the United States, it is entirely understandable that U.S. trade deficits not only continue, but now involve U.S. firms importing more into the U.S. consumption sink that they export.

The large and growing disparity between the multinational sales/export ratios of U.S. firms and those of rivals reflects both the translation effects of a secularly declining dollar and the lead-in character of U.S. multinational capital dating back to the Bretton Woods period. Yet, despite the wide disparity between the multinational sales/export ratios, what is noteworthy is that foreign-based affiliates within the United States generate sales in large multiples of their imports. This is particularly true for European-based firms but also for Japanese firms whose reputation for the establishment of U.S. import bases is notorious.

Figures 7.3 and 7.4 show that whether in consideration of U.S. multinationals or rivals, trade is now secondary to the main sales effort, with overseas production taking the significant lead. U.S. deficits associated with multinational firms—both foreign and U.S. based—have expanded greatly over the last 30 years. In the period of 1982–99, U.S. multinational corporations exhibited a positive balance in reference to "associated" exports and imports that included not only the balance with their own affiliates but with customers and suppliers generally. This export

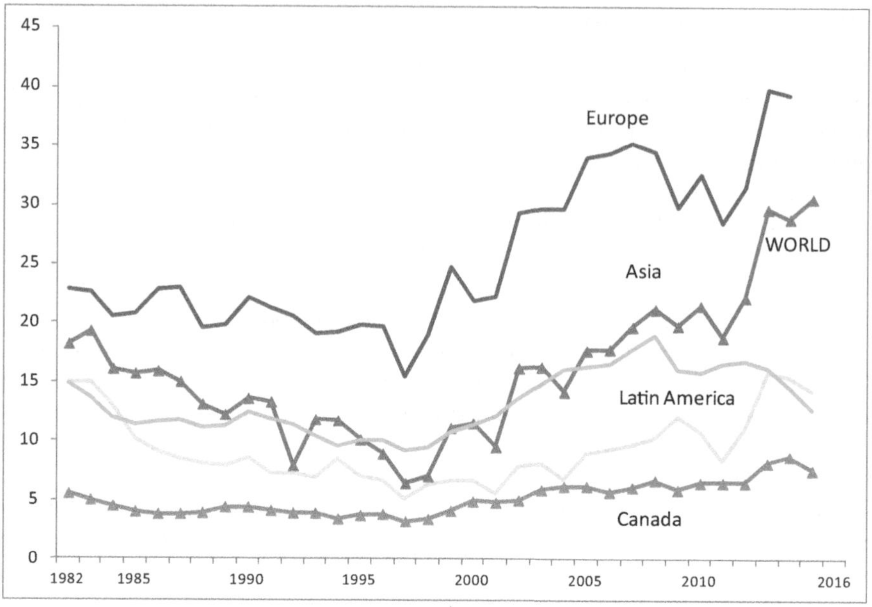

Figure 7.3 Multinational sales/U.S. exports (goods) to affiliates

Source: Department of Commerce.

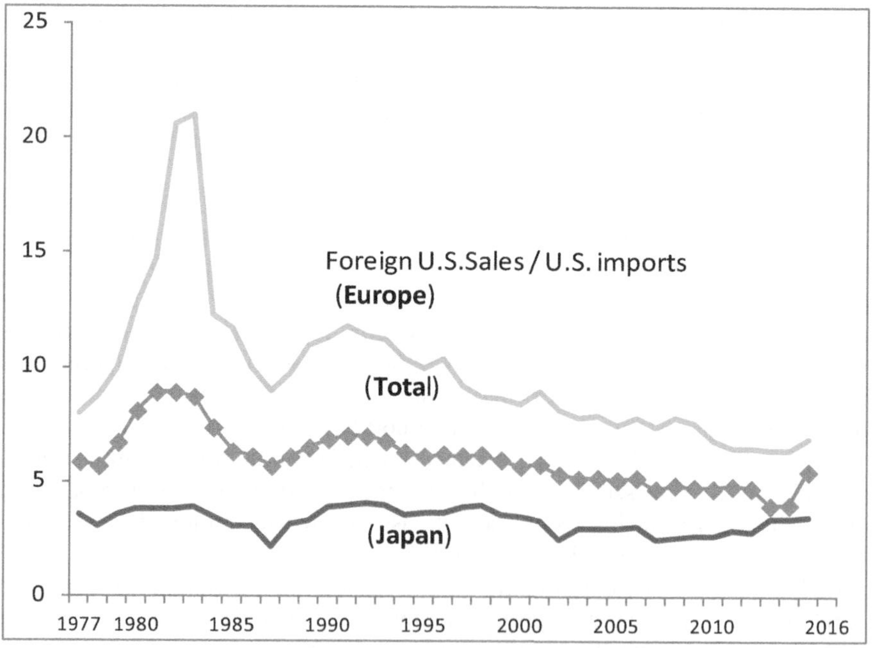

Figure 7.4 Foreign U.S. sales/U.S. imports

Source: Department of Commerce.

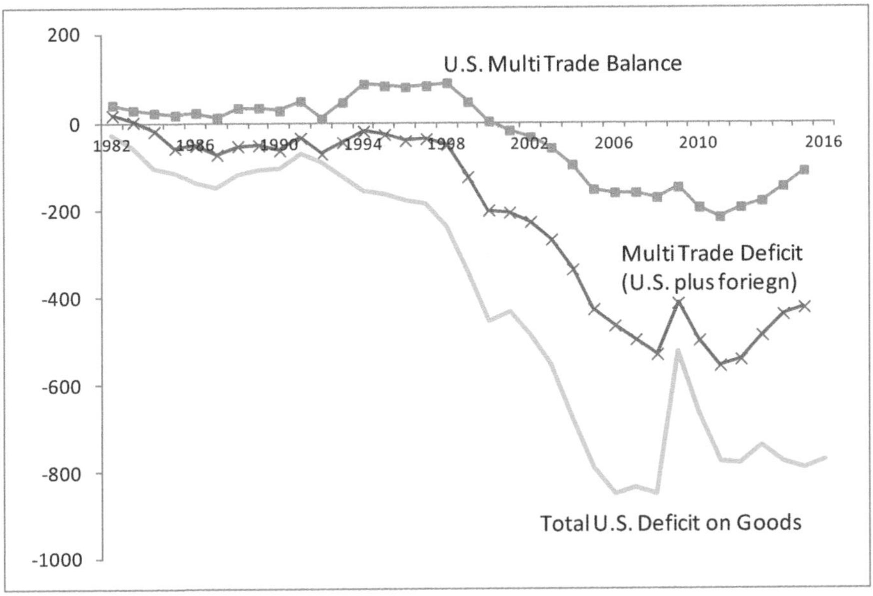

Figure 7.5 The multinational trade deficit

Source: Department of Commerce.

surplus helped counter the ongoing deficit of U.S. affiliates of foreign parents and helped keep the consolidated multinational deficit on goods to an average of 29 percent of the overall deficit on traded goods. However, in the period of 2000–14, the surplus trade balance of U.S. firms turned to deficit. On a consolidated base, the proportion of the total deficit on traded goods associated with all multinational firms more than doubled to over 60 percent.

Figure 7.5 shows the breakdown of the trade deficit on goods, and the narrowing proportion of the non-multinational trade deficit to the total. Notice that the bulk of the multinational deficit is attributable to foreign-owned U.S. affiliates. This large foreign-affiliated component reinforces the general perception that export-based economies are largely responsible for U.S. trade imbalances. Yet as depicted in Figure 7.3, these imports are (in total) but one fifth of U.S. sales by foreign affiliates.

The absence of self-correction

Mainstream economy theory has it that trade deficits would self-correct with a long-haul decline in the value of the dollar. Significant spikes have interrupted the secular decline in the dollar after 1971, notably the spike originating in the late 1970s, the spike associated with the high-tech bubble and Asian crisis of the late 1990s, and the spike of the last few years. Nevertheless, the long secular decline of the dollar should have ameliorated or corrected the U.S. trade deficit.

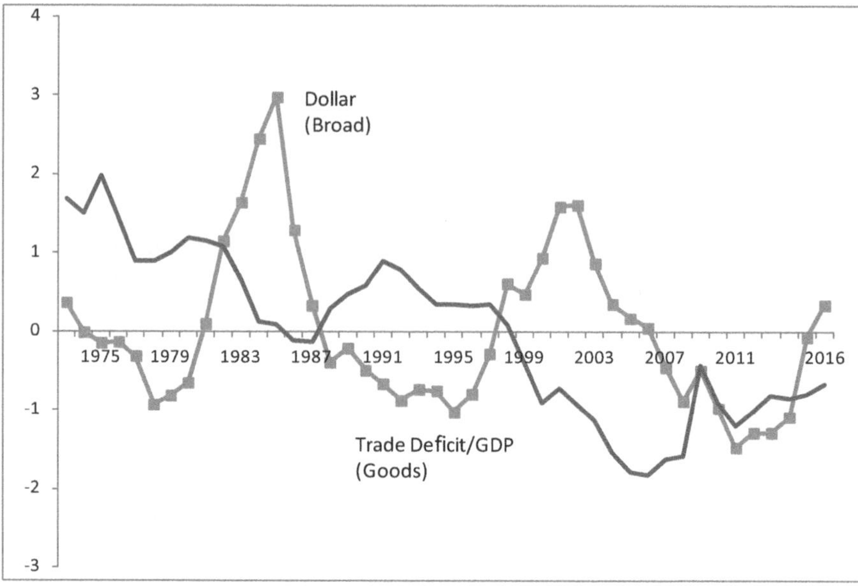

Figure 7.6 Trade deficit (goods) and the decline in the dollar

Source: Department of Commerce.

However, as Figure 7.6 shows, the trade deficit has not only increased in absolute value but relative to the overall U.S. economy[16] (I use normalized data so as to be able to display disparate series on the same Y axis.)

This inability to self-correct is not surprising, given the multinational context of trade and the asymmetry of U.S. capital in relation to rivals. In concentrating on how U.S. multinational production abroad substitutes for U.S. exports, the above discussion complements a much larger literature on how U.S. corporations use imports, both from arm's-length suppliers and foreign affiliates to supply U.S. markets. Global import supply chains have been extensively researched as they are *directly measurable*.[17] The evidence for the multinational production substitution effect and its growth, however, is readily at hand. The massive expansion of multinational sales to parents' exports—particularly in Europe where the multinational sales–parents' exports-to-affiliate ratio almost doubled since the late 1990s to now reach 30 times U.S. exports—suggests that export substitution is not only alive and well but has greatly expanded. This conclusion is fully in line with the growth of virtually every relevant statistic relating to the multinational presence of U.S. firms compared to their domestic counterparts—assets, labor, value added, sales, capital expenditures and net income. Moreover, the fall-off of multinational firms' associated exports relative to total U.S. exports also argues for a multinational escape by the biggest players within the U.S. economy. As I document in Appendix 2, the relative decline of multinational "associated" exports relative to total exports has not been due to a relative decline in the domestic U.S. dominance of U.S. multinational firms. Although there has been a small relative decline in the value added of non-bank parent to U.S. businesses in general since the late 1970s—possibly due to the increased level of non-tradable services on the home front—the relevant data on research and development, and capital expenditures shows that multinational firms still play the key role domestically. This is particularly true in the important tradable manufacturing sector where multinational firms have accounted for over 60 percent of multinational sales of goods abroad. Research and development by multinational firms in manufacturing accounted for over 80 percent of the total R&D within the U.S. since the 1980s, and for over 90 percent of U.S. domestic capital expenditures since the late 1990s. In manufacturing proper, multinational firms still account for over 60 percent of manufacturing value added—a ratio that has been relatively constant since the late 1970s.

As I document in Appendix 2, the multinational component of the trade deficit is most closely correlated with trend as measured by time, with exchange rate changes making a relatively small contribution towards explaining residuals on trend. I interpret this finding to mean that institutional arrangements—formed over decades of multinational expansion—now dictate the ongoing and seemingly uncorrectable trade deficit. In contrast, there is no trend associated with the increasingly smaller non-multinational component of the trade deficit. Perhaps surprisingly, the correlation of this non-multinational deficit with exchange rate changes is even less than the correlation of the multinational component.

The question of trade imbalances and the inability of the U.S. trade deficit to self-correct have motivated scholars to advance a myriad of explanatory factors. Apart from the offshoring of production, such factors include the rise of export-based nations such as China bent on rapid growth rates, the manipulation of exchange rates including the "fixing" of currencies such as the yuan to the dollar, the rise of global capital flows disengaged from any explicit relationship to trade and the low U.S. saving rate. These explanations are often integrated: export led growth, like that of China and Japan has been (and is) fed by currency manipulation (Feldstein, 2008, pp. 113–125). The high level of consumption is facilitated by an expansion of debt underpinned by the influx of foreign monies (D'Arista and Erturk, 2010, p. 66). Such high consumption is the reverse side of a low U.S. saving rate, which, in turn, prevents correction. According to a now-familiar analysis, inadequate U.S. saving draws in foreign monies from export-based nations and oil exporters keeping the dollar from falling to levels that would correct the U.S. trade deficit.[18]

Apart from offshoring and the observation that massive capital flows may well arrest any self-correcting tendencies on trade imbalances (Liang, 2012, p. 355), these explanations harbor the notion that if only the dollar were permitted to fall enough, the U.S. trade deficit could be cured. Some scholars hold that a substantial decline is highly likely. Foreign central banks have a strong incentive to maintain dollar holdings: a devaluation of significant size would bring about massive capital loses. But the reverse side of this reluctance to dump is the "giant gift" that will come to an end when foreigners refuse to accept paper in exchange for goods (Feldstein, 2008, p. 115). The prospect of a rush to the exit has motivated scholars to advocate rebalancing of trade surpluses and deficits along the lines of increasing the U.S. saving rate, enhancing the attractiveness of the euro as a reserve currency and exercising fiscal constraint (Mann, 2002, p. 150). Such rebalancing, along the lines of expanding saving and fiscal constraint—even if such could be achieved—could only crimp an already stagnating growth rate.

Any prescription that neglects the multinational dimensions of trade appears today as a throwback to an earlier age and an honorific bow to mainstream economic theory.

Free cash and the trade deficit

In producing approximately 70 percent of their value added within the United States, U.S. multinational players are still firmly ensconced within their home turf. But they have taken on a globalized dimension whose tentacles have grown into virtually every part of the globe. The outreached arms of the affiliates are, for the most part, attached to the largest firms. In 2014, of the over 30,000 majority-owned affiliates abroad, multinational parents that employed over 1,000 workers had roughly two-thirds of the total affiliates. Those parents with over 10,000 employees had roughly one-half.[19] The employment of affiliates abroad topped 13 million, more than all U.S. workers employed in domestic manufacturing, over double that of construction and 1 million less of all U.S. workers employed in the retail trade.[20] Of the national profits earned by U.S.-headquartered parents, the fraction accounted for by foreign operations has steadily grown. In the late 1940s, roughly 5 percent of national profits derived from receipts derived from the rest of the world; in the 1970s, roughly 10 percent. But by 2016, almost one-third of national profits—inclusive of profits of totally domestic firms—came from overseas operations.[21]

Paul Krugman once commented that economic competition involves businesses not nations (Krugman, 1998, p. 120). The U.S. trade deficit, however, is the deficit of the nation, not of the giant firms that make up the foundation of the U.S. economy. World competition has motivated U.S. firms to become integral parts of the markets that they serve and to import product for sale to the U.S. market—the single largest national market in the world. As I have argued above, U.S. firms have acquired a built-in incentive to taper off on exports and to expand imports to the detriment of domestic investment. Cutting back on investment is tantamount to cutting back on profit, but (again) with sufficient deficit spending by both households and the government, such cutbacks on investment allow free cash to appear. The free cash dispersed to shareholders through dividends and stock repurchases and to consummate mergers is thus dependent on a long and deepening institutional cybernetic involving both domestic and international debt. The larger question involves the limitations on debt stimulation. The expansion of household debt was largely dependent on expanding the collateral base related to housing. The crisis of 2008 demonstrated conclusively that such collateralization has limits. The federal debt has shown an extraordinary ability to expand relative to production and to the political tolerance of the underlying population to tolerate repeated tax declines for the rich. This ability to expand federal debt has also been dependent on the surplus cash derived from export-based nations that are in a position to dump their near-cash. They are reluctant to do so for fear of capital losses and the loss of export markets. Just how far this reluctance extends is a question for the future. Any such dumping would drive up U.S. interest rates and make existing debt piles increasingly difficult to service.

Notes

1 Mira Wilkins's works (1970, 1974), are certainly the most complete reference works to consult for detailing the historical outgrowth of U.S. multinational expansion. For a colorful description of Wall St. bankers seeking U.S. capital's involvement with German enterprise prior to World War II, see Phillips, 2004, pp. 37–40.
2 World Investment Report, 2016, Annex Table 2, p. 200; Percentage of "total capital invested abroad" for 1971 and 1976 are given in Beaud, 2000, Table 6.7, p. 226.
3 In 2010, the sales of the top U.S. firms were 31 percent of the global total: *Fortune*, July 25, 2011; figures for 1971 from *Fortune*, August 1972.
4 The "snake" was a first and somewhat failed attempt by Germany and France to jointly float their currencies against the dollar. The "snake" was designed to avoid a currency war between Germany and France.
5 *Historical Statistics of the United States*, Series U 41-462, U.S. Department of Commerce, Bureau of the Census, 1975.
6 *Survey of Current Business*, July 2016, Table C, p. 3.
7 *Survey of Current Business*, various issues. Continuous data starts from 1982; there is a gap between 1978 and 1982 and only periodic disclosures after 1966.
8 Summaries of studies maintaining the *net* positive trade aspects of U.S. foreign direct investment are to be found in Kujawa, 1973. These offerings were sponsored by the National Foreign Trade Council Inc. (originally published in 1971: Kujawa, 1973, pp. 153–157); the National Association of Manufacturers (1972: Kujawa, 1973, pp. 172–178); The Emergency Committee for American Trade (1972: Kujawa, 1973, pp. 178–185) and the U.S. Department of Commerce in conjunction with Harvard University Graduate School of Business Administration (1972: Kujawa, 1973, pp. 165–172).
9 See Musgrave, 1975, for a succinct summary of Horst's studies (1974a, 1974b) on the complementary nature of exports to multinational sales. Also, see the qualified remarks of Epstein, 1993, p. 207.
10 The tipping point was the pressure exerted by Germany and France "and the Bank of England's need to convert $700 million into gold to alleviate pressure on sterling" (D'Arista, 2009, p. 643).
11 In his famous debates with Milton Friedman, Robert V. Roosa did not discuss the multinational aspect of falling exchange rates, but he did indicate the possibility of U.S. export-based inflation consequent on the dollar's fall (Friedman and Roosa, 1967, p. 46). The implementation of dollar-based pricing systems gives an alternative explanation to Ronald I. McKinnon's view that the differential inflation rates between the U.S., Europe and Japan was due to a rebound effect consequent on a "flight from the dollar." According to McKinnon, the "flight" resulted "in a fall in the demand for money with no offsetting reduction in supply. Combined with a lower dollar in the foreign exchanges, the stage was set for the great U.S. inflation of the 1970s" (McKinnon, 2013, p. 51). This understanding may help explain the 1970s, but the differential inflation rates continued. See McKinnon's Figures 3.3, p. 35 and 4.4, p. 49). Refusal to see outside particular market boundaries is another widely used tactic to avoid intra-company competition. Grey markets are the predictable result.

12 Most apparent in the rapidly growing economics of Eastern Europe, China, India, Brazil, Africa and the Middle East (Barefoot and Mataloni, Jr., 2011, pp. 35–39).
13 Ranked by revenue, of the top 100 largest businesses in 1964, "sixty-five were American, eighteen belonged to the EEC, eleven were British and five were Japanese" (Mandel, 1970, p. 30). In 1971, U.S. firms had 63 percent of the revenues of the top 300 industrial firms. Expanding the universe to all firms, this ratio fell off to around 40 percent in the early to mid-2000s (Medlen, 2005, p. 554) and to 31 percent in 2010. In the same year, 29 of the top 100 firms were U.S. based (*Fortune*, July 25, 2011).
14 In 2013, parent-owned foreign-affiliate U.S. imports accounted for less than 13 percent of parent imports into foreign-owned U.S. affiliates.
15 Neglecting the transitory component of inventory change, the foreign content includes value added abroad plus other foreign inputs. Foreign content can therefore be calculated as multinational sales minus U.S. exports to affiliates. Calculations are made on majority-owned affiliates.
16 This four and a half decade decline needs to be emphasized. In accordance with Marshall-Learner conditions, J effects might well explain short-term lags involving corrective adjustments and may well explain the insensitivity of certain demand-inelastic imports to dollar devaluation. Most modern trade, however, involves fairly homogeneous substitutes. Short-term J effects cannot possibly explain how U.S. deficits could expand in the face of the long-term decline in the dollar over nearly half a century.
17 As noted above, see Houseman et al., 2011; Milberg, 2004; Milberg and Winkler, 2013 and Timmer et al., 2014.
18 A retrospective view, endorsed by the last two heads of the Federal Reserve, had it that surplus foreign saving—consequent on trade surpluses—helped explain the large volume of U.S. consumption recently collateralized by inflated home prices. And by a circular implication, such large consumption helped explain the low U.S. saving rate.
19 *Survey of Current Business*, December 16, 2014, p. 7.
20 Domestic employment figures from the *Economic Report of the President*, February 2015, Table B-14, p. 400.
21 Bureau of Economic Analysis, Tables 6.16A, 6.16B, 6.16C 6.16D.

References

Adelman, Morris A., *The World Petroleum Market*, Resources for the Future Inc., John Hopkins University Press, 1972.

Baily, Martin Neil and Barry P. Bosworth, "U.S. Manufacturing: Understanding Its Past and Its Potential Future," *Journal of Economic Perspectives*, Vol. 28, No. 1, Winter 2014.

Barefoot, Kevin B. and Raymond J. Mataloni Jr., "Operations of U.S. Multinational Companies in the United States and Abroad," *Survey of Current Business*, November 2011.

Barker, Betty L., "U.S. Foreign Trade Associated with U.S. Multinational Corporations," *Survey of Current Business*, Vol. 52, No. 12, Department of Commerce, December 1972.

Beaud, Michael, *A History of Capitalism*, 1981, Reprint, Monthly Review Press, New York, 2000.

Cohen, Stephen D., *Multinational Corporations and Foreign Direct Investment: Avoiding Simplicity, Embracing Complexity*, Oxford University Press, Oxford, 2007.

Cutler, Fred and Samuel Pizer, "Foreign Operations of U.S. Industry: Capital Expenditures, Sales and Financing," *Survey of Current Business*, U.S. Department of Commerce, October 1963, Table 9.

D'Arista, Jane, "The Evolving International Monetary System," *Cambridge Journal of Economics*, 2009, Vol. 33, pp. 633–652.

D'Arista, Jane and Korkut Alp Erturk, "The Case for International Monetary Reform," *Real World Economics Review*, Issue 55, 2010, pp. 58–81.

Eichengreen, Barry, *Globalizing Capital: A History of the International Monetary System*, 2nd edition, Princeton University Press, Princeton, NJ, 2008.

Epstein, Gerald, "The United States as a Debtor Country," in *Creating a New World Economy*, edited by G. Epstein, J. Graham and J. Nembhard, 1993, pp. 199–220.

Feldstein, Martin, "Resolving the Global Imbalance: The Dollar and the U.S. Saving Rate," *Journal of Economic Perspectives*, Vol. 33, No. 3, Summer 2008.

Frank, Robert H. and Richard T. Freeman, *Distributional Consequences of Direct Foreign Investment*, Academic Press, New York, San Francisco, CA and London, 1978.

Friedman, Milton and Robert Roosa, *The Balance of Payments: Free versus Fixed Exchange Rates*, rational debate seminars, American Enterprise Institute for Public Policy Research, Washington, DC, 1967.

Grimm, Alexis N. and Charu S. Krishnam, "Trade in Services in 2014 and Services Supplied through Affiliates in 2013," *Survey of Current Business*, October 2015.

Horst, T., "The Impact of U.S. Investment Abroad on U.S. Foreign Trade," working paper, Brookings Institute, 1974a.

Horst, T.,"American Exports and Foreign Direct Investment," Discussion paper no. 362, Harvard Institute of Economic Research, May 1974b.

Houseman, Susan, Christopher Kurz, Paul Lengermann and Benjamin Mandel, "Offshoring Bias in U.S. Manufacturing," *Journal of Economic Perspectives*, Vol. 25, No. 2, Spring 2011, pp. 111–132.

Krugman, Paul, *Pop Internationalism*, MIT Press, Cambridge, MA and London, 1998.

Kujawa, Duane, ed., *American Labor and the Multinational Corporations*, Praeger Publishers, New York and London, 1973.

Liang, Yan, "Global Imbalances and Financial Crisis: Financial Globalization as a Common Cause," *Journal of Economic Issues*, Vol. XLVI, No. 2, June 2012.

Mandel, Ernest, *Europe vs. America*, Monthly Review Press, New York and London, 1970.

Mann, Catherine, "Perspectives on the U.S. Current Account Deficit and Sustainability," *Journal of Economic Perspectives*, Vol. 16, No. 3, Summer 2002, pp. 131–152.

Mataloni, Jr., Raymond, "Real Gross Product of U.S. Companies' Majority-Owned Foreign Affiliates in Manufacturing," *Survey of Current Business*, April 1997.

McKinnon, Ronald I., *The Unloved Dollar Standard: From Bretton Woods to the Rise of China*, Oxford University Press, Oxford, 2013.

Medlen, Craig, "Two Sets of Twins? An Exploration of Domestic Saving-Investment Imbalances," *Journal of Economic Issues*, Vol. XXXIX, No. 3, September 2005.

Milberg, William, "The Changing Structure of Trade Linked to Global Production Systems: What Are the Policy Implications?" *International Labor Review*, Vol. 143, No. 1–2, 2004, pp. 45–90.

Milberg, William and Deborah Winker, *Outsourcing Economics: Global Value Chains in Capitalist Development*, Cambridge University Press, New York, 2013.

Musgrave, Peggy, B., *Direct Investment Abroad and the Multinationals: Effects on the Unites States Economy*, Subcommittee on Multinational Corporations of the Committee on Foreign Relations United States Senate, August 1975.

Phillips, Keven, *American Dynasty*, Penguin Books, New York, 2004.

Polk, Jude, Irene W. Meister and Lawrence A. Veit, "U.S. Production Abroad and the Balance of Payments: A Survey of Corporate Investment Experience," *The Conference Board*, 1966.

Rowthorn, Bob, "Imperialism in the 1970s—Unity or Rivalry?" *New Left Review*, No. 69, September–October 1971, pp. 31–51, reprinted in *International Firms and Modern Imperialism*, edited by Hugo Radice, Penguin Books, Harmondsworth, [1971] 1975.
Servan-Schreiber, Jean-Jacques, *The American Challenge*, Discus Books, Avon, NY, 1969.
Timmer, Marcel P., Abdul Azeez Erumban, Bat Los, Robert Stehrer and Gaaitzen J. de Vries, "Slicing Up Global Value Chains," *Journal of Economic Perspectives*, Vol. 28, No. 2, Spring 2014.
Wilkins, Mira, *The Emergence of Multinational Enterprise: American Business Abroad from the Colonial Era to 1914*, Harvard University Press, Cambridge, MA, 1970.
Wilkins, Mira, *The Maturing of Multinational Enterprise: American Business Abroad from 1914 to 1970*, Harvard University Press, Cambridge, MA and London, 1974.
Yanaga, Chtoshi, *Big Business in Japanese Politics*, Yale University Press, New Haven, CT and London, 1968.

Appendix 2

Multinational deficits and parents' embeddedness

The entanglement of trade and multinational sales is reflected in the high correlation of trade deficits to "trend" rather than to alterations in exchange rates. The first line of Table A2.1 below records the correlation coefficients (r^2) on trends (i.e. time, 1982–2012) relating to the overall deficit balance on goods, the deficit associated with U.S. "Associated" exports and imports, the U.S. affiliate deficit, the foreign-owned U.S. affiliate deficit, and the deficit not associated with multinational trade ("Other"). Notice the relatively high explanatory power of trend in the deficits associated with multinational capital in contrast to the low trend correlation of the deficit not associated with multinational connectedness, i.e. "Other."

The second line of Table A2.1 records the correlation coefficients of the residuals around trend to changes in the dollar exchange rate, with annual lag numbers associated with the highest r^2 attached in parentheses. These correlation coefficients indicate that at least some explanatory power can be attributable to exchange rate changes, with the highest correlation being associated with the "Overall" category. Noteworthy is the fact that foreign-owned U.S. affiliates demonstrate the highest correlation of the subcategories in reference to alternations in exchange rates. I attribute this fact to the higher import content of foreign-owned U.S. affiliates relative to U.S. capital with its higher reliance on multinational sales. That the "Other" category shows a somewhat lower correlation than others is somewhat surprising and begs explanation.

As noted in Chapter 7, there has been a steep fall-off in the ratio of multinational "Associated" exports of goods relative to U.S. exports of goods in general. This decline might be accounted for if the non-multinational sector of the U.S. economy grew in a significant way relative to multinational parents. As shown in Table A2.2a below, time slice comparisons from the late 1970s do show a relative rise in value added for the non-multinational sector. But they also show a relative

Table A2.1 Trade deficit components: correlations on trend

	Overall	*Associated U.S.*	*Affiliate U.S.*	*Foreign-owned*	*Other*
Trend	.65	.68	.52	.63	.12
Residual on $	.61(lag2)	.35(lag2)	.35(lag2)	.48(lag3)	.30 (lag1)

constancy in the important manufacturing sector, with multinational firms predominating. This sector is most important in reference to the current topic of substitutability. As a fraction of multinational sales of goods abroad, manufactured goods have risen and fallen, but the general trend has been upward and in recent years has accounted for over 60 percent of the multinational sales of goods. The comparative story on capital expenditures and research and development between U.S. multinational parents and U.S. business shows even a higher predominance by multinational parents. The data on capital expenditures comes in very late as Census data on total capital expenditures within the U.S. was first initiated in 1993. But what data we have indicates that multinational firms have acquired a significant rise in their relative dominance, with capital expenditures within manufacturing now in excess of 90 percent of the total (Table A2.2b). The large proportion of research and development (Table A2.2c) carried out by multinational firms also shows a relative dominance and is no doubt based on their *comparatively* large size relative to U.S. businesses in general.

In sum, there is little or no evidence that the sharp relative fall-off in multinational "Associated" exports is due to a decline in multinational firms' dominance within the United States. The fall-off is best explained by the production abroad of multinational firms and the substitution of such production for exports.

Table A2.2 Multinational parents' embeddedness: value added, capital expenditures, R&D

	1977	*1982*	*1989*	*1995*	*1999*	*2009*	*2012*
a. Percentage of **value added** of non-bank parents to U.S. businesses							
All industries	32	33	26	23	24	20	20
Manufacturing	67	68	62	60	68	61	64
b. Percentage of **capital expenditures** of non-bank parents to U.S. businesses							
All industries				44	43	40	44
Manufacturing				62	97	91	*
c. Percentage of **R&D** of non-bank parents to U.S. businesses							
All Industries			78	91	86	97	95
Manufacturing			84	*	92	*	81

Sources: *Survey of Current Business*, August, 2014; November 2011: 3. Table 3; July 2000: 31; February 1994: 45, Table 3; statistics on capital expenditures from the Census Bureau Annual Capital Expenditure Surveys, Table 4a. Total Research and Development figures from U.S. Department of Commerce, Table 5.6.5.

*For the years noted, reported data on capital expenditures and research and development for the parents were in excess of the total. Inquiries at the Department of Commerce and the Census Bureau suggest that these anomalies may well be due to sampling error and inconsistent classification of various firms within manufacturing and other categories such as the wholesale trade. The Census Bureau Survey's total capital expenditure figure of $204.4 billion for 2012 was less than parents' reported capital expenditure figure of $220.2 billion. Reported multinational parent manufacturing R&D expenditures were in excess of the total for 1995 and 2009.

8 Free cash, relative valuation and inequality

Given the precariousness of labor employment and labor's increasingly fractured composition, it is no mystery as to why capital's share of income should have risen relative to that of wage and salary employees over the last four decades. As understatement, one might say that the bargaining strength of capital has expanded relative to the laboring class. A more accurate assessment, with a possible tilt to overstatement, would assert that the bargaining power of labor—understood as an economic class—has simply disappeared.[1]

The rise in capital's share of income has also driven wealth inequality. Higher incomes translate into a higher level of saving among the rich which, in turn, translate into rising wealth disparities. Moreover, as noted in Chapter 5, the expansion of capital's share expands the *relative* valuation of older capital. This expansion of relative valuation has been a major force driving mergers, the concentration of capital and the associated stock speculation surrounding the valuation of targets and stock buybacks. Stock buybacks and merger premiums have expanded stock valuation and rising wealth inequality. This increasing preference for older capital has been part of the same stagnation tendencies that have undercut growth, the wage share of income and the deficit spending utilized to counter stagnation. In turn, the free cash derived from deficit spending has driven mergers and stock buybacks to the point that the number of listed firms in the United States has shrunk from around 8,000 firms in the mid-1990s to a total somewhat less than 4,000 in the spring of 2017.[2] Each decline in the taxation of corporations and the wealthy has expanded the deficits. The causal chain has been (and is now) self-reinforcing, as expanded deficits expand free cash spillage resulting in higher stock valuations. In a cybernetic loop, higher stock valuations drive more and more stock buying.

Stockholder valuation

Recently, there has been an extensive controversy over managers' concerted effort to enhance short-term stock values through stock buybacks and dividends.[3] These expanded payouts are understood to have diverted monies away from real investment that generates growth. In an analysis that typifies a number of others, William Lazonick holds that "wide-spread economic prosperity" is being held back by the "allocation of corporate profits to stock buybacks" (Lazonick, 2014, p. 48). According to Lazonick, this sabotage of prosperity is largely due to managers' concern with their own remuneration. Since "[s]tock-based instruments make up the majority of their pay, and in the short-term buybacks drive up stock prices," managers have every incentive to engage in the short-term thinking that "can enable the company to hit quarterly earnings per share (EPS) targets" (p. 48). Although conceding that "tender" offers can place additional power in the hands of managers looking out for long-term interests, the larger amount of stock buybacks through open-market purchases "often come at the expense of investment in productive capabilities" (pp. 50–51).

In addition to managerial remuneration, scholars have advanced other reinforcing arguments to explain the increasing concern with stockholder value. In a study involving asset inflation, financial derivatives and pensions, Jan Toporowski (2000) notes that stock valuations have inflated due to increasing amounts of pension monies flowing into the market (p. 81). With limited supplies of stock, expanded flows of stock demand drive up the price of assets. Toporowski's study of pensions is mainly concerned about the longer-term prospects of pension cash-out due to an aging work force and the split of institutional investments between mature markets and the periphery. But the large -scale involvement of institutional investors that he documents suggests an additional reason for managers to target short-term stock valuation. Large amounts of money can move quickly out of any one or more companies, devastating stock values. Being ever-present, such threats keep managers aware of current stock valuations and shorten time horizons. As William Lazonick and Mary O'Sullivan have noted

> by the 1980s the deregulated financial environment and the rise of the institutional investor as a holder of corporate stocks encouraged top managers to align their own interests with external financial interests rather than with the interests of the productive organizations over which they exercised control.
> (Lazonick and O'Sullivan, 2000, p. 27)

Financial pressures expand when non-financial firms extend financial credits and take on financial debt obligations. Julie Froud and colleagues (2006) understand stockholder value concerns as reflective of differing financial arrangements accorded to different industries and firms. Yet, in their examination of three case studies including Ford and General Electric, commonalities overshadowed differences. The authors document the increasing indebtedness of the firms, the concern for growth by acquisition, and the establishment of financial lending subsidiaries. The acquisition of higher levels of both credit and debt involved the corporations more intimately in financial markets. In this involvement, stock price was a primary concern.

The case studies illustrate certain general truths. Debt is easier to acquire and service when corporate valuations are high. To the extent that stock valuations reflect high profits, high stock valuations allow more borrowing. This is not to say that those firms with higher profits will necessarily expand borrowing. Indeed, up until the last few decades and adjusted for industry differences, "the more profitable a firm [was], the less it borrow[ed]" (Mott, 2010, p. 71).[4] But taken over the whole economy, the enlargement of profits has allowed a higher level of debt, a higher level of expansion in terms of acquisition, and a higher level of payout through stock buybacks and dividends. In the post-1980 era, the larger firms have been the major players. As Leila Davis has documented, relative to smaller firms, large firms have accumulated an ever-larger share of financial assets relative to fixed assets, have become relatively more leveraged and have been responsible for a disproportionate share of stock buybacks (Davis, 2016, p. 116).

Stock valuation and stagnation

The concern with managerial short-term stock targeting is question begging. Scholars, like Lazonick (2015), Lazonick and O'Sullivan (2000) and Orhangazi (2007), hold that such short-termism is largely responsible for the decline in productive growth. Lazonick and O'Sullivan even hold that maximizing shareholder value constitutes "a new ideology for corporate governance" (Lazonick and O'Sullivan, 2000, p. 13).

But what accounts for such a shift in viewpoint? The most straightforward answer is the resurgence of stagnation, driving down corporate growth rates since the late 1960s. The arrow of causality needs to be reversed. Short-termism is largely the result rather than the cause of stagnant growth. Managers will respond to the possibility of short-term value extraction when long-term prospects for growth turn bleak. As argued previously in Chapter 6, understanding the forces of long-term stagnation is to understand the rise of deficits—both public and private—and free cash generation. As this free cash provides a collateral base through which additional capital can be raised through financial markets, one can understand the enlarged use of debt for merger expansion, dividends and stock repurchases. In short, understanding free cash generation allows for a deeper understanding of the financialization of the non-financial firm.

Figure 8.1 shows the upward movement of free cash and total capital spillage. Figure 8.2 shows the composition of the spillage in the form of dividends, mergers and stock buybacks expressed as a cumulative fraction of new corporate fixed investment. As shown in Figure 8.1, total spillage exceeds free cash. That there is no direct one-to-one correspondence is not surprising. The high volatility of profits and investment commitments dictate a high volatility of free cash. This volatility, combined with corporate access to capital markets and a variety of independent factors surrounding dividends, mergers and stock repurchases, sever any direct connection between free cash and capital disgorgement. Mergers involve changing industrial considerations, anti-trust enforcement policies and significant lags between merger announcements and consummations. Stock buybacks involve not just free cash but tax considerations and changing laws involving stock option allowances (Reich, 2015, pp. 102–103). Dividend payouts tend to fall into patterns that managers are reluctant to change, even when cash flows fall short (Schiller, 2005, pp. 188–191).

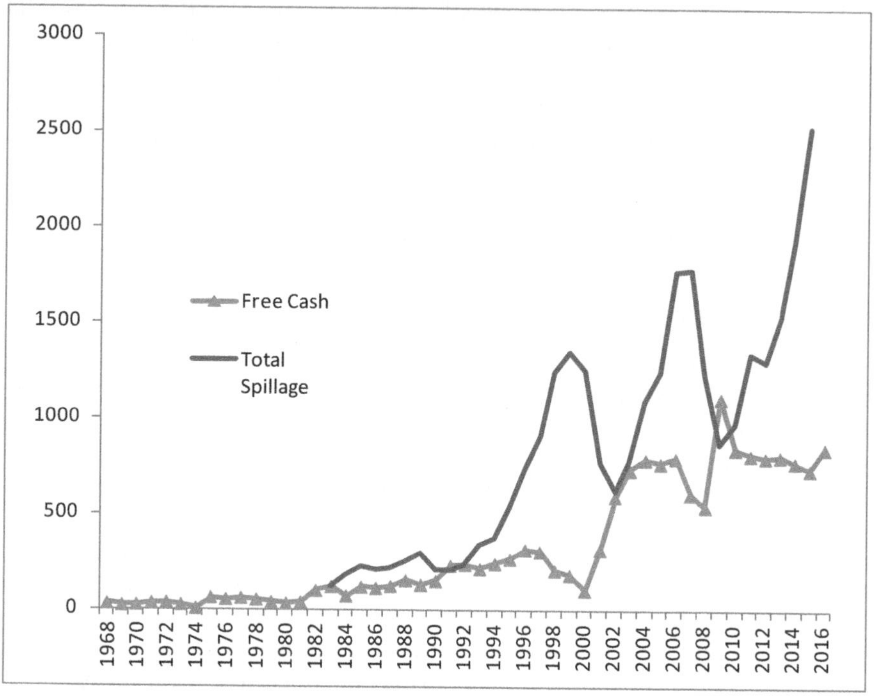

Figure 8.1 Free cash and spillage

Sources: Department of Commerce; Federal Reserve, *Flow of Funds*, Standard and Poor's, *Mergerstat Review*.

Nevertheless, free cash should be understood as a structural underpinning driving capital gains. The spectacular growth of free cash, rising into the neighborhood of $500 million to $1 trillion in recent years certainly has certainly been the major factor involved in the spillage. In recent decades, corporations have filled in the gap between free cash and total spillage primarily by issuing bonds. Over the last three decades (1984–2016) $6.25 trillion of net stock retirements of non-financial corporations were largely offset by corporate bond issues of $5 trillion.[5] In short, corporations have traded bonds for equity. As interest is tax deductible, this trade has not only bolstered stock prices, but has allowed corporate taxes to shrink. Such tax shrinkage has contributed to the federal deficit and, as an unintended consequence, more free cash.

In expressing capital spillage as a fraction of new corporate investment, Figure 8.2 implicitly contains a normative message. It suggests how much investment growth might have expanded were such spillage directed towards new investment growth. Such spillage has routinely exceeded 50 percent of new investment and has averaged over 80 percent since the mid-1990s. Together, Figures 8.1 and 8.2 also give a partial look into how stagnant investment growth has been coupled

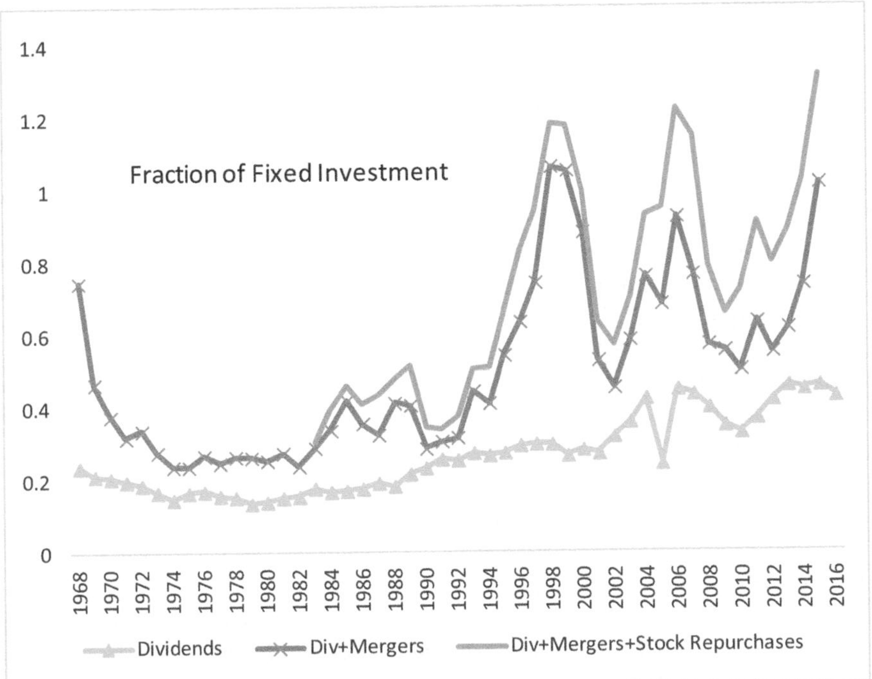

Figure 8.2 Capital spillage

Sources: Department of Commerce; Federal Reserve, *Flow of Funds*, Standard and Poor's, *Mergerstat Review*.

with expanded wealth and income inequality. That such free cash generation and its spillage derive from stimulatory deficits also gives reflective pause on how Keynesian deficit pump priming generates an increased level of wealth disparity. Of course, higher taxes could claim such spillage and rectify such disparity. But in the present political context, where lower taxes allegedly sponsor growth, such an argument is simply unacknowledged, or, more exactly, not even brought into political consciousness.

Thomas Piketty and inequality

In recent years, the relationship of stagnation and inequality is most often connected with Thomas Piketty and his associates.[6] I will show below how free cash spillage helps to elucidate certain aspects of Piketty's scholarly endeavors. But first it is necessary to briefly review Piketty's central thesis. As free cash is directly associated with corporate income and equity, I begin with Piketty's own summary of the most recent rise in inequality in reference to capital income and capital gains:

> a very substantial and growing inequality of capital income since 1980 accounts for about one-third of the increase in income inequality in the United States—a far from negligible amount. Indeed, in the United States, as in France and Europe, today as in the past, *income from capital always becomes more important as one climbs the rungs of the income hierarchy.*
>
> (Piketty, 2014, pp. 300–301; emphasis added)

Thomas Piketty's *Capital in the Twenty-First Century* is the main book associated with a world project involving a number of scholars documenting the disparities in wealth and income across a variety of nations over significant historical time periods. The book is also associated with a central thesis that relates wealth and income inequality to a long-run tendency for the rate of return on capital (designated as r) to outpace the growth of income (g). Piketty breaks down capital's share of Y (the total income stream) into the rate of return on capital times the capital/income ratio). He designates this breakdown as the "first fundamental law of capitalism" (p. 52).

(1) $\frac{\pi}{Y} \equiv \frac{\pi}{K} * \frac{K}{Y}$ In Piketty's symbolic notation $\propto \equiv \boldsymbol{r\,x\,\beta}$

Where π = *Returns to Capital* ***(K)***

Piketty's "First Fundamental Law" is an identity. It is important to note that as an identity, *it can be associated with any theory of inequality* that specifies the rate of return on capital in reference to the capital/income (output) ratio.

Piketty gives content to his "fundamental law" by an empirical observation that r > *g*. This is equivalent to asserting a long-term tendency of the capital/income (output) ratio to rise through time. This ability of the economy to absorb more and more capital relative to the level of the economy is, of course, question begging and, as I will discuss below, has brought forth an extended controversy. Piketty's association of capital/output growth with an expanded level of capital's share also requires an explanation of how such capital expansion could co-exist without a corresponding percentage decline in the rate of return of capital. Piketty's fundamental assumption concerning expanded inequality is that the rate of return on capital will remain relatively constant—or at least not decline in percentage terms more than the capital/output ratio expands.

Piketty also links expanded income inequality to expanded wealth inequality through the capital/output ratio. In experiencing an increasing amount of income returns, the wealthy few that disproportionately own the vast bulk of the capital stock will redeploy such returns into investment and therefore own more capital from which more income can be extracted. Wealth concentration will intensify at the same time as income inequality expands. Piketty specifies this mechanism of expanded wealth concentration in his "Second Fundamental Law" where the capital/output ratio approximates the saving/income ratio, divided by the income growth rate g. For the recent slowdown in the growth rates of the United States and other advanced countries, the "Second Fundamental Law" has a particular meaning. In Piketty's words:

> a country that saves a lot and grows slowly will over the long run accumulate an enormous stock of capital (relative to its income), which can in turn have a significant effect on the social structure and distribution of wealth . . . in a quasi-stagnant society, wealth accumulated in the past will inevitably acquire disproportionate importance.
>
> (p. 166)

Like all quick renditions, the above sketch of Piketty's overall vision does not do justice to the nuances and qualifications of Piketty's 650-page tome. At times, Piketty understands the inequality of r > g as "the fundamental force for [income and wealth] divergence" (Piketty, 2014, p. 424), but in other writings sees it as a simple heuristic allowing for the data on income and wealth inequality to be organized in a central way (Piketty, 2017, p. 553). Concerned as he is with the long view and the major institutional changes that have been part of societal changes over a hundred years, Piketty provides ample warning against reductionism. At one point, he notes that r > g is not to be conceived as "a logical necessity," but rather as an historical fact dependent on "many technological, psychological, social and cultural factors" (p. 361). Piketty also asserts that this tendency for r > g applies to an amalgamation of capital inclusive of land, housing, and net domestic and net foreign capital. Piketty measures capital by monetary value and so conflates capital with wealth. As will be argued below, this conflation of operating capital with monetary values of wealth is not simply a measurement problem. Asset inflation needs to be taken into account if one is concerned with the operational basis of inequality.

Piketty is also concerned with the social aspects of inequality, particularly with the possibility of society evolving into a modern version of an older Gilded Age where inheritance of wealth and income flows predominate. This is Piketty's projected dystopia. Under such a dystopia, democratic forms of government and meritocratic aspirations fade before plutocratic dominance of politics, culture and economics. For Piketty, this dystopia is not some fantastic made-up projection. One of the true virtues of Piketty's work is the long-term approach that he takes. In his view, the shrunken inequalities of wealth and income of the Great War, the Depression and the decades immediately after World War II should not be understood as normalcy. On the contrary, Piketty understands the long-term tendency of r > *g* as the normal tendency and suggests that the return to heightened inequality after 1970 may well be a return to a long-term trend (p. 372).

Free cash spillage and Piketty's modeling

According to Piketty, capital deepening—understood as a rise in the capital/output ratio—is the essential key for understanding the long-term tendency for inequality to expand in reference to both income and wealth. Applied to the short run, however, a rise in the capital/output ratio with stagnant growth undermines any firm contention that income would be redistributed towards high-saving capital owners. The Kaleckian notion that "capitalists earn what they spend" suggests that the rate of return on capital might fall sufficiently under stagnant growth to overpower any rise in the capital/output ratio. This would be particularly true if the rise in the capital/output ratio was accompanied by large amounts of excess capacity. Indeed, if the capital/output ratio expands, it is hard to envision how excess capacity could be avoided under stagnant growth particularly in light of the fact that capital becomes ever more efficient. As shown earlier in Figure 5.5, excess capacity has indeed expanded along with the secular decline in corporate investment growth rates since the late 1960s. Piketty's "Second Fundamental Law" roots inequality in a long-term rise of the capital/output ratio where capital is understood as a factor of production. But in measuring (conflating) capital with wealth, Piketty's meaning of the capital/output ratio becomes blurred. If capital is measured by wealth, a rise in the capital/output ratio might well occur when stock bubbles appear. Piketty's brief discussion of Tobin's Q (p. 191) certainly shows his awareness of the difference between capital valuation as the accumulated value of net investments and their stock value. But in reading Piketty, one gets the sense that he conceives of the different capital valuations as largely incidental—determined by measurement problems, stock appreciation and decline, but without larger theoretical implications.[7] But as shown by the dramatic expansion of Tobin's Q (Figure 5.1), this disparity in the measurement of wealth is not something to be casually dismissed.

If capital is measured by accumulated net investments, a rise in the capital/output ratio is inherently one with recessions and with slow growth. Idle capacity is unprofitable capacity, but is nevertheless part of the capital stock. Here it is useful to recall Roy Harrods's and Evsey Domar's "knife edge"[8] whereby a decline in the rate of investment beneath the rate necessary to maintain full capacity leads to further declines in investment and depression. Piketty mentions Harrod and Domar (p. 231). But he largely discounts their theory as reflective of the Great Depression, rather than crediting their contribution as a theoretical advance capable of explaining the inherent instability of a capitalist order with government stabilization measures.[9]

Figure 8.3 shows the enormous difference in the corporate capital/output ratios when capital is measured by stock valuation as opposed to fixed net investments. In his major treatise, Piketty does not break out corporate capital from his far more inclusive category whereby all types of capital are amalgamated. But the disparity shown in Figure 8.3 certainly illustrates the hazards of substituting the current monetary valuation of capital for historical outlays minus depreciation. Under discounted streams, stock valuation records the presumed discounted expected streams of all capital under the corporate mantle. But in Piketty's understanding, such valuation is supposed to reflect capital's contribution to production. Although Piketty explicitly warns against an over-reliance on simple modeling, he nevertheless endorses Solow's growth model where capital, labor and technology combine to produce output (p. 231). Piketty's contention, that the capital/output ratio rises through time leading to an expanded share of income flowing towards capital, led him to the conclusion that the elasticity of substitution of capital for labor "has apparently been greater than one over a long period of time" (p. 231). This assertion is in stark contradiction with the vast bulk of elasticity estimates suggesting an elasticity of less

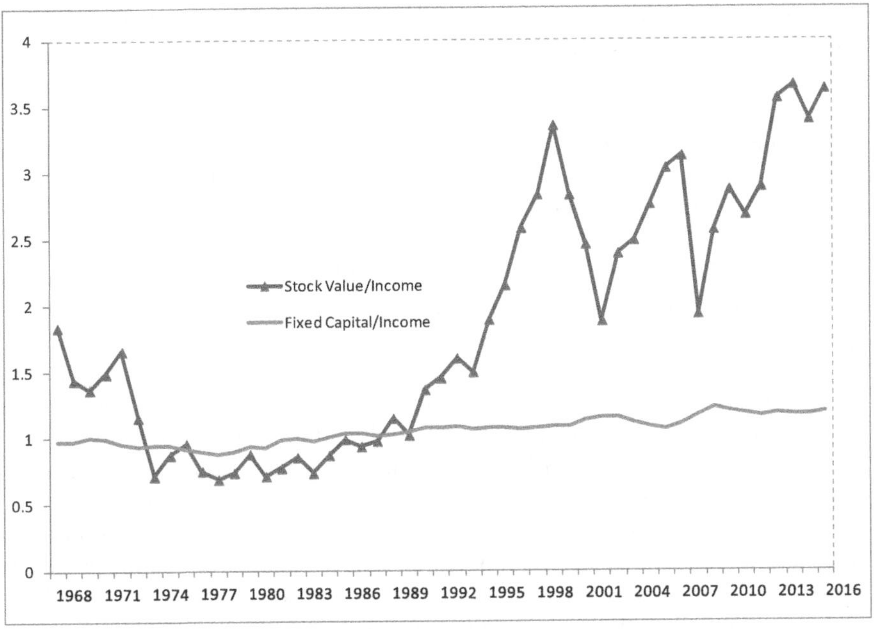

Figure 8.3 Capital/income (output) ratios

Sources: Department of Commerce, *Flow of Funds*, Federal Reserve.

than one.[10] Piketty's elasticity problem is that he must accept an elasticity greater than one if he wants to understand the rise in capital's share in terms of a production function while measuring capital's contribution by a monetary measure.

In light of Piketty's "First Fundamental Law," such measurement differences over capital might seem to be a matter of indifference. The data on capital's share can be fed back into the identity relating the rate of return to the capital/output ratio with the rate of return determined by the "definition" of capital. But productive capital has a direct operational meaning in terms of the expansion and contraction of production. As constructed, Piketty's "Second Fundamental Law" understands the rise of capital emanating out of saving and production rather than capital gains. Subsuming productive capital under financial capital—as Piketty does—obfuscates the operational basis of his inequality thesis and begs the question concerning the divergence between capital valuations.

Stock valuation vs. net investment valuation

Understanding the rise of free cash and its spillage gives at least a partial understanding of why stock valuation has risen so much relative to operational capital as measured by accumulated net investments.[11] To remind: the direct disgorgement of capital into the hands of the rich encouraged further stock purchases and stock appreciation.

Moreover, as discussed in Chapter 6 in reference to the theory of discounted streams, such cash spillage has tended to compress interest rates with the ancillary consequence of expanding capital gains, making for a bubbly economy subject to blowups such as those in 1987, 1991, 2001 and 2008. (Refer to Figure 6.6 for a look at the synchronous decline of equity returns and Moody's long-term interest rate.) Expected returns to equity may be unobservable, but the discounting factor as reflected in current interest rates has been quite explicit. The long thirty-some-year sector decline made for a predictable trend that was both anticipated and self-fulfilling.

Such a self-driving trend made for an amplification and feedback effect. A simple example illustrates the point. A capital asset returning $1 a year in perpetuity and capitalized at 10 percent equals $10 in capital value. An expectation that the discount rate will fall to 8 percent (a 20 percent decline) will raise the value of the capital asset to $12.50 (a 25 percent expansion in capital gains). Any decline in rates, whether propelled by a decline in equity returns due to free cash spillage, or a Greenspan Put drives further expectations of equity expansion which then amplifies stock valuations and drives further declines in equity returns.

Under such expectations, the corporate capital/output ratio will rise by a greater percentage than the discount factor declines. This is because the decline in the rate of return on equity (as displayed in Figure 6.6 above) contributes to a lowered rate of discount by which the present values of assets are determined. Consequently, inequality expands. Piketty does not examine this phenomenon because, for him, capital exists as a factor of production only. But in monetary terms, capital is more than a factor of production. In terms of equity valuations, capital responds to discounted streams of uncertain future returns, amplified by anticipated capital gains driven by expectations of lowered rates of discount. In a feedback loop, these lowered rates of discount depend, in turn, on lowered rates of return to equity.

There has been a roughly 66 percent decline in the cash rate of return on equity (Figure 6.6 above) over the period from 1970 to 2016 as stock values have expanded. This would seem to contradict Piketty's assumption of a roughly constant rate of return accruing to capital. There is no contradiction. Piketty takes the long view. Moreover, his assumption of a relatively constant rate is calculated on total capital as opposed to corporate capital. But this recent corporate decline in the cash rate on equity does speak to the differences between the most recent bout of inequality and those associated with the past. Unlike the Gilded Ages of the past, the most recent inequality has been associated with an increasingly stagnant economy combined with an increasing amount of public and private deficit spending. The resultant free cash spillage and the expansion of stock wealth has been superimposed on a stagnant economy resulting from a decline in the growth rate of investment.

Piketty's "First Fundamental Law" of capitalism is the multiplicative result of the rate of return times the capital/output ratio. Although from the early 1970s to 2014, the rate of cash return on equity fell by roughly two-thirds, the capital/output ratio rose roughly 200 percent. Correspondingly, as Figure 8.4 shows, corporate capital's share of output rose roughly 45 percent.

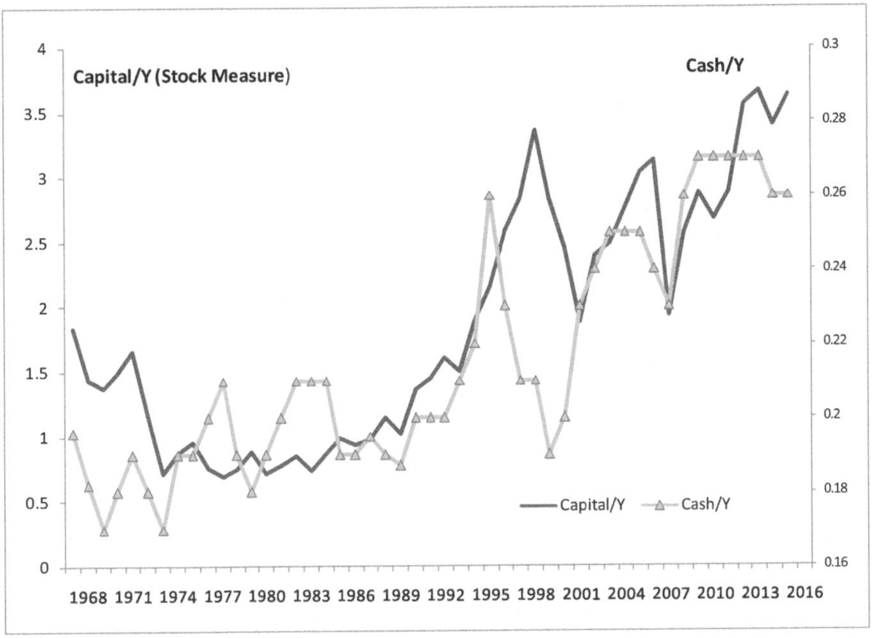

Figure 8.4 Capital/Y; Cash/Y

Source: Department of Commerce, Table 1.14; Federal Reserve, *Flow of Funds*, Table L.223.

It is important to remind again that Piketty's "First Fundamental Law" is an identity. Combined with the given data on capital's share, any specification of the capital/output ratio will generate a corresponding rate of return and vice versa. Piketty's warning against reductionism should be taken to heart. As a organizing principle, Piketty's "First Fundamental Law" may well be useful. But by itself, it explains nothing. The rise in capital's share of output is best understood as a combination of forces involving free cash spillage, the globalization and automation of production and the reduction of labor's power, both in politics and in the workplace.

Piketty's wealth measurement of capital, however, does make sense in a project involving the long-term distribution of wealth and the role of asset appreciation. Understanding the relationship between deficit spending, free cash and capital gains elucidates Piketty's hierarchical depiction of income and expanded wealth through capital gains. In assessing the top income gains, Piketty finds that the higher the income category, the more that capital gains figure into income (2014, Figures 9.7, 8.8, pp. 299–300). Piketty notes that "without capital gains, salaries would be the main source of income up to the .01 percent level of the income hierarchy" (p. 301). In highlighting the newer forms of income inequality, he points particularly to the advent of "supermanagers" "who have managed to obtain extremely high, historically unprecedented compensation packages for their labor" (p. 302). This new development ceases to be surprising in light of the free cash that is now disgorged through dividends, stock buybacks and mergers that pump up stock prices and allow the easy cash-out of options and grants.

Piketty describes the lopsided expansion of income surrounding the "super-managers" since the 1970s as primarily an Anglo-Saxon phenomenon (p. 315). This phenomenon may—at least in part—be culturally rooted. Unlike a large part of continental Europe and Japan, whose late development retained a large element of feudal communalism, the English had a long incubatory period developing the self-interested individuals associated with the growth of markets. The frontier lands of the United States, Canada and Australia were born capitalist.

Along different lines and as a suggestion for further inquiry, it might be instructive to derive free cash estimates for corporations located in other countries. A working hypothesis: the Anglo world has had a higher free cash spillage component than continental Europe and Japan.

Notes

1 Recently, there has been a outpouring of books addressing the topic of inequality. To cite a few: James K. Galbraith, *Created Unequal* (2000); *Inequality and Instability* (2012); Edward N. Wolff, *Top Heavy* (2002); Joseph E. Stiglitz, *The Price of Inequality* (2012) and *The Great Divide* (2015); Les Leopold, *Runaway Inequality* (2015).

2 *Economist*, May 27, 2017, p. 16. Some part of this shrinkage has been due to an increasing preference for going private. But some other part has been due to the ongoing expansion of mergers and acquisitions that—as imperfectly gauged by "Net Announcements" of both listed and unlisted firms—have been running at the rate of 3,000–12,000 a year from 1995 to 2015 (*Mergerstat Review*, various issues). Expressed as a fraction of total market capitalization, merger capitalization—that is, the aggregated value of firms absorbed through mergers and acquisitions—appears modest. For the late 1960s, the ratio of merger capitalization to stock capitalization was around 2 percent per annum, and for the mid-1980s and late 1990s around 3 percent (Andrade, Mitchell and Stafford, 2001, p. 105). Since 1980, merger activity has picked up. Nevertheless, over the period 1980–2015, the average annual ratio still remained under 5 percent. These ratios, however, do not illuminate the changes in market capitalization driven by merger-induced changes in capitalization. Under the assumption that acquisition premiums are distributed independently of the level of merger capitalization and industry, estimates can be constructed of both the total stock gains due to mergers and their contribution to changes in stock capitalization. For any given year, the effect can be dramatic because oftentimes the total market capitalization either goes negative or changes very little. But if we construct "rolling-ten-year" ratios of merger premiums to changes in stock market valuation, we arrive at a larger view of the contributing merger phenomena. As measured by this ten-year rolling ratio of "acquisition premiums" to changes in stock valuation, such activity has accounted for a substantial fraction of stock value expansion. From the ten-year ratio beginning in 1968 (1968–78) to the ratio begun in 1990 and ending in 2000, the ratio averaged around 13 percent. But averaging over the ten-year periods from 1990–2000 to the ten-year period, 2005–15, the average ratio expanded to 42 percent. This higher ratio needs to be taken in context as this latter period encompassed the dramatic collapse of equity prices during the Great Recession. Nevertheless, this ratio expresses how the mergers and the premiums associated with them helped enormously in maintaining equity expansion in recent years (premiums from *Mergerstat Review*, various issues; stock capitalization from the *Flow Funds*, Federal Reserve, Table L.223.

3 Mergers do enhance stock values, but as noted in Chapter 5, such enhancements typically accrue to investors in targeted firms rather than to investors in acquirers.
4 Here, Mott summarizes the conclusion of Myers, 1993.
5 Federal Reserve, *Flow of Funds*, Tables F. 223; F. 213.
6 Unless otherwise noted, all page references are taken from Piketty, 2014.
7 In commenting on Piketty, Robert Solow endorses this view, at least in reference to the long run: "as long as we stick to longer-run trends, as Piketty generally does, this difficulty [the conflation of capital with wealth] can safely be disregarded" (Solow, 2005, p. 52).
8 Robert Solow's metaphor that Harrod was later to protest. See Hagemann, 2009, p. 84.
9 Piketty also asserts that large variations in the capital/output ratio confirm a flexibility that the Harrod-Domar thesis denies.
10 In collecting 47 elasticity estimates from the literature, Devesh Raval shows that 41 are one or less (Raval, 2017, p. 84).
11 This is not to suggest that measuring capital by accumulated net investments is without super-problems. To amalgamate heterogeneous items into an aggregate figure is question begging at best. Moreover, the problem of obsolescence and depreciation is a problem that even in theory has not yet been solved. Current measurements rely on prices of used capital equipment, but the mix and match amalgamation problem remains. Piketty mentions the Cambridge controversies over the meaning of capital and comes out on the side of Robert Solow and his colleagues who maintain that capital can be amalgamated and treated as a "factor" or production along with labor and technology (p. 231).

References

Andrade Gregor; Mark Mitchell and Erik Stafford, "New Evidence and Perspectives on Mergers," *Journal of Economic Perspectives*, Vol. 15, No. 2, Spring 2001, pp. 103–120.

Davis, Leila, E., "Identifying the 'Financialization' of the Nonfinancial Corporation in the U.S. Economy: A Decomposition of Firm-Level Balance Sheets," *Journal of Post-Keynesian Economics*, Vol. 39, No. 1, 2016.

Froud, Julie, Sukhdev Johal, Adan Leaver and Karel Williams, *Financialization and Strategy: Narrative and Numbers*, Routledge, Oxford, New York and Canada, 2006.

Galbraith, James K., *Created Unequal*, University of Chicago Press, Chicago, IL, 2000.

Galbraith, James K., *Inequality and Instability: A Study of the World Economy Just Before the Great Crisis*, Oxford University Press, Oxford, 2012.

Hagemann, Harald, "Solow's 1956 Contribution in the Context of the Harrod-Domar Model," *History of Political Economy*, Annual Supplement, Duke University Press, Durham, NC, 2009.

Lazonick, William, "The Problem with Stock Buybacks," *Harvard Business Review*, September 2014.

Lazonick, William and Mary O'Sullivan, "Maximizing Shareholder Value: A New Ideology for Corporate Governance," *Economy and Society*, Vol. 29, No. 1, 2000, pp. 13–35.

Leopold, Les, *Runaway Inequality: An Activist's Guide to Economic Justice*, Labor Institute Press, New York, 2015.

Mott, Tracy, *Kalecki's Principle of Increasing Risk and Keynesian Economics*, Routledge Studies in the History of Economics, Routledge, Taylor and Francis Group, London and New York, 2010.

Myers, Stewart, "Still Searching for Optimal Capital Structure," *Journal of Applied Corporate Finance*, 1993, pp. 4–14.

Orhangazi, Ozgur, "Financialization and Capital Accumulation in the Non-Financial Corporate Sector: A Theoretical and Empirical Investigation of the U.S. Economy: 1973–2003," Working Paper Number 149, Political Economy Research Institute, Amherst, MA.

Piketty, Thomas, *Capital in the Twenty-First Century*, Belknap Press of Harvard University Press, Cambridge, MA and London, 2014.

Piketty, Thomas, "Toward a Reconciliation with the Social Sciences," in *After Piketty: The Agenda for Economics and Inequality*, edited by Heather Boushey, J. Bradford Delong, and Marshall Steinbaum, Harvard University Press, Cambridge MA and London, 2017.

Raval, Devesh, "What's Wrong with Capital in the Twenty-First Century's Model?" in *After Piketty: the Agenda for Economics and Inequality*, edited by Heather Boushey, J. Bradford Delong and Marshall Steinbaum, Harvard University Press, Cambridge, MA and London, 2017.

Reich, Robert, *Saving Capitalism: For the Many Not the Few*, Alfred A. Knopf, New York, 2015.

Shiller, Robert J., *Irrational Exuberance*, Princeton University Press, Princeton, NJ, 2005.

Solow, Robert, "The Rich Get Richer Dynamic," *New Republic*, Vol. 245, No. 8, May 12, 2014, pp. 51–55.

Stiglitz, Joseph E., *The Price of Inequality*, W.W. Norton and Company, New York and London, 2012.

Stiglitz, Joseph E., *The Great Divide*, W.W. Norton and Company, New York and London, 2015.

Toporowski, Jan, *The End of Finance: Capital Market Inflation and Pension Fund Capitalism*, Routledge, Taylor and Francis Group, London and New York, 2000.

Wolff, Edward N., *Top Heavy*, Century Foundation, The New Press, New York, 2002.

9 Crossing the boundary line

The recent association of expanded inequality and stagnation involves a myriad of contributing factors: the globalization of production and financial flows, the new high-tech environment, the sustained attack on labor, the consequent insecurity of working people and the flattening of wages, the restriction of investment due to monopoly power and multinational production, the petering-out of countervailing forces offsetting stagnant investment and the near-exhaustion of debt stimulation from both government and households. Using a neo-Kaleckian model, I have argued that the rapid expansion of debt-stimulation—in the face of investment growth slowdown—has expanded free cash flows which have made a large contribution to inequality and the speculative and financial bubbles that now surround us.

Contemplation of remedial responses challenges imaginative limits.[1] But the lack of collective control over the investment process certainly ranks towards the top of the list. Uncertainty in reference to future profitability, lack of coordination between industries and offshoring of productive facilities hampers the magnitude of investment while in-place corporate platforms largely determine the ends towards which investment is directed. This latter point needs to be stressed. Ongoing patterns of investment depend on the existing distribution of wealth, income, economic and political power. This complex of wealth, income and political power is a legacy complex descended from history. As John Kenneth Galbraith has repeatedly stressed,[2] the corporation stands at the heart of a "planning system" which constantly injects needs and wants into the underlying population so as to maintain existing markets, while providing the necessary ad-driven excitement for the purchase of new products of questionable utility. Far from being sovereign, consumers become receptacles for a barrage of want creation, tailored to the existing industrial structure with its appended distribution of income and wealth, and where the process of production manufactures the very wants upon which production depends.[3] In stark contrast to the corporate mandate for growth and the accompanying corporate need for advancing its cause through advertising and public relations, the public sector, apart from its military component, has no built in mechanism for public commitment and expansion.

Any progressive program to provide economic security, rectify the massive inequality around us, and counter investment stagnation requires a general assessment of basic human needs and an explicit recognition that, for millions of households, the market system cannot deliver on these needs. Apart from food, a bare bones list includes health, housing, transportation and secure income derived from useful employment. Racially segregated neighborhoods, industrially devastated areas, and job-abandoned small towns, with their high rates of unemployment and low rates of labor participation, are the most obvious signs of distress. But problems associated with working people are now apparent across a wider spectrum of the laboring classes. This spectrum includes the working poor, construction workers subject to the most volatile component of investment, those engaged in routine trade functions and civic and white-collar employment subject to automated displacement. Where ample job opportunities abound, living is often unaffordable. For the millions of households locked in debt and subjected to more and more rapid job turnover and stagnant wages, the prognosis for a rise in the standard of living is bleak.

The for-profit system serves the bulk of human needs for those who can afford to satisfy them. Indeed, it is remarkable that, in the absence of macro-planning, the economy can supply so much for so many. But the for-profit system is also a boundary line that restrains progress. Existing political arrangements are such that this boundary line is not to be crossed by government encroachment on private markets. The boundary line mandates that government not produce any product that private markets currently serve, even when such service is totally inadequate for millions.

In mainstream economics, there is no distinction between "needs" and "wants." Commodities are produced in accordance with "demand," where consumers exercise their sovereignty through consumer voting power as measured by money. As the sovereign consumer is both the start and the end point of inquiry, the entire historical backdrop of resource endowments is conveniently removed from view. The implicit assumption is that the existing nexus of purchasing power is to be taken for granted. This deflection of inquiry has powerful ramifications, particularly in reference to societal maintenance requirements. Civilized society requires ample employment opportunities and security for the general population. The current "consumer-sovereignty" economy requires a far larger amount of investment and growth for the provision of general needs than a planned economy that actually targeted such needs.

Below, I take up the possibilities of government production in the areas of health and energy to illustrate how government ownership of productive facilities and government investment could significantly enhance human welfare. These examples are industry specific but at least in the case of energy have a much wider application in regards to other basic needs regarding transportation and housing. These examples of health and energy should be understood as illustrative, but not exclusively so. They provide rock-bottom pillars of productive activity and consequently the basis of a larger collective responsibility for the welfare of the many.

Intrusion into industrial areas now served by private industry involves breaking the boundary line that prohibits direct government production. A first look at the boundary line is prefatory to an argument that such a boundary line should be crossed.

The boundary line

The boundary line is most vividly shown by the long and uneven history surrounding the advocacy for public works and by current budgetary expenditures. Federal government expenditures are geared almost exclusively to defense expenditures and transfer payments. Defense expenditures may well expand aggregate demand and inject funds for research and development, but they carefully avoid encroaching on private markets. Spending hundreds of billions injects purchasing power and holds up an existing for-profit economy as it currently exists. Nuclear submarines and F-35 bombers inject billions of dollars into the economy for domestic purchases of homes, transportation and food. Such expenditures, however, do nothing in the way of producing such needs.

In a similar way, transfer payments to social security recipients, to those medically entitled, to those currently unemployed and to the indigent involve a shuffling of monetary cards but leave the basic for-profit boundary line intact. Health is provided by a for-profit industry. Social security and food stamp recipients spend their monies within the all-encompassing for-profit system. Unemployment benefits are dispensed to maintain a socially acceptable society that allows people to eat when in distress. A standard textbook will also remind readers that such benefits automatically "stabilize" the for-profit economy when plunged into downturn.

The financing of government and subsidies are similarly supportive of the for-profit boundary line. Subsidies to solar energy might entice new private ventures, whereas oil depletion allowances and restrictive quota systems are props to existing industries. But these types of subsidies—and literally scores of others—undergird the for-profit system. Lowering corporate taxes may well sabotage growth but is routinely and ironically undertaken in its service. Substituting deficit spending for taxes creates free cash and a top-heavy wealth distribution. But such deficit spending is universally recognized as a stabilizing force even when accompanied by obligatory expressions of regret. Nowhere, outside of the Tennessee Valley Authority, and assorted municipal utilities and land leases, does government-owned productive facilities produce revenues in sufficient measure to make a dent in government receipts. This is primarily because the government, outside a considerable land mass, the public school system, the U.S. Postal Service and toll-free roads, owns essentially nothing.

Breaking the for-profit boundary line in reference to investment is the first requirement for major progress in providing economic security for the many. The way forward is through government ownership of productive facilities geared to satisfying basic human needs. "Socialization of investment"—to use Keynes's phraseology, is, of course nothing new. But to date, such socialization has been largely confined to infrastructure projects, public edifices and a war-making apparatus that either serve the larger for-profit economy or leave it alone. In solidifying monopoly pricing arrangements during the Depression, the codes of the National Industrial Recovery Act (1933) did little or nothing to enhance employment opportunities. But the job-producing investments associated with the Public Works Administration (an offspring of the NIRA), the Civil Works

Administration and Works Progress Administration gave rise to a large expansion of public works. Thousands of new bridges and public buildings, nearly 500 new airports, expanded hydroelectric works, water purification networks and viaducts, flood control and reclamation projects, hospitals, old-age homes, harbor facilities, sewer systems, schools, roadways, improved railway facilities, a modest attempt at slum rebuilding and an enlarged military apparatus with a swollen naval component constituted a new commitment to public investment. These projects were in addition to the many cultural and educational programs of the CWA and WPA that brought theater, art and adult education to millions. Apart from the "force account" government projects of the Works Progress Administration where government directly controlled production and investment, projects were contracted out to private construction companies. Most importantly from the standpoint of business, the projects directly avoided competition with private firms and markets, and often served businesses in the sense of providing increased infrastructure.

New Deal socialization of investment certainly augmented employment, both directly and indirectly. Public investment also

> helped to promote a series of striking innovations and technical changes in such fields as civil and structural engineering, transportation, distribution, machine production, electric-power generations and aeronautics [playing] . . . a key part in advancing U.S. economic productivity in a variety of sectors, setting the stage for postwar economic growth.
>
> (Smith, 2006, p. 88)

But despite such depression-fighting and productivity-enhancing efforts, the Depression continued until swallowed up by World War II. It was the enlarged scale of government war intervention and its financing that provided for the full employment of the war economy. On an annual basis, government expenditures during the height of the war effort (1941–44) grew roughly three times over government expenditures during the latter part of the 1930s (1935–39) with the federal government share expanding over seven times. During the Depression, particularly in the early years of the 1930s, federal deficits ranged from half to 40 percent of federal expenditures. As percentages these deficits were quite high, but the limited expenditures of the New Deal relative to what was required for recovery limited the efficacy of this high-powered spending. Moreover, direct taxation hit only the very rich, with direct taxation of income actually declining in percentage terms from the level of the late 1920s (Leff, 1966, pp. 11–13). As a percentage of federal expenditures, the deficits of World War II were in the same neighborhood as the deficits of the mid-1930s, but had as their context the multifold expansion of expenditures associated with the War. Moreover, they were backed up not only by the carry-over of very high taxes on the rich, but an excess corporate profits tax and a broadened income tax base swollen by full employment. For those who lived through the back-to-back crises of the Depression and the War, it was obvious that the Depression could have been remedied if only enough government expenditures had been forthcoming.[4]

The larger question brought forth by the sequential crises of depression and war was why the government could spend so much on the War without a similar commitment to fighting the unemployment of the Depression. As Lord Beveridge put it in 1943, "Unemployment has been practically abolished twice in the lives of most of us—in the last war and in this war. Why does war solve the problem of unemployment which is so unsolvable in peace?" (cited in Bailey, 1959, p. 9). The answer, briefly sketched out by Paul Baran and Paul Sweezy (1966, pp. 142–177), is that unlike war expenditures which invoke virtually no economic opposition from private parties, government peacetime expansion is narrowly constrained by markets already served by business enterprise and to which the political apparatus is beholden.[5] In reference to the New Deal programs, this deference accorded to private interests was quite explicit. Harry Hopkins, chief administrator of the WPA, wrote that

> Policy from the first was not to compete with private business. Hence we could neither work on private property, set up a rival merchandising system, nor form a work outlet through manufacturing, even though manufacturing had contributed to relief rolls hundreds of thousands of workers.
>
> (Hopkins, 1936, p. 163)

In short, the boundary line was fully operational. And so it remains.

The secular slowdown of investment and income growth over the last forty-some years suggests a needed new role for enlarged government production. I emphasize government production as opposed to expenditures. The lack of any discussion surrounding the for-profit "boundary line"—let alone the crossing of such a line—indicates how the political commitment to markets by the governing class blinds that same class as to the possibilities of satisfying human needs outside of private for-profit criteria. The absence of discussion as to the possibility of government production is testimony to the importance of the boundary line. The market system is not just a supplier of goods and services, but a quasi-religious totem commanding a deference bordering on holy writ. Public expenditures in support of the existing economy are clearly admissible as items for political dialogue. But government production is not.

In recent years, this inadmissibility is particularly striking given the political distress surrounding government financing with sequestering, debt-limitation debates and government shut-downs. Government production need not be self-financing but could be partially so. Unlike defense expenditures and transfer payments where government either "consumes" production (defense) or transfers purchasing power, direct government production would garner in revenues. Self-financing, however, need not be rigorously pursued. In consequence, government production threatens private markets. Put in the starkest terms, government production and the garnering of revenues is without any strict break-even constraint. For sustaining the economy, this lack of constraint is the essential advantage of government production over private production. Unlike private industry whereby profitability is necessary for survival and where uncertain future profitability hampers current production and investment, government production can proceed without any necessity for breaking even. Government production can thus provide for societal needs without any strict monetary constraints.

The lack of a strict break-even point derives from the taxing and borrowing power of the state. Such powers allow government production to proceed on an uninterrupted basis whether the economy is in a boom phase or otherwise. Like current expenditures devoted to defense and transfers, government production expands income. And government production would do so with a certainty of outcome not available to presently structured government expenditures whose effect is indirect and consequently uncertain. Revenues from government production could be redeployed within governmental structures without the payout to stockholders that now provides the speculative amphetamine of free cash and mergers.

Yet, there is one commonality in reference to government production and expenditures. Monetary outlays derived from government deficits—whether created in the course of government production or simple expenditures—generate free cash. Sufficiently high taxes on the wealthy, however, would eliminate this outpouring.

Crossing the boundary line

A Keynesian "socialization of investment" in health and energy could make substantial progress towards satisfying human needs. In concentrating on health and energy below, I address political opposition to government production and assess how such opposition might be minimized. A large part of my sketch involves a "buyout" of vested interests. Another part involves a mobilization of political interests. Health and energy are concerns that involve virtually everybody. Increasing their supply at lower costs serves the larger public interest, including business interests. Obviously, the myriad complexities of health and energy cannot be addressed here. Only the general line of increasing supply and the ramifications of such expansion will be formulated. Ideally, initial start-up monies directed towards government investment would come from the top of the wealth and income pyramid. As has been stressed, this too invites opposition, perhaps insurmountable opposition. But any line of progress involves bucking up against vested interests, and not just in finance. Putting government production in competition with existing for-profit structures invites opposition not just from the industries in direct competition with government enterprise but across the entire for-profit business system. This is true even when particular cases, like health and energy, could enhance the bottom line for the bulk of business enterprises. Healthy workers are productive workers. Cheap energy reduces costs across the entire business spectrum. But governmental competition in one industrial area—particularly if successful—invites the imagination to roam over the entire industrial and financial landscape for possible extension. This possible extension, of course, is the main threat to business enterprise and from which political opposition is to be expected.

Health: creating a parallel government health system

Gauged in terms of cost and health outcomes, the United States has one of the worst health systems among advanced capitalist countries. This general assessment is notorious. Whether measured by life-spans, infant mortality, preventable deaths through timely medical care, respiratory infections, heart disease, kidney failure, or divergence of health outcomes by income category, the United States is either at the bottom or ranks towards the bottom among OECD countries. This collective failure is reinforced by the fact that the United States spends nearly twice the average as a percentage of GDP—16.9 percent as opposed to 9 percent for the 35 member countries.[6] As a percentage of total U.S. consumption, health expenditures rose from around 6 percent in 1965 to around 17 percent in 2015.[7] Some part of this rise is due to much improved health care, for those who can afford it. But the largest part has to do with the increased commercialization of health. Among the most flagrant deficiencies is the idea that health—far from being considered a human right and a public good—is treated as an individual matter to be purchased and consumed like any other commodity.

The case of insurance coverage is a case in point. The largest part of health insurance is offered through employers, with a predictable falling-off of such offerings with diminished business size. But insurance expense is ultimately tied to health care charges. The recently enacted Affordable Care Act has put a much larger percentage of low-income persons under insurance. But some 10 percent of the non-elderly population still remains uninsured. The overwhelming reason is expense, both in terms of smaller businesses being unable or unwilling to offer plans, and the inability of low-income families being able to afford insurance even with subsidies tied to income level and newly formed insurance exchanges. Medicaid and Medicare offer aid to the elderly, disabled and indigent. But here the case is quite uneven, as Medicaid is tied to state funding. Most importantly, in the absence of government health production, government funding is reduced to stipulating caps on various medical procedures (which are often declined by medical personnel) and simply paying the bills for the procedures that aren't.

Inequality of health outcomes is the result both of inequality of income and the outsized inflationary component of health traceable to the structure of the health industry. Health is provided by an industry encompassing medical schools, pharmaceutical companies, health equipment suppliers, hospital networks, insurance companies, law services, the American Medical Association, and a host of specialty trade associations reflecting an increasingly diverse group of medical specialists devoted to keeping doctors and medical personnel in sufficiently short supply so as to bolster salaries. Long ago, Milton Friedman spoke of the American Medical Association as "the strongest trade union in the United States" (Friedman, 1962, p. 150). Only about one in four doctors belongs to the Association, but kindred associations are part of specialty occupations and have a similar pecuniary interest. The restrictionist tendencies of medical schools have kept the supply of U.S. physicians and surgeons to roughly one in three hundred people and the number of dentists to one in fifteen hundred.[8] Adding to the shortage problem, more medical students are contemplating another career option, such as advising health care companies and being part of medical care start-ups (Mostue, 2017, p. 34). Some part of this abandonment is due to the expense associated with medical training. Of course, figures on doctors and dentists do not include the numerous nurses, medical practitioners, home-care specialists and others. But the paltry numbers of physicians and dentists give some idea of why U.S. physicians in general practice receive some 40 percent more pay than their European counterparts, with some U.S. specialists receiving roughly double (Rosenthal, 2017, pp. 56–57). U.S. pay disparities between general practitioners and specialists also explain some part of why much-needed general practitioners are in such short supply.[9]

Monopolistic practices cross the entire health industry. In part, these practices reflect the fact that health services are—and have to be—provided locally. Health facilities need to be widely dispersed, which increases local concentration and exempts these facilities from larger competitive pressures. Hospitals, ambulatory services, doctors, dentists and orthopedic practitioners are part and parcel of communities. These local monopoly conditions, however, combine with nationally located oligopoly structures in insurance, medical devices, for-profit hospitals and pharmaceuticals to produce a complex mixture of monopolistic power. Insurance carriers in general are relatively deconcentrated, but "direct health and medical insurance carriers" are very concentrated with the top four national providers accounting for approximately one-third of total revenues in 2012, the top eight for one-half.[10] Local health insurance concentration is much higher. If states are ranked by concentration of insurance providers, the median state has two providers accounting for two-thirds of the total market.[11] In pharmaceuticals, the top four accounts for almost one-third of shipments, the top eight for almost half.[12] The monopolistic power of the pharmaceutical industry is notorious. Major drug companies justify high prices on the basis of the need for research and development monies and the monies needed for the rigorous tests imposed by the FDA; but promotional expenses in 2012 were fully three-quarters of private pharmaceutical funding, with all levels of government and universities contributing roughly the same as private funding (Askin and Moore, 2014, pp. 110, 132). Moreover, apart from generics, specific drugs are patented. So, doctor-prescribed medicines are funneled into sales of one or another companies. By the nature of the case, large amounts of drugs are quite literally prescriptions for monopoly as well as prescriptions for health.[13]

Non-profit community hospitals make up over half of community hospitals calculated on 2015 data.[14] Although exempt from the profits tax, these non-profits operate largely on the same commercial basis as for-profit facilities, with large CEO compensation packages, high-priced private rooms and other amenities tailored to customer choice. Profit is called "operating surplus." Tax-exempt status is to be justified by charity work but, as usual, the devil is in the details. Accounting for the costs of such charity allows for a host of pecuniary rewards directed towards hospital complexes and personnel (Rosenthal, 2017, pp. 46–52). Government hospitals—primarily state and local—make up roughly one-fifth of community hospitals—a slightly larger number than for-profits. Among the latter, the top four accounted for over half of 2012 revenues; the top eight accounted for nearly three-quarters.[15] National concerns, like the HCA group having 177 hospitals in 20 states,[16] exemplify some of the larger concerns. But quasi-monopoly combines are often geographically concentrated. So national statistics often minimize the problem of concentration. For example, in 2014, there were 95 hospital mergers with locally dominated oligopolies making up many of the complexes. Sutter Health of California, comprising "twenty-four hospitals, thirty-four outpatient surgicenters, nine cancer centers . . . [and] . . . thousands of affiliated doctor practices" is but one example (Rosenthal, 2017, pp. 207–209).

The enormous complexity of the U.S. health system might suggest that it is beyond repair. But the complexity is perhaps the largest part of what is driving health inflation. Employment and billing of medical "extenders" (i.e. assistants), outsourcing dialysis treatments with appropriate markups, restricting drug formularies by particular insurance providers, testing for pre-existing conditions, hogging medical information, padding administrative costs, unbundling fees so as to maximize total return, codifying the pricing of various medical procedures according to "usual" inflationary practice, over-testing to inflate bills and prevent malpractice lawsuits—all are in the mix. To this, we should add the entrepreneurial practice of outsourced billing for services rendered by firms owned by the very doctors whose primary employment is with the hospitals that they bill. Claims as to over-treatment are, of course, disputable in any particular case, but when revenues depend on it, there is the ever-present suspicion of its presence, particularly in the absence of safeguards. Drug testing and approval by the FDA is largely done by comparing drug outcomes to placebos rather than comparative testing by value. Approval by value would require new drugs to be price-competitive with equally effective alternatives. This would, of course, entail regulatory restrictions on pricing in general.

Private insurance companies and government personnel associated with the Medicare and Medicaid programs have an interest in keeping costs in line. But given the lopsided medical expertise of the health industry, arguments surrounding medical costs run in one direction—the direction of increasing costs. This one-way dialogue is reinforced by the political power of the medical and pharmaceutical industries, which prevents government bidding on drugs and government interference in the production of medical care. Even the insurance industry—with its interests in keeping health care costs in line—reverses course when its own interests are at stake. Lobbying by the insurance industry was the main force in eliminating the possibility of a "public option" under the Affordable Care Act with which private industry would have had to compete.

The politically powered health market is a "free market" in the sense that it is uncontrolled. But it is certainly not price competitive. Nor is competition a panacea. Like natural monopolies, health facilities should not be needlessly duplicated through competition. Competing insurance packages with their "out-of-network" constraints are often so confining that more of the same is not necessarily more of what is necessary and good. Cherry-picking of youthful and healthy applicants and the attempt to dump those associated with "pre-existing" conditions make insurance expensive whether more insurance companies enter the fray or not. Drug competition is virtually impossible when discovery is protected by patent rights. As long as malpractice awards are a significant portion of health expenses and are essentially unlimited, more competition from lawyers means more lawyers and consequently more health expense. Medical schools limit the supply of medical personnel at least nominally to maintain quality. But to ask them to expand the supply is to ask them to act against the pecuniary interests of their graduates. More personnel begs the question of how the supply is to expand and who is to do it.

Constructing a parallel public option

Constructing an effective public health system entails government health *production* across the board—from medical schools, pharmaceutical production, hospitals and care facilities and insurance. The existing for-profit complex makes up some 17 percent of the national economy. As such, overwhelming opposition to government health production might appear as inevitable. This opposition is currently reflected not in the long-standing discussion surrounding health care, but in the *silence* surrounding the possibility of addressing the essential health problems of the United States at its source—in the for-profit nature of the existing health complex. In sketching out a skeletal public health system below, I have no illusions as to the ease of political enactment. The sketch is laid out so as to emphasize that making progress on the health front is not so much a technical issue but a political one.

The political problem is the boundary line of for-profit production.

A sketch

The government would build and operate medical schools in the service of increasing the supply of physicians, surgeons, dentists, nurses and associated medical personnel. Increasing the supply of medical practitioners would lower the salaries and wages of such personnel in both public and private facilities and thus lower health costs generally. Quality need not be compromised if sufficient resources are devoted to the effort. Initially, of course, existing medical personnel would have to be procured from private markets and such procurement would be expensive. But given the taxing and deficit-spending power of the state and the eventual return measured in terms of the nation's health, such expenditures could certainly anticipate a substantial public backing. Like any large-scale investment expenditure, they would be amortized over time.

Applications to government-owned and operated medical training facilities would be enlarged by granting free or extremely low tuition to qualified applicants. Currently, the large amounts of money and debt necessary to complete medical training discourages the pool of potential recruits. It is often argued that, given the long-term payback, student medical expenses are well worth it. This argument has the limitation that a good many qualified students and potential applicants shy away from debt burdens in general, whether such debts are for medical education purposes or otherwise. The argument has the additional limitation that financial considerations should not discourage persons wanting to devote their lives to health improvement. Free or extremely low tuition to government medical schools would be granted on the basis of stipulated service in government hospitals and care facilities upon graduation. If graduates eventually were to decide to pursue other options, then tuition—based at least partially on market criteria—would be imposed. Of course, such contractual arrangements would be set forth upon initial entry into government educational facilities.

Government hospital and care facilities would have to be expanded. As noted above, government community hospital facilities account for roughly one-fifth of the over 5,000 or so hospitals across the nation, mainly at the state and local levels. State and local finance is severely limited. So, an expansion of federal facilities would have to do the job. Apart from construction of new facilities, one possibility would be for the federal government to actively acquire some portion of the non-profits that now account for over half of community hospitals. Non-profits enjoy tax-exempt status and putting legalized caps on the "costs" associated with executive pay, "costs" associated with private rooms, "costs" of medical procedures and "costs" and markups associated with outsourced medical services, might encourage those in charge of existing facilities to allow the federal government to take them over on favorable terms. A less desirable but perhaps more feasible alternative would be to allow continued tax-exempt status contingent on governmental control. Such acquisition and control would allow the pricing of hospital services to fall, providing a standard that would cross the nation. It is a rare U.S. family that has not encountered a $2,000–5,000 a night hospital bed for one or more of its members. Government-owned facilities would end such practices. Double billing, often disguised by the "unbundling of medical costs" so as to allow add-ons and markups would end. Unnecessary testing would also end, as there would be no incentive to pad bills. Patients would acquiesce, upon entering such facilities, to a limitation on medical malpractice claims. Such limitations would discourage the legal industry from pursuing outsized awards accruing from accidents and misfortune.

In addition, government pharmaceutical production facilities would be established, pricing drugs in accordance with family income and production costs. Such facilities would, like private pharmaceutical firms, hire chemists and trained personnel to further product development and research. New drugs would be subjected to the same strict testing standards now in place. In addition, new drugs would have to pass a value test that would assess benefits against the cheapest alternatives. New discoveries would be offered without patent rights and be available to the larger private distribution chains. Such chains, however, would have to compete with government facilities that would price in accordance with production costs and, as mentioned, be available to low-income recipients at perhaps even lower costs.

If governmental health care were sufficiently broad-based and ubiquitous in nature, it is not even clear that insurance, let alone a "public option" would be necessary.

People would have health care as a right, not as a commodity purchase. Such a system, might, of course, invite abuse. In the absence of a price system of rationing, hypochondriacs and others might over-extend the use of government facilities. These and many other details and assorted problems would have to be worked out. But government production of health is certainly a way forward in helping people have access to what should be considered a basic right and a public good.

The cost-reducing features of government health production also demonstrate the limitations of any finance system severed from health cost considerations. A single-payer system operating through general government receipts would certainly be preferable to what is now available—particularly in reference to the problem of "adverse selection." But health costs need to be addressed. A single-payer system—however progressive in intent—needs to couple its progressive features with the lowering of health costs. Increasing the supply of health services is the key to lowering costs. Only governmental production can carry this out.

People of all income classes need health care. Making such care widely available would not only make the U.S. population healthier but would—*in real terms*—lessen the current rise in income inequality. Income inequality is generally measured in money terms. In the case of necessities like health care, there is a strong argument for measuring inequality in terms of actual outcomes.

Energy

Addressing any complex of needs entails addressing society as a whole. Energy provides *the* key example. Energy is intimately linked to housing, job location and transportation. The high-speed electrical railroads now widely available in the developed world outside the U.S. serve to illustrate the obsolescence of the U.S. train system that currently carries 40 percent of the freight miles.[17] Current meager mass transit facilities need to be massively extended to allow expanded housing placement and ready access to job hubs without the dreaded commute.[18] Government electrification of new mass transit facilities together with the electrification of the auto could use renewables (particularly solar) that would not only provide employment in implementation but counter the destructive and dangerous use of nuclear power and fossil fuel reserves. Solar installations would be placed in the Sun Belt areas where the fuel is free and where large amounts of federal land is currently unused. Such energy could then be placed on an expanded national grid unencumbered by overlapping regulatory jurisdictions that currently hinder the wider dispersal of energy across the nation. This transmission of energy from the Sun Belt into northern climes would require more networks for electrical traffic. Their establishment would provide useful employment. The actual hardware associated with mass transit and solar paneling could be produced in high unemployment areas like Detroit devastated by de-industrialization, offshoring and automation. Solar electrification of transit would sharply lower the cost of housing by making more land available. Government housing projects would also be beneficial. In sharp contrast to the paltry expenditures devoted to housing development during the Great Depression, a new government emphasis on government production of prefabricated housing could expand the supply of housing, lowering house prices and mortgage debt. Housing across various income classes now accounts for roughly 35–40 percent of consumer expenditures (Medlen, 2008, p. 860). Any substantial lowering of this housing percentage would give more mass purchasing power for other industries and raise the standard of living for millions.

Solar energy is now cost-competitive with existing utility-generating facilities and will, if current projections continue, be more than cost-competitive. Given that the fuel is free, the real problem is the fixed costs of installation. In 2008, Ken Zweibel, James Mason and Vaasilis Fthenakis projected a Grand Solar Plan that would cost $400 billion over forty years. They assumed that the 2008 installed cost of $4 per watt would, in an unspecified but short amount of time, decline to $1.40 (Zweibel, Mason and Fthenakis, 2008). Their projections might have seemed optimistic at the time, but, retrospectively viewed, were quite pessimistic. In 2017, the "average silicon solar module spot price" per watt was below $.50, a reduction from just under $2 in 2010.[19] More recent projections envision another 30 percent reduction by 2022 (Ball, 2018, p. 90). The Grand Plan involved the installation of direct current (DC) lines for long-distance transmissions and a series of pressurized caverns for the storage of compressed air across the nation that would be released to power electrical turbines during off-hours. The authors of the Grand Plan calculated that with such an installation, U.S. carbon dioxide emission would be 62 percent below 2005 levels by 2050. This projection assumed a 1 percent growth in energy consumption, achieved partly through improved conservation. According to projections, the plan would supply 69 percent of electricity and 35 percent of all energy at mid-century (Zweibel, Mason and Fthenakis, 2008, p. 71).[20]

There is certainly enough land to accommodate the Grand Plan Currently, the federal government owns roughly 28 percent of the entire U.S. land area, mostly in the West, with a good percentage in states that are sun-drenched, such as California (45.9 percent), Arizona (38.7 percent), Nevada (79.6 percent) and New Mexico (35.4 percent) (Argueta, Hanson and Vincent, 2017).

Solar energy is by far the fastest growing source of net electrical generation, with wind generation just behind. But total wind and solar are still just a miniscule fraction of electrical power generation. In 2014, total renewables of wind and solar were about 5 percent of the total, with solar beneath 1 percent.[21] Existing utilities are committed to legacy assets. For these utilities, long-term contractual pricing provides the necessary certainty for investment commitment and assurance for debt holders. These long-term pricing commitments are being undermined by ever-cheaper renewables. Developers of solar are deluging existing utilities with power that they don't want and if accepted would only lower prices below a profitable level for energy across the board.[22] This is what the *Economist* has called "Clean energy's dirty secret,"[23] sometimes dramatically referred to as the "utility death spiral."[24] Utilities understandably prefer to phase out legacy assets judiciously over time so as to maximize returns.

Government subsidies are now being utilized to sustain the profitability of these legacy assets. Such monies would be better used if directed towards government ownership of electrical facilities. Significant inroads could be done directly by government purchase of private facilities. According to the 2012 Business Census, the top twenty firms in "Electric Power generation, transmission and distribution" had over half of the revenues and controlled about half of the over ten thousand establishments in the private sector; the top fifty had roughly three-quarters of the revenue and controlled about two-thirds of the establishments. Given that concentration ratios remain relatively constant over short periods, a provisional estimate can be made on the amount of monies necessary for the government to dominate the utility field. The market capitalization of the top twenty firms (April, 2017) was $564 billion.[25] Under the assumption that the same market capitalization-revenue ratio held for the top fifty firms as for the top twenty, the total market capitalization for the top fifty would approximate $760 billion, a total approximating the military budget in one year. Or, to use another comparative yardstick, the free cash flow of a typical recent year; less by over $400 billion than the $1.19 trillion wealth holdings of the top fifty wealth holders in the U.S. and one-third of the $2.4 trillion of the top four hundred in 2016.[26]

If the government were to procure bond financing at 2½ percent, annual service charges on borrowings equivalent to the total market capitalization would be less than $20 billion a year. Procurement might well entail an acquisition premium. But even assuming a 40 percent premium, the financing of such government acquisitions would appear more like a statistical error in government outlays than an actual expenditure for the procurement of perhaps the most important industry in the U.S.

In addition to private for-profit firms, municipals and cooperatives also produce electricity. But they produce a minority share and often purchase from larger suppliers. On 2015 data, such state and local government owned municipals and cooperatives produced about 30 percent of electrical revenues with private investor-owned utilities producing the rest.[27] Municipals and cooperatives have a vested interest in keeping costs to an absolute minimum. Piped-in low-cost federal energy would be more than welcome.

Large-scale government production of solar energy has another advantage which relates to inequality. Some proponents of solar energy suggest that solar will be installed "one rooftop at a time"[28] and give kudos to "micro-grids" and "sustainable communities" that allow local production (Worland, 2017, p. 22; Kammen, 2017, p. 38). Given the no-carbon footprint of solar, such installations are to be welcomed. Yet home and commercial installations are expensive. In consequence, those who can afford solar energy will escape paying utilities, reducing scale at existing companies and forcing regulators to apportion costs over a smaller and less affluent customer base. Such reduction in scale would operate to maintain high prices upon those less able to afford them. Utilities are already pushing back on those installing rooftop farms. For example, the Arizona Public Service, the Phoenix area utility, recently proposed a $100 monthly surcharge on each solar homeowner in the name of other utility users who pay for the grid and its maintenance (Biello, 2014, p. 68). This is just another instance of how for-profit ownership gets in the way of solar progress.

In the last half-decade, there has been debate among energy experts as to the optimal mix of renewables and more traditional sources of energy. Leading the charge into a renewable future is Mark Z. Jacobson and three co-authors who argue that Wind, Water, Sun (WWS) and derived hydrogen could give us 100 percent of energy production in a few decades were modern energy technologies employed today in a momentous start towards a non-carbon, non-nuclear future (Jacobson et al., 2015).[29] Against Jacobson and his colleagues, 21 scientists have critically assessed this futuristic plan indicating the presence of modeling errors, unjustified assumptions and a total disregard for the numerous political, environmental and economic obstacles involved in the transformation into an optimal energy mix (Clack et al., 2017). That such a wide array of experts can disagree about energy technologies is in no way surprising. But what is clear is that without collective control—that is to say, government control—over energy possibilities, such a debate, even if resolved, can get side-tracked by existing utility companies and their political power. Clearing the deck by instituting government ownership and control allows for progress without the hindrance of for-profit criteria dictating future prospects.

This last point cannot be over-emphasized. Government purchase of existing utilities would allow a breakdown of the various conflicting regulatory areas and bodies so as to provide for a national plan. Energy is the life-blood of the whole economy. A unified national grid would be much easier to effect were the government to own as well as control the bulk of the existing lines. New Direct Current (DC) lines would be hooked up to existing lines without the for-profit complications involved in negotiations with private parties. Cheaper energy, like cheaper health, would have a wide base of political support not just from residential parties, but from a large swath of business enterprise where energy is a major input.

As noted above, a government energy network would also provide the basis for the installation of electrified mass transit facilities whose hardware could be produced in government fabrication facilities located strategically to give meaningful jobs in economically depressed areas. As a term, "idle capacity" should not be reserved for underutilized capital installations. If not voluntarily carried out in self-directed pursuits or leisure, idle human capacity is sheer waste. In making for fuller employment, government production costs money. But in absorbing idle capacity, government production also expands economic output that would not have otherwise come into being. Expanded national income and an expanded tax base is the reverse side of an absorption of idle capacity. In addition to generating fuller employment, government production facilities could also be utilized to give job chances to those "out of the labor force," including those released from prison[30] and the long-term unemployed.

Government production of all types constitutes a large reservoir of latent possibilities. Among various needs, housing should be near the top of the list. The case of post-War Britain demonstrates the possibilities. Until reversed by the privatization moves of the Thatcher government, British production of municipal housing was quite extensive. From "the late 1940s through the early 1950s, municipal homes constituted more than three-quarters of all new properties built, and they continued to outnumber private-sector developments in absolute terms until 1958" (Matthews, 2017, p. 48). In 1979, they still housed 42 percent of the population. Municipal ownership and rent collection were locally based and tailored to local conditions. In time, however, ownership increasingly reverted to private parties and the commitment to government sponsorship waned along with the relative supply of new government housing. In ways approximating the housing problem in the U.S., British housing has become increasingly expensive, particularly in areas that provide for higher levels of employment.

Electrified mass transit facilities in the U.S. would extend housing possibilities enormously, as the U.S. is a nation of paltry population relative to land area. A U.S. national housing plan would increase the supply of *affordable* housing. Government fabrication of pre-fab housing could be accomplished, with a variety of differing housing designs based on standard architectural platforms. Final assembly, of course, would be carried out at locations accessible to jobs. But, like mass transportation hardware, the pre-fabrication of housing parts could be located in high unemployment areas, which, in itself, would create local demand for such housing. Affordable housing would free up purchasing power for millions and allow for a much higher standard of living while providing security as well.

Projects, jobs and income

Projects create jobs, and useful projects create useful jobs. Government production directed towards basic needs also provides income maintenance.

Income maintenance for those in need is now generally accomplished through tax credits and direct public assistance. Social security, Medicare, Medicaid, food stamps and assorted welfare payments like Temporary Aid to Needy Families (TANF) are income receipts directed towards for-profit ends. I stress "for-profit ends," because such payments stand quite apart from government production. In our earlier illustrative examples, parallel government health and energy systems would not only be production systems but income maintenance systems as well. They would provide income through job creation. They would also increase the real income of the population by providing health and energy at reasonable cost.

In consideration of a much larger role for government production in a variety of fields, solar electrification and modernization of transportation facilities would have first priority. Made sufficiently cheap through solar, such transportation would have the considerable advantage that government jobs could be brought to people and their communities, rather than the reverse. Under market conditions, migratory exit patterns arise out of industrial devastation. Those who have exited have had to find new housing and jobs in areas where skill sets were often mismatched and where housing prices undercut potential income and employment gains. Migratory dislocation has impacted not just those who have left, but family and community connections across the board. Those left behind in such areas as Detroit, Flint, Braddock and Scranton inhabit industrial areas approximating wastelands. Families, social contacts through voluntary associations and friendships have often been torn up in the process.

National planning could significantly mitigate such human suffering. Under current market economics, such suffering is simply understood as collateral externalities.

Government production would have the added benefit of establishing wages and working-hour conditions that could—over sufficient time—establish new benchmarks that private industry would have to match. The reduction of necessary labor hours brought about by the advance of technological displacement and artificial intelligence (AI) could be countered by a reduction in working-day hours. Under present conditions of private employment, a reduction in working hours constitutes a reduction in take-home pay. Such reduction is understandably resisted by working-class members. But under the auspices of government employment, if wage increases accompanied working-hour reductions, pay could be kept up and opposition minimized. Reduction in work-day hours would also allow an increased sharing of work, allowing for both a meaningful contribution to output by more persons and sufficient income for economic security.

This forward march would have to be instituted through government employment. In the private sector, reduction in working hours for private routine jobs is often met by additional temporary personnel. But for jobs requiring high levels of skill, the private sector cannot be expected to train employees for temporary employment. Again, government employment has the advantage. The government is not profit-constrained. Moreover, if government jobs were sufficiently secure, government training costs would tend to translate into expanded training costs by private employers, as the latter would have to match the labor conditions of government employment. This is, of course, another case where societal maintenance and expanded welfare would invite opposition from business interests. But the upside is many-fold: combined with higher employment and wages, the spread of education and training—instigated initially through government production but spread into the private sector—would not only be valuable in and of itself but would counter at least some of the forces generating rising inequality.

Government production across a variety of industries would also constrain inflation brought about by tighter labor markets and expanded wage concessions. Sufficiently dispersed across industries, government productive entities could set price benchmarks that would extend to private industry. These "public options" need not be large to effectively police pricing behavior. Government production would only need to be widely available to consumers as an alternative to privately produced goods. In reference to pricing, government enterprises would act as policing agencies not by fiat or explicit price control but by controlled market competition. Such government competition would tend to nullify oligopoly pricing and the consequent investment restriction accompanying oligopoly formations. The tradeoff between inflation and unemployment, etched out in A.W. Phillip's famous curve, would no longer appear as inevitable. High employment and high wages have been generally associated with higher increases in prices. Government pricing across numerous industries could break such an association.

Production versus income maintenance

In terms of implementation, direct government production in a variety of fields appears as entirely unrealistic. This unrealism derives not so much from technological feasibility but from political entrenchment of what Thorstein Veblen termed the "Vested Interests." Competition from government production entities entails encroachment on the profitability of private enterprise, encroachment on oligopolistic pricing, encroachment on the ability of the few to extract large portions of income from the many. Government production geared towards needs in the form of home, health, transportation and the collective welfare also challenges the invested frivolity of production for its own sake and for the income maintenance provided by such production. In confronting an obsolete commitment to more and more production of dubious service, John Kenneth Galbraith once observed that such critical exposure brings about a challenge to the "greatest of vested interests, those of the mind" (Galbraith, 1958, p. 3).[31]

There is also the important question of public control over government enterprises. The long history of regulatory capture, the business dominance of the NRA codes and assorted public subsidies of private parties might suggest the inevitable dominance of business over any governmental productive enterprises. The historical record provides little basis for optimism. Progressive movement along the governmental control front would involve the necessity for democratic sensibilities and a collective vision of production for human needs and income security. The obstacles pitting private markets against government production might well seem insurmountable. But however difficult the obstacles, the articulation of ultimate results is certainly a necessary condition for a forward movement along a democratic political front.

The linkage of government production and income generation would have to balance government production with traditional solutions to unemployment which accord compensation to those displaced. There is no necessary incompatibility. As usual, details matter. John Kenneth Galbraith recommended that such compensation be geared to the level of unemployment and its duration. Unemployment compensation would rise with the severity of downturns which would bolster or at least stabilize purchasing power when it was most needed. Temporary unemployment would be met with lower compensation under the presumption that the unemployed would soon be back at work (Galbraith, 1958, pp. 298-–304). The details themselves would be hammered out with regard to local employment conditions. Such cyclical variation in compensation would certainly be preferable to the present condition where unemployment benefits are rigidly specified with periodic legislative alternations dependent on circumstances.

Among a variety of challenges, government production would have to attend to the availability of government projects and the differential income between government work, private employment and unemployment grants. High government wages would not only motivate private employers to raise their rate of remuneration but put a higher penalty on non-participation in the labor force. The concept of non-participation has become a new focus for those who project a future "jobless" world where machines, robots and artificial intelligence increasingly reduce labor requirements outside of a high-tech sector. The most extreme form of severance of income maintenance from production is the proposal for a basic income whereby individuals would be entitled to a certain stipend independent of current and previous employment. For proponents, a basic income would permit people to use their free-but-paid time to pursue dreams, hobbies and whatever their minds conceive within budgetary constraints. A basic income would also alleviate the income maintenance problems of a projected imagined world without jobs.[32] This understanding of an income-maintained robotized future is, in some sense, the end point of a much older understanding that goods and services must be purchased as well as produced. Henry Ford's implementation of a $5 a day payday was a way to keep artisan mechanics from sabotaging machines. But it was also a signal to other capitalists that high pay allowed high consumption and high profits. In a similar way, the outpouring of federal monies on military projects permitted (and permits now) an extension of consumption power amplified by Keynesian multiplier effects. In that military items are quite useless for the satisfaction of human needs, the military outpouring of monies sustained (and sustains now) the consumption vision that the basic income proposal puts center stage.

Proponents of a basic income generally recommend a universal stipend, suggesting that any targeting of the poor inevitably entails degrading "means" tests. Monies allotted to the rich could be clawed back through higher taxes. If untaxed, a basic income would allegedly maintain incentives to work, a decided improvement over current means-tested welfare where work often involves an extremely high tax as welfare recipients lose benefits. The effect on wages is uncertain: for the working poor, a basic income involves the same type of subsidy to business as earned income credits. Correspondingly, wages might drop as employers recognize that lower wages would still allow sufficient income maintenance. Others suggest that wages might increase to entice people to work. This might well be the case, particularly if the basic income were high enough to allow a reasonable and secure standard of living. On the negative side, a basic income might create a large number of people with nothing to do—a society encapsulated within a culture of uselessness—and, depending on the level of a basic income stipend, dictate wage rate hikes incompatible with the existence of smaller businesses that now employ a large part of the workforce. In addition, there is a preponderance of evidence that useful employment is psychologically healthy and that all types of individual maladies are associated with severance from useful endeavor (Blustein, 2008, pp. 230–232). This is not to deny the possibility—even the likelihood—that there are large numbers of individuals who, under a basic income, would thrive. The uncertain outcomes of a basic income make existing pilot programs something to watch.[33] But at the level of current knowledge, the outcomes of a universal basic income are quite uncertain.

Another, and increasingly written about, solution to unemployment is a government job guarantee program that would act as a buffer stock that feeds government employees into and out of the private sector in accordance with general economic conditions. Job skills markedly deteriorate when the unemployed sit out too long. In addition, depressed conditions often lead to the failure of firms with obsolete equipment that are skill specific. A job guarantee program would absorb displaced workers exiting from whatever source. Like unemployment insurance, a job guarantee program maintains demand when it is most needed and without the possible negative consequences of a universal basic income.

Proponents of the buffer-stock concept also maintain that correct use of the buffer stock could restrain inflation:

> the government offers a fixed wage (that is a price) to anyone willing and able to work, and lets market forces determine the total quantity of government spending that would be required to satisfy the demand for public sectors jobs under the Job Guarantee . . . [W]hen the private sector is inflating, a tightening of fiscal and/or monetary policy can shift workers into a fixed-wage Job Guarantee sector to achieve inflation stability without causing costly unemployment. This program both anchors the general price level to the price of employed labour of this (currently unemployed) buffer and can produce useful output with positive supply side effects.
>
> (Mitchell, Wray and Watts, 2016, p. 245)

Economists, like Mitchell, Wray and Watts, who propose a job guarantee program, are most often associated with Modern Monetary Theory (MMT), which maintains that a sovereign government with access to its own money supply is without financial constraint in providing jobs. But the virtues of such guaranteed full employment are tempered by the level of the Job Guaranteed wage imposed on working-class people. Presumably, the wage would be set in accordance with income maintenance criteria. However, unlike a system based on extensive government pricing of final output, the pricing policies of business firms would be constrained by the same harsh fiscal and monetary policies advocated by traditional mainstream economics. In fighting inflation, the contemplated filling-up of the buffer stock of labor would be the result of a spillover effect where employees previously employed in higher-wage jobs empty into the lower-wage employment of the guaranteed job.

The higher the guaranteed wage, the larger the proportion of the labor force employed by government. Set high enough, the guaranteed wage would either squeeze profits as firms were forced to match the government benchmark or be translated into inflation. The larger the government buffer stock, the more the demand for government projects. Such demand would beg the question of what the government would produce. If carried far enough, such projects would certainly bump up against the boundary line surrounding privately produced goods. In tightening labor markets, government projects would also ramp up the inflation that the job guarantee program was designed to counter. So a type of balancing act would have to be imposed: a lower guaranteed wage would allow a higher expansion of output and vice versa. Some advocates of the Job Guarantee have suggested a revitalization of the type of nationalized industrial development that was part of Europe after World War II. For example, William Mitchell and Thomas Fazi advocate a return to the extended government ownership of utilities, railroads, airports, state banks, airlines, public hospitals and other public enterprises which became increasingly privatized beginning in the mid-1970s. For these theorists, the way forward is to go back, calling for a reclamation of the state in the interests of public welfare (Mitchell and Fazi, 2016, pp. 248–249). So MMT theorists have broached the for-profit boundary line. However, the government projects upon which the buffer stock would be employed have not as yet been fully specified.

The proponents of MMT bring to the limit the idea that the government is unconstrained as to monetary means. They correctly maintain that the U.S. government—understood as the nexus of the Treasury and Federal Reserve—can produce money in whatever quantities are necessary to maintain full employment. They also maintain that spending is what generates inflation—not just money creation. But they are apparently unaware of how increased monetary spending over and above taxes—either through deficits or direct deposit to recipients of government contracts—would create free cash in equal measure. To prevent free cash spillage leading to expanded inequality, asset appreciation and speculation high taxes on corporations and the rich would have to complement the full employment monetary expansion central to MMT theory.

The perimeter of the boundary line

Thorstein Veblen once surmised that the only real chance for significant change in the economic system was to have the economic system completely collapse. In his *Engineers and the Price System* (1921), Veblen hinted as the possible arrival of a new society whereby valuation in terms of price and profit would be supplanted by a rational industrial system made "on the initiative and under the direction of the country's technicians taking action in common and on a concerted plan." The "Vested Interests" would move over, not by forcible dispossession "[but] . . .involuntarily after the industrial situation gets quite beyond its control" ([1921] 1990, p. 132). This new order—visionary but vague in its dimensions—would put industry in the service of human welfare, not business.

Veblen's death prevented him from witnessing the various global salvage attempts to resuscitate the economic system during the Depression. The fascist policies of the 1930s that aligned business interests with war preparedness and the worship of the state might well have given him pause as to the viability or desirability of any technocratic vision of national planning. Had Veblen lived to witness the New Deal, he would have encountered a variety of commentators who feared a similar devolution of a U.S. national recovery movement into fascism.

This dystopian vision did not happen. That it need not happen was perhaps best argued by Mordecai Ezekiel (1939, pp. 259–270), who argued that a bottom-up industrial plan aimed at human economic welfare need not involve the glorification of the state, exaggerated nationalism, dismemberment of labor organizations, or coercive management typified by fascist regimes. Labor and consumer representatives would complement business representatives in constructing "democratically formulated" industrial plans that would fit into a coordinated national plan. Extending the state-buying programs of agriculture into industries would insure that planned production would in fact get purchased. Such state-sponsored buying would take the uncertainty out of the investment equation and provide a basis for industrial expansion. Recalcitrant industries might have to be forcibly put into alignment with national output plans but Ezekiel optimistically thought that such cases would be the exception.

The New Deal programs never rose to a national plan. So it is unclear as to whether plans along Ezekielian lines could have ever functioned, even at a minimal level. But it is not surprising that Ezekiel's "democratic" plans never evolved out of talking points. The economic and political power of business was too strong. Moreover, the all-encompassing nature of Ezekiel's plan, corresponding to the depths of the Depression, was too much to even assess how it could be implemented. Only a comprehensive plan could rise to the occasion of countering the Depression. But given the existing political and economic realities of the time, such totality of planning was beyond extended discussion, let alone practical effect.

Today, any movement towards government production would be best facilitated in stages and directed towards the most basic of needs. It is in this spirit that I have chosen health and energy as starting points for violating the current perimeter of the boundary line. Such demarcation, however, could be (and would be) subject to events and circumstances. The most recent downturn of 2007–10 is suggestive. A time-traveling Veblen would have been disappointed that the most recent crisis did not lead to any significant restructuring of the economy. But he would not have been surprised. Veblen was fully aware of the political power of business and how business ideology seeps into the underlying population. The most recent collapse caught the political and economic elites by complete surprise. But they quickly regained composure. The rescue efforts surrounding the banks and auto companies demonstrated their commitment to a reestablishment of the economy along pre-crisis lines. Instead of nationalizing the investment banks that were at the center of the crisis, the Federal Reserve and the Congress bailed them out and restructured them along the same "pre-crisis for-profit" lines. An alternative scenario would have been for the government to take over these failed banks (a virtually costless endeavor given the collapse in bank stock prices) and rationalized these conduits of capital so as to funnel monies into productive investments such as health and energy. Such nationalization would have also had the added benefit of closing down or at least policing the proliferation of financial instruments that were central to the downturn.

Instead of bailing out the auto firms, the government could have transformed them into government-owned mass transit production facilities. Given the collapse in auto shares, this transformation would have cost virtually nothing. Fundamentally, the auto firms are simply mass organization firms capable of producing anything. This was shown concretely during World War II when auto production was halted and former auto workers were transformed into workers producing military hardware. In a similar way, government construction of synthetic rubber plants and steel plants during the War was not held up by considerations of the for-profit boundary line. There was the War to fight and production took precedent over concerns about the proper sphere for government production.

The differential monetary commitments surrounding the sequential crises of the Depression and the War demonstrated the overwhelming constraints holding back government production directed towards useful ends. By itself, the War also demonstrated the productive capabilities of government investment and employment—capabilities that could be extended into useful production today. The War siphoned off free cash through very high taxes imposed on the wealthy and corporations. Today, this precedent of production and finance needs a refreshment of memory. The historical record shows that high production is fully compatible with a redistribution function whereby income is spread more evenly and where significant government productive facilities are commonly owned. Any expansion in the perimeter of the boundary line would, of course, invoke increasing opposition from business interests. But production targeting basic human needs would provide for at least a start.

Notes

1 The problems associated with the offshoring of production and finance translate into demands for a home-spun retraction of offshore activities equivalent to the familiar metaphor of transforming omelets back into eggs. New digital technologies dispense with routine jobs. Inexpensive education for new job-ready skills might seem a worthwhile goal. But to fashion educational objectives around ever-changing job slots is to fit human material into ever-changing Procrustean beds and to discount education aimed towards critical thinking and other ends. Limiting the hours of the working day, combined with a higher wage, could spread the work, and I examine below the possibility of government initiatives in this regard. Expanded inequality can be reversed through higher taxes on the wealthy combined with restrictionist policies on offshore accounts and international transfers. Demands for higher taxes on the wealthy, however, bump up against the disproportionate, if not all-encompassing, political power of the wealthy and their apparent commitment to the view that higher taxes on them spell lower economic growth and lower employment opportunities for all.

2 Most particularly, in his *The New Industrial State* ([1967] 2007.

3 In Galbraith's view, these created wants are often only peripherally related to what is actually needed for a better life. A better life goes beyond buying things. A better life requires security of income and health, the possibility of independent thinking, an expansion of leisure and public goods such as education, easily accessible parks and a non-polluted and aesthetically pleasing environment. Galbraith holds that any real progress towards a better life would require a much larger expansion of the public sphere. He does, however, respect the private property boundary line. Although he maintains that the paucity of resources devoted towards public ends stands in stark contrast to the abundance of resources devoted to private ends, his recommendations for expanded public expenditures do not encroach on markets already served by business.

4 As a symbol of this manifest truth, one might point to the Employment Act of 1946, often misleadingly labeled the Full Employment Act. The War constituted the benchmark by which the failed efforts of the New Deal could be gauged. The War raised the question as to why the government could not have spent the same amount of monies during the Depression to affect the same full-employment result of the War. The Employment Act of 1946—where the government was nominally charged to maintain employment—constituted the answer to the question. Nevertheless, the fear that an enlarged government—freed from war production—would compete with private

enterprise served to qualify the "fullness" of employment objectives of the Act. The federal government was obligated to promote (not guarantee) "maximum employment, production and purchasing power" in the context of promoting "free competitive enterprise and the general welfare CONDITIONS UNDER WHICH THERE WILL BE AFFORDED *useful employment*, FOR THOSE able, WILLING, and seeking to work" (quoted in Bailey, 1950, p. 228; original emphasis). (For a history of the establishment of the Employment Act, see Bailey, 1950).

5 Baran and Sweezy maintain that "*given the power structure of United States monopoly capitalism*, the increase of civilian spending had about reached its outer limits by 1939" (1966, p. 161; original emphasis). They maintain that under modern conditions, formal democracy rules but that the political power structure reflects business interests in general, with particular regard to the megaliths of corporate power. Political power is thus plutocratic in content (p. 155).

6 National Nurses United and the Sanders Institute, 2017, pp. 6–7.

7 Bureau of Economic Analysis, Table 2.4.5.

8 U.S. Bureau of Labor Statistics, CPS Tables, in Table 633, ProQuest Statistical Abstract of the United States, 2016, p. 408.

9 In Germany, the Netherlands, Canada, France and Australia, over 30 percent of doctors are general practitioners whereas in the U.S. general practitioners constitute around 12 percent (Askin and Moore, 2014, p. 12).

10 2012 Economic Census, NAICS code, 524114.

11 *Economist*, November 4, 2017, p. 14.

12 2007 Economic Census, NAICS code 3254.

13 The abuse of patent protection is widespread. One illustrative case involves Humira, a treatment for inflammatory diseases, made by AbbVie. The drug is protected by over a hundred patents, some part of which have to do with the processes necessary to carry out production. Costs to patients reputedly can run up to $50,000 a patient. Challenges to Humira involve lengthy legal battles, which in themselves drive up health costs (Koons, 2017, pp. 17–18).

14 "Fast Facts on U.S. Hospitals," American Hospital Association.

15 2012 Economic Census, NAICS code 622.

16 *Forbes*, September 5, 2017 p. 31.

17 *Economist*, February 13, 2016, p. 61.

18 It is often contended that more urban density through high-rise facilities would cut transportation costs and provide for better living arrangements. Such high-density arrangements would also fight suburban sprawl. As portrayed by advocates of high density, workplace and residence would be close in proximity, reducing transportation costs, time and energy waste (McDonough, 2017 pp. 44–48). On strictly technical merits, such density arguments make sense, and might, in time, come to partial fruition. However, given the seemingly insuperable problems associated with transforming already high-density metropolitan areas into still higher-density arrangements, such transformations appear, at least for now, quite problematic.

19 *Bloomsberg Businessweek*, June 19, 2017, p. 49. Estimates of costs vary widely as some cost specifications include compressed air facilities, new transmission lines and the like. The recent dramatic lowering of solar costs, however, are not in doubt.

20 The Grand Plan envisions using government subsidy systems to incentivize private utilities to modify, modernize and scrap existing facilities. The long-distance DC current would run primarily along interstate highway corridors and then converted into AC at regional hubs. It would then be transmitted to customers along existing routes. Financing would come from a carbon tax and a vaguely stipulated national renewable energy plan. It is not clear how the authors came to the 40-year, $400 billion figure. But the fact that they think $400 billion over 40 years is a lot of money suggests that they have not looked at federal finances where, for example, the current military budget is double their 40-year subsidy figure *on an annual basis.*

21 Earth Policy Institute, "U.S. Net Electricity Generation by Selected Sources 1950–2014," posted April 16, 2015.
22 A case in point is the utility structure under Berkshire Hathaway Energy, a Warren Buffett group. Buffett himself is a fan of renewables, but his utility complex is resisting any obligation to purchase solar energy "when states determine the extra electricity isn't needed": *Bloomberg Businessweek*, August 14, 2017, pp. 25–26.
23 *Economist*, February 25, 2017, p. 11.
24 See Gavin Bade's discussion of an Edison Electric Institute's White Paper utilizing this term (Bade, 2015, p. 6).
25 From *Statista*: https://www.statista.com/statistics/237773/the-largest-electric-utilities-. . . .
26 *Forbes*, October 25, 2016, pp. 128–212.
27 Federal Government Office of Electricity, Renewables and Uranium statistics.
28 See Brian Dumaine's discussion of Solar City, a large rooftop installer (Dumaine, 2014, pp. 96–102).
29 Jacobson and Delucchi (2009, pp. 58–65) calculate that on a world scale, some $100 trillion would have to deployed over twenty years, quite apart from transmission costs. They also note that some forms of WWS renewables would in the transition period be more costly than fossil fuels, indicating the temporary necessity for "feed-in-tariffs," carbon taxes and a removal of subsidies directed towards fossil fuels.
30 Currently U.S. prisons and jails house over 2 million people, whose chances for employment upon release are, at best, problematic. Recidivism could potentially be cut by dramatic amounts were the government to offer meaningful employment. Prison tabulation for 2013 from Tables 374, 375, pp. 240–241, in *ProQuest Statistical Abstract of the United States*, 2016.
31 Over a half century ago, John Kenneth Galbraith maintained that the normative nexus of production and income—"by thy sweat thou shalt eat"—evolved from the condition of universal poverty across ages. In the new affluent society where marginal increases in production were devoid of any large measure of utility, production was valued primarily by the income so derived. As Galbraith put it: "The income men derive from producing things of slight consequence is of great consequence" (Galbraith, 1958, p. 292). In Galbraith's view, ideas were not so much eclipsed by other ideas, but by events, trends and happenstance that made older ideas not so much wrong as obsolescent. The new affluence of the U.S.'s post-WWII experience operated to render the tight nexus of production and income somewhat obsolete. New beginnings oriented towards income security could commence once there was a general recognition that increased production was of marginal benefit.
32 Forward-looking explorers of a basic income—like Mark Zuckerberg—envision community based projects of saving the planet and providing better health where learning occurs through trial and error. According to Zuckerberg, such projects have a better chance of success if individuals had a safety net to fall back upon when and if failure occurred (Zuckerberg, 2017). The socially disruptive impact of the new high-tech world is now widely discussed. See Ford, 2015; Srnicek and Williams, 2015; Mason, 2015.
33 On pilots, see Standing, 2017, Chapter 11.

References

Argueta, Carla N., Laura A. Hanson and Carol Hardy Vincent, "Federal Land Ownership: Overview and Data," *Congressional Research Service*, March 3, 2017.

Askin, Elisabeth and Nathan Moore, *The Health Care Handbook: A Clear and Concise Guide to United States Health Care System*, Washington University in St. Louis, MO, 2014.

Bade, Gavin, "The Top 10 Trends Transforming the Electric Power Sector," *Utility Dive*, September 17, 2015.

Bailey, Stephen Kemp, *Congress Makes A Law*, Columbia University Press, New York, 1950.

Ball, Jeffrey, "Shell Faces 'Lower Forever,'" *Fortune*, February 1, 2018, pp. 85–93.

Baran, Paul and Paul Sweezy, *Monopoly Capital: An Essay on the American Economic and Social Order*, Monthly Review Press, New York, 1966.

Biello, David, "Solar Wars," *Scientific American*, November 2014, pp. 68–71.

Blustein, David L., "The Role of Work in Psychological Health and Well-Being: A Conceptual, Historical and Public Policy Perspective," *American Psychologist*, Vol. 63, 2008, pp. 228–240.

Clack, Christopher T.M., Staffan A. Qvist, Jay Apt, Morgan Bazilian, Adam R. Brandt, Ken Caldeira, Steven J. Davis, Victor Diakov, Mark A. Handschy, Paul D. H. Hines, Paulina Jaramillo, Daniel M. Kammen, Jane C.S. Long, M. Granger Morgan, Adam Reed, Varun Sivaram, James Sweeney, George R. Tynan, David G. Victor, John P Weyant and Jay F. Whitacre, "Evaluation of a Proposal for Reliable Low-Cost Grid Power with 100% Wind, Water, and Solar," *Proceedings of the National Academy of Sciences*, June 27, 2017, pp. 6722–6727.

Dumaine, David, "Mr. Sunshine," *Fortune*, October 27, 2014.

Ezekiel, Mordecai, *Jobs For All*, Alfred A. Knopf, New York, London, 1939.

Ford, Martin, *Rise of the Robots: Technology and the Threat of a Jobless Future*, New York: Basic Books, 2015.

Friedman, Milton, *Capitalism and Freedom*, University of Chicago Press, Chicago, IL, 1962.

Galbraith, John Kenneth, *The Affluent Society*, Houghton Mifflin Company, Boston, MA, 1958.

Galbraith, John Kenneth, *The New Industrial State*, Princeton University Press, Princeton, NJ and Oxford, [1967] 2007.

Hopkins, Harry, *Spending to Save: the Complete Story of Relief*, New York: W.W. Norton, 1936.

Jacobson, Mark Z. and Mark A. Delucchi, "A Path to Sustainable Energy," *Scientific American*, November 2009, pp. 58–65.

Jacobson, Mark Z., Mark A. Delucchi, Mary A. Cameron, and Bethany A. Frew, "Low-Cost Solution to the Grid Reliability Problem with 100% Penetration of Intermittent Wind, Water, and Solar for All Purposes," *Proceedings of the National Academy of Sciences*, Vol. 112, No. 49, December 8, 2015, pp. 15060–15065.

Kammen, Daniel, M., "Sustainable Communities," *Scientific American*, December 2017, pp. 28–39.

Koons, Cynthia, "Guarding Big Pharma's Crown Jewel," *Bloomberg Businessweek*, September 11, 2017, pp. 17–18.

Leff, Mark, *The Limits of Symbolic Reform: The New Deal and Taxation, 1933–1939*, Cambridge University Press, Cambridge, London, New Rochelle, NY, Melbourne and Sydney, 1966.

Mason, Paul, *Postcapitalism: A Guide to Our Future*, London, Allen Lane, 2015.

Matthews, David, "The Struggle for Shelter: Class Conflict and Public Housing in Britain," *Monthly Review*, Vol. 69, No. 4, September 2017, pp. 43–52.

McDonough, William, "How Cities Could Save Us," *Scientific American*, July 2017.

Medlen, Craig, "Galbraith's Preference Mappings: Needs and Wants, Evidence from the 2005 Consumer Budget Study," in *Notes and Communications, Journal of Economic Issues*, September 2008, pp. 853–862.

Mitchell, William and Thomas Fazi, *Reclaiming the State: A Progressive Vision of Sovereignty for a Post-Neoliberal World*, Pluto Press, London, 2016.

Mitchell, William, L. Randall Wray and Martin Watts, *Modern Monetary Theory and Practice: An Introductory Text*, CreatSpace: An Amazon Company, 2016.

Mostue, Anne, "Doctors Without Patients," *Bloomberg Businessweek*, September 11, 2017.

National Nurses United and the Sanders Institute, "Medicare for All vs. All the Healthcare That Each Can Afford," June 2017.

Rosenthal, Elisabeth, *An American Sickness: How Healthcare Became Big Business and How You Can Take It Back*, Penguin Press, New York, 2017.

Smith, Jason Scott, *Building New Deal Liberalism: The Political Economy of Public Works, 1933–1956*, Cambridge University Press, New York, 2006.

Srnicek, Nick and Alex Williams, *Inventing the Future: Postcapitalism and a World without Work*, Verso Press, London, 2015.

Standing, Guy, *Basic Income: And How We Can Make It Happen*, Pelican-Penguin Books, 2017.

Veblen, Thorstein, *The Engineers and the Price System*, Transaction Publishers, New Brunswick, NJ and London, [1921] 1990.

Worland, Justin, "A Small-Scale Power Solution Could Pay Big Dividends Across the U.S.," *Time*, August 21, 2017, p. 22.

Zuckerberg, Mark, "Harvard Commencement Address, 2017," May 10, 2017.

Zweibel, Ken, James Mason and Vasilis Fthenakis, "A Grand Plan for Solar Energy," *Scientific American*, January 2008, pp. 64–73.

Index

1920s stock bubble 38–50; consumer deficit spending 47–48; Federal Reserve 45–47; financialization 44; free cash ratios 41–42; Kaleckian analysis 47–48; mergers 40–43
1960s, profit squeeze 67–68
1970s, "The Great U-Turn" 69–70
1980s, equity retirements 64

Accelerated Cost Recovery System 94
acquisition premiums 64
affiliate employment/investment 120–123
Affordable Care Act 155
aggregate demand, Kalecki 15
aggregate totals, Kalecki 13
Arnold, T. 54
"art of self governance" 28
Autor, D. 71

Baran, P. 3, 84, 85
basic income 165
benefits of governmental production 162–163
bond issuance 90–91, 95–96, 136–137
bond markets, rates of return 101–102
the boundary line 149–152; crossing 152; energy investment 153, 158–162; health systems 153–158; income maintenance 164–167; perimeter of 167–169; wages 163–167
Brainard, W.C. 56–58
"Brain Trust" 53–54
Bretton Woods system collapse 113–115
buffer-stock concept 165–166
"Build or Buy": marginal Q 65–67; relative valuation 60–64

Cairncross, A.K. 24–25
capacity: cash expansion 82; idle 161–162
capital accumulation: Keynes 22–23; militaristic expansion 32–33; profit rate theory 69; rate of 68, 74–75
capital exports: European growth 26–27; Hobson 24–34; Keynes 23; market expansion 25, 27; United States 113
capital imports, United States 25–26, 34–35
capital/output ratios 65–72; 1960s 67–68; "The Great U-Turn" 69–72; Piketty 138–144; recessions 140; underutilization 72–73; "zapping labor" 70–72
capital spillage 135–137
capital taxation, Kalecki 97
Capital in the Twenty-First Century 138–139
cartels 31–32
cash expansion through new investment 82
cash flow/output ratios 62–63
cash spillage 105, 107
Civil Works Administration (CWA) 149–150
class-based consumption 17–18
Cold War 86
Collateralized Debt Obligations (CDOs) 103–104
colonialism 18–19; *see also* imperialism
comparative advantage 27
competition: 1960s profit squeeze 67–68; health systems 155–156
consumer debt/equity ratios 101
consumer debt/income ratios 98–99
consumer deficit spending: 1920s stock bubble 47–48; stagnation 97–101
consumption, Kalecki 14, 17–19
corporate free cash ratios 41–42
corporate investment, free cash as a fraction 88–89
corporate restructuring 69–72

corporate taxes 92–97
"crowding out" 102, 106
current account balances: 1920s stock bubble 47; Kalecki 14–15, 18–19
CWA *see* Civil Works Administration

debt/equity ratios, consumer 101
debt/income ratios, consumer 98–99
degree of monopoly 17
Democracy after the War 28–29, 33
dentists 153–154
depressions: capital/output ratios 140; foreign markets 26; Hobson 24; investment 17–18; monopolies 53–55; war 150–151
derivatives trading 103–104
derived income from capital exports 25
digitization 70–72
direct governmental production 147–173; benefits 162–163; boundary line 149–152; energy investment 152, 158–162; health systems 152–158; industrial plan 167–169; New Deal 150; self-funding 151–152; vs. income maintenance 164–167; wages 163–167
distributive shares, Q theory 62–64
dividends 40–41, 43, 135–137
double billing 157
duty of saving 22–23

Earned Income Tax Credit (EITC) 92
earnings dispersion: government borrowing 96; since digitization 71–72
Economic Consequences of the Peace 22–23
"education race" 71–72
efficiency: marginal Q 66–67; new investment 82; relative valuation 62–63
EITC *see* Earned Income Tax Credit
elasticity 140–141
electricity generation 152, 158–162
electrification 158–159
EMU *see* European Monetary Union
energy investment 152, 158–162
Engineers and the Price System 167
equity retirements, 1980s 64
Europe: Bretton Woods collapse 114–115; capital exports 26–27
European Monetary Union (EMU) 115
evidence for relative valuation 74–75
The Evolution of Modern Capitalism 30–31
exceptionalism, U.S. 34–35
excess capacity 15
excess savings and imperialism 24
exchange rates 118–120
executive compensation 72, 143–144
expanded Kaleckian model 87–90
exports: multinational sales ratios 115–123; surpluses 18–19
Ezekiel, M. 54, 167–168

fat-tails 104
Federal Reserve: 1920s stock bubble 45–47; stagnation 103, 104, 106–107; Volker 107
financialization and 1920s stock bubble 44
floating rates 118–120
food imports 26, 35
Foreign Direct Investment (FDI), U.S. 113
foreign markets, depressions 26
for profit boundary line 149–152; *see also* government production; the boundary line
Foster, J.B. 86
free cash ratios 41–42, 88–89
free cash spillage 139–141
Friedman, B.M. 106
Friedman, M. 45–46

Galbraith, J. 71
Galbraith, J.K. 9, 147, 164
General Theory 29–30
gentrification 101
Germany, cartels 32
globalization 67–72; 1960s 67–68; digitization 70–72; exchange rates 118–120; "The Great U-Turn" 69–72; multinational production and sales 115–123; post-Bretton Woods 117–120; self-correction, absence of 123–126; underutilization 72–73; U.S. Trade deficit 124–127; "zapping labor" 70–72
Golden Age 69–72
Gordon, R. 85–86
governmental production 147–173; benefits 162–163; boundary line 149–152; energy investment 152, 158–162; health systems 152–158; industrial plan 167–169; New Deal 150; self-funding 151–152; vs. income maintenance 164–167; wages 163–167
government deficit spending: the boundary line 149–152; Kalecki 14–15, 18–19; as stimulus 90–91, 95–96; Twin Deficit debate 105–107
government-sponsored entities (GSEs) 103, 105

Grand Solar Plan 159
"Great Divergence" 99–100
"Great Leap Forward" 85–86
Great Merger wave 40–43
"Great Moderation" 83
Great Recession of 2008-9 83–84, 89, 98–101, 103–105
"The Great U-Turn" 69–72
Greenspan, A. 103
gross profits, Kalecki 14–15
GSEs *see* government-sponsored entities

Hawley, E.W. 54, 55
health inflation 155
health insurance 153–156
health systems 152–158; competition 155–156; insurance 153–156; medical training 153–154; monopolies 154; non-profits 154–155; sketch 156–158
Heilbroner, R.L. 3, 4
high-tax relative comparison 97
Hobson, J.A. 22–37; colonialism 24–29; depression 24; historiography of industry 29–34; *Imperialism* 24–29, 31–34; monopolies 31; redistribution 33–34; underdevelopment 28; United States 34–35
horizontal equity 93
household debt: equity ratios 101; income ratios 98–99; stagnation 97–101
housing 161–162; bubble 100–105

idle capacity 161–162
Imperialism 24–29, 31–34
imperialism: Hobson 24–29, 31–34; Keynes 23, 29–30; military expansion 26, 32–33; parasitism 26–27; Schumpeter 32–33; surplus capital 24
income distribution: capital gains 143–144; capital/output ratios 138; government borrowing 96; taxation effects 92
income growth rates and investment 73
income maintenance 164–167
income redistribution 33–34
Indian railways 28
indirect effects of Great Merger Wave 42–43
The Industrial System 30–31
industry, Hobson 29–34
inequality, Piketty 137–139
insurance, health 153–156
interest rates and stagnation 101–103
investment: cash expansion 82; corporate taxation 94–95; income growth rates 73; Kalecki 16–19; Keynes 16–17; marginal Q 65–67; as self-funding 16–19; socialization of 149–167; underutilization 72–73

Jacobson, M.Z. 161
Japan and Bretton Woods collapse 114–115
job guarantee programs 165–167

Kalecki, M. 13–21; 1920s stock bubble 47–48; capital taxation 97; derivations 14–15; export surpluses 18–19; investment 16–19; Principle of Increasing Risk 15–16; wages 14–15, 18
Keiretsu 114
Keynes, J.M.: capital accumulation 22–23; capital exports 23; colonialism 23; imperialism 29–30; investment 16–17, 18; over-saving 29, 31
Krugman, P. 126

labor: precariousness 71; "zapping" 70–72
legacy assets in energy generation 159–160
loans on securities and 1920s stock bubble 46

McKinnon, R.I. 118
manager compensation 143–144
manufacturing, decline of 99
marginal advantage 27
marginal Q 64–75; evidence for 74–75; "The Great U-Turn" 69–72; underutilization 72–73; "zapping labor" 70–72
market expansion and capital exports 25, 27
medical training 153–154, 156–157
Meltzer, H. 45, 46
Merger/New Investment ratios 63–64
mergers: 1920s stock bubble 40–43; "The Great U-Turn" 69–72; marginal Q 64–69; Q theory 56–60; relative valuation 60–64
migratory dislocation 162–163
military expansion 26, 32–33, 150–151
Modern Monetary Theory (MMT) 166–167
Money Market Funds 104
monopolies: depressions 53–55; Great Merger Wave 40–43; health services 154; Hobson 31; New Deal 53–56; obsolescence 52; technological change 31
monopolistic pricing power 13, 17
Monopoly Capital 84

Moretti, E. 99
mortgages, stagnation 97–101
multinational deficits and parents' embeddedness 131–132
multinational escape 112–132; affiliate investment 120–123; Bretton Woods collapse 113–115; exchange rates 118–120; post-Bretton Woods 117–120; production 115–123; sales/export ratios 115–123; self-correction, absence of 123–126; trade deficits 123–127, 131–132
multinational production and sales 115–127; affiliate investment 120–123; post-Bretton Woods 117–120
multiplier effect 18, 96
Mummery, A.F. 29

National Industrial Recovery Act of 1933–35 (NIRA) 54, 55, 149–150
net investment valuation vs. stock valuation 141–144
New Deal 53–56, 150
new investment, cash expansion 82
newly industrializing countries (NICs) 70
NICs *see* newly industrializing countries
NIRA *see* National Industrial Recovery Act of 1933–35
non-profit healthcare providers 154–155

obsolescence 51–52
offshoring 115–123; affiliate investment 120–123; post-Bretton Woods 117–120; self-correction, absence of 123–126; trade deficits 123–127
oligopoly: Great Merger Wave 40–43; Kalecki 13, 17–18; New Deal 53–56; stagnation 84–87
output/investment ratios 65–75; 1960s 76–78; "The Great U-Turn" 69–72; marginal Q 65–69; underutilization 72–73; "zapping labor" 70–72
over-saving, Keynes 29, 31

parasitism 26–27
parents' embeddedness 131–132
pharmaceuticals 154–156, 157
The Physiology of Industry 29
Piketty, T. 137–144; elasticity 140–141; free cash spillage 139–141; inequality 137–139; stock vs. net investment valuation 141–144; wealth measurement 143–144
precarity of labor 71
pricing power, monopolistic 13, 17
Principle of Increasing Risk 15–16
The Problem of the Unemployed 31, 33–34
production: governmental 147–173; multinational 115–123; vs. income maintenance 164–167
productivity advances 15
profit rate theory 68–70
profit squeeze 67
prospective revenues 62

Q theory 56–75; concepts 56–60; distributive shares 62–64; marginal Q 64–69; relative valuation 60–64

railway building 23–26, 28
rate of capital accumulation 68, 74–75
rates of return: bond/stock markets 101–102; on capital vs income growth 138–139
redistribution, Hobson 33–34
Reed, H.L. 45
regulatory reform and stagnation 103–105
relative equality, U.S. exceptionalism 34–35
relative valuation: acquisition premiums 64; cash flow/output ratios 62–63; evidenc8e for 74–75; marginal Q 64–69; Merger/New Investment ratios 63–64; profit rate theory 68–70; Q theory 60–64; stagnation 135–137; stocks 133–137; underutilization 72–73; "zapping labor" 70–72
renewable energy investment 158–161
The Revenue Act of 1936 55
The Rise and Fall of American Growth 85
risk: Kalecki 15–16; securitization 104

sales/export ratios 115–123; affiliate investment 120–123; post-Bretton Woods 117–120
savings, investment-driven 16–19
Say's Law 83
Schumpeter, J. 32–33
Schwartz, A.J. 45–46
Second Industrial Revolution 85–86
"Second Machine Age" 72
securitization 103–105
self-correction, absence of 84, 123–126
self-funding: governmental production 151–152; investment as 16–19
Servan-Schrieber, J. 114
serviceability 52
"sham self-government" 33

shareholder value and stagnation 135–137
social compact, breakdown of 67–68
socialization of investment 149–151; energy 152, 158–162; health systems 152–158; *see also* governmental production
solar power investment 158–161
speculation: 1920s stock bubble 40–47; financialization 44
stability and government deficit spending 15
stagnation 83–111; Great Recession 83–84, 89; high-tax relative comparison 97; household debt 97–101; interest rates 101–103; oligopolies 84–87; Piketty 137–144; regulatory reform 103–105; securitization 103–105; stimulation 87; stock valuation 135–137; taxation 91–97; Twin Deficit debate 105–107
Steindl, J. 3, 84, 85, 86
stimulants, stagnation 87, 90–91, 95–96
stock bubble of 1920s 38–50
stock markets, rates of return 101–102
stock repurchases 64, 134
stock valuation 133–144; free cash spillage 139–141; marginal Q 64–69; stagnation 135–137; Veblen 52–53; vs. net investment valuation 141–144
subprime loans 100, 105
Summers, L. 83–84
"supermanagers" 143–144
'super profits' 23
surplus capital and imperialism 24
Sweezy, P. 3, 84, 85, 151

TANF *see* Temporary Aid to Needy Families
tariffs, 19th century 27
taxation: of consumption 92; corporate 92–97; horizontal equity 93; investment effects 94–95; Revenue Act of 1936 55; stagnation 91–97; "Territorial Option" 96–97; top marginal income rates 91–93
technological change: monopolies 31; obsolescence 51–52; productivity advances 15
Temporary Aid to Needy Families (TANF) 162
Temporary National Economic Committee (TNEC) 54–55
territorial expansion 22–34; Hobson 24–29, 31–34; Keynes 23
"Territorial Option" 96–97
Theory of Business Enterprise 52
Thorp, W.L. 41–42
TNEC *see* Temporary National Economic Committee
Tobin, J. 56–58
top marginal income tax rates 91–93
Toporowski, J. 134
trade deficits: and free cash 126–127; multinationals 123–127, 131–132; *see also* sales/export ratios
transport electrification 158–159
trustification 31–32, 35
Tugwell, R.G. 53–54
Twin Deficit debate 105–107
two-earner households 99–100

underdevelopment 28
underinvestment and stagnation 86–87
underutilization 72–73
United States (U.S.): capital imports 25–26, 34–35; Earned Income Tax Credit 92; exceptionalism 34–35; exports 115–127; Federal Reserve 45–47, 103, 104, 106–107; Foreign Direct Investment 113; health system 153–158; New Deal 53–56, 150; "Territorial Option" 96–97; trade deficits 123–127, 131–132

Veblen, T. 51–53, 167
vested interests 164, 167
Volker, P. 107

wages: 1920s stock bubble 47; basic income 165; Earned Income Tax Credit 92; earnings dispersion 71–72; executive compensation 72; governmental production 163–167; Hobson 24, 33–34; job guarantee programs 165–167; Kalecki 14–15, 18; two-earner households 99
war spending 150–151
Wicker, E.R. 45
Works Progress Administration (WPA) 150

"zapping labor" 70–72

For Product Safety Concerns and Information please contact our EU representative GPSR@taylorandfrancis.com Taylor & Francis Verlag GmbH, Kaufingerstraße 24, 80331 München, Germany